A Christian
Response to
Horror Cinema

A Christian Response to Horror Cinema

Ten Films in Theological Perspective

PETER FRASER

McFarland & Company, Inc., Publishers
Jefferson, North Carolina

Frontispiece: Father Karras (Jason Miller) confronts the cold truth in *The Exorcist.* 1973. Warner Brothers.

LIBRARY OF CONGRESS CATALOGUING-IN-PUBLICATION DATA

Fraser, Peter, 1957–
    A Christian repsonse to horror cinema : ten films in theological perspective / Peter Fraser.
      p.   cm.
    Includes bibliographical references and index.

    ISBN 978-0-7864-9824-6 (softcover : acid free paper) ∞
    ISBN 978-1-4766-1972-9 (ebook)

    1. Horror films—History and criticism.   2. Motion pictures—Religious aspects—Christianity.   I. Title.
PN1995.9.H6F745 2015
791.43'6164—dc23   2015009371

BRITISH LIBRARY CATALOGUING DATA ARE AVAILABLE

© 2015 Peter Fraser. All rights reserved

No part of this book may be reproduced or transmitted in any form or by any means, electronic or mechanical, including photocopying or recording, or by any information storage and retrieval system, without permission in writing from the publisher.

Front cover: Jason Miller as Father Damien Karras in *The Exorcist*, 1973 (Warner Bros./Photofest)

Printed in the United States of America

McFarland & Company, Inc., Publishers
  Box 611, Jefferson, North Carolina 28640
    www.mcfarlandpub.com

To the Kingdom of Daylight's Dauphin

Contents

Introduction   1

1. *What Lies Beneath* the Horror Genre   5
2. Monster and Man: Guillermo del Toro's *Pan's Labyrinth*   26
3. Modern Paralysis and Ancient Faith: Carl Dreyer's *Vampyr*   42
4. Carnival Pleasures: Karl Freund's *The Mummy*   60
5. Lawless Men and Beasts: Jacques Tourneur's *Night of the Demon*   78
6. Kill Thine Enemy: Howard Hawks' *The Thing*   95
7. The Return of Molech: Robin Hardy's *The Wicker Man*   113
8. The Corruption of the Virgin: William Peter Blatty's *The Exorcist*   132
9. No Pleasure but Cruelty: John Carpenter's *Halloween*   152
10. Lord of the World: Hideo Nakata's *Ringu*   168

Conclusion   191
Chapter Notes   195
Bibliography   201
Index   205

Introduction

More than a decade ago I slept through an alarm and found myself speeding down Interstate 94 from Milwaukee to Chicago for a morning meeting with a publisher's representative at an academic convention. I wanted to cancel and go back home, and might have done just that if cell phones had been more common then. It was grey, cold, and snowy, and my thoughts swirled around the impossible task of finding legal parking downtown and how far the slushy jog to the hotel would be.

"Do not despise these small beginnings," an Old Testament prophet once wrote. That cold start now seems strangely suitable for the project the representative pitched to me. I had recently written a book about how Western filmmakers give shape to divine presence in religious films, and she thought the perfect complementary work would address the other side of the subject: horror film, the genre designed around the incarnation of evil. I felt awkward enough at the meeting, with snow dripping off my boots onto the carpet and my nose red and wet, that I probably would have agreed to anything reasonable. The woman was engaging, the project seemed doable, and I was very young; someone ought to write a credible book on horror from a theological position. It might as well be me, I thought.

My main point of reference, beyond many Saturday nights trying to stay awake with my brother through *Creature Features* when we were boys, came via a graduate course in horror film at the University of Illinois. But that was a miserable experience. The overlay of critical theory was cumbersome, and the timing could not have been worse. My mother was dying from cirrhosis of the liver in a hospital in Chicago, and visiting her meant missing the one scheduled group showing of the films we were to watch. I saw a double feature of *The Night of the Living Dead* and *The Texas Chainsaw Massacre* alone one afternoon in a concrete-walled, eight-by-eight projection cell with the old machine clicking

Introduction

through those unspeakable grotesqueries while its bulb slowly heated the suffocating air. Horror films have always gotten under my skin and never more so than during that term.

Still, the opportunity to take a few steps toward tenure beckoned. I told friends that I had made up my mind to walk past the sign that warned sojourners to abandon all hope along the way. The book was designed to match the previous one: an introduction that laid out the inner workings of the genre followed by a series of chapters that advanced the conversation point by point, each analyzing a landmark film. Simple enough. At least it seemed so until midway through the introduction when, while studying a Robert Zemeckis film called *What Lies Beneath*, I started to experience what Freud would have called "dread," but what my more old-world wife termed "night terrors." At night or when working alone, I began to sense a dark presence outside and around me. If I'd had an inkwell handy, like Luther did, it might have hit the bedroom door a few times. Those terrors inclined me to put the project down for more than a year.

In 2002 I tried again but experienced more of the same and with more nightmares and chills, and no one to help buffer the experience— we were raising four young children. The situation just didn't seem safe, especially at that stage in our family life, so one day I gathered from my study the books and tapes I had on the subject and carried them out to the trunk of our family car, and that was that. Still, it took weeks to regain a sense of well-being, and although I was able to move on to other projects, when standing in line or scanning the titles at our local Blockbuster, the horror shelves seemed always slightly to be hovering in my peripheral vision.

Some years later, while doing volunteer work with a teen group in Milwaukee's inner city, I found myself agreeing to watch Gore Verbinski's *The Ring*, despite the clench in the belly just from seeing the trailers that were running during breaks of *Monday Night Football*. I saw *The Ring* on a Saturday night in a mall theater full of urban teens screaming and talking back at the screen—one of the most memorable aesthetic experiences of my life. But not mine alone. In the lobby I met a young man from the neighborhood who asked for a ride home. He wasn't about to stand on the corner and then ride the bus, and worse still walk the

Introduction

four blocks from the bus stop to his apartment. That's when I determined to go back to the horror book and finish.

The moment presented itself during my first year at Regent University, where I met a colleague who had been involved in exorcisms and who agreed to keep me in mind, so to speak. What was needed then from me was a schedule and routine. I found I could study and plan in the relative security of my office and then write while traveling by train to visit relatives and friends who live in Chicago, a trip I still make every couple months. Still, all did not go easy. The book threatened to come to a final halt the month I was researching demonic possession and sketching chapter 8 on *The Exorcist*. That old dread followed me home some days and into my bed. Several times I had to wake my wife.

It could be said that some of us are simply more impressionable. And while that is certainly true, horror film surmises that the easiest victims of the diabolic are those who have no healthy fear and respect for the subject. The Church has taught for centuries that the Devil and demons prey on the foolish, and a prevalent motif in horror film reminds us that the goal of Evil with the capital letter is to incarnate itself within the foolish.

Readers can decide for themselves how to measure these metaphysics and interpret this short account. My intention is to open or reopen a serious conversation about the *what* and the *why* of horror and how sensible people, and especially sensible people who believe in things that go bump in the night, might respond. I want to explain where the horror genre came from, how it works, and what it suggests about the trajectory of the culture through the twentieth century. This book in no way attempts to validate the genre; the market has already done that. Horror films grossed nearly a half billion dollars in the United States just last year.

What I hope comes across as unique here is the blending of two seemingly disparate approaches. One analyzes the remarkable achievements of several major artists working in this very dark genre, and does so in a sophisticated way. The other acknowledges the source of horror from the position of historical theology; that is, as the old faith assumed very specific things about the inner workings of this world and the unseen world that circles it, so this book begins with the older assump-

Introduction

tion that the human race was lost by a choice which followed a temptation, and that behind the temptation was a spiritual presence. The tension between those two approaches might be best resolved in a truism that both saints and artists have embraced through all centuries, that in the workings of our mysterious creation there remains something fundamentally inexplicable about human experience, alternately joyful and terrifying, something that makes obedience along the way both a cause for wonder and a necessity for survival and salvation.

1

What Lies Beneath the Horror Genre

> *My thanks! I find the dead no acquisition,*
> *And never cared to have them in my keeping.*
> *I much prefer the cheeks where ruddy blood is leaping...*
> —Mephistopheles in Goethe's *Faust*

During the opening credits in Robert Zemeckis' thriller *What Lies Beneath* (2000), the camera hooks and draws us through a murky pool of water, past ripples of seaweed toward an object hidden in the distant deep. Briefly a young woman's ghostly face flashes over the watery images; moments later, it returns more vividly, eyes closed then suddenly opening wide at the sound of haunted whispers, as if demons have been awakened from their infernal sleep. But, before we can discern anything further, the shots dissolve into a different reality as the film's protagonist, Claire Spencer, rises from the water of a bath having momentarily dozed and slid under.

It's an effective sequence, both as mood-setter and jump-starter, in a film deeply indebted to Alfred Hitchcock's virtuosity in matters of mood and surprise. But beyond these immediate and pleasing nods to suspense classics like *Psycho* and *Vertigo*, Zemeckis' film proves to be a textbook exploration of the mechanics of a different genre, the horror film, and a thoughtful response to the often inadequate attempts of modern critics to explain away the real dread underneath that genre. The wide-eyed viewer shocked at the sudden appearance of the ghost woman and the demonic voices in the opening sequence of *What Lies Beneath* is told moments later that this narrative journey was only a nightmare after all. A woman fell asleep in her bath and had a bad dream before the water forced her back up to reality; perhaps a dream prophetic of some coming trouble, yes, but still just a dream. Any experienced film viewer, however, realizes instantly that this sequence is only act one, scene one of the longer play, which by the rules of narrative invention and in particular the tease-and-reveal narrative invention of the horror genre cannot maintain so pat an explanation. Something else must be going on, something far less easy to explain.

Ever since the glib psychiatrist in Hitchcock's *Psycho* tried to dismiss Norman Bates' aberrant behaviors by waving a thurible of pop Freudianism, easy explanations and clean resolutions have become self-aware clichés in the dark corridors of horror film. Michael Myers with his doll's eyes is not dead on the cold ground after Donald Pleasence empties his pistol into him in John Carpenter's memorable *Halloween* (1972). Somehow, Myers disappears without even leaving a bloody trail, a stunning repudiation of the easy answer that he was just a troubled boy after all. Troubled boys die when shot repeatedly and dropped fifteen feet. The savvy horror viewer knows this, and expects some such false conclusion to arrive several minutes too early. Samara isn't set free by the heroic journalist protagonist to roam some heavenly countryside for abused children in Gore Verbinski's *The Ring* (2002); rather she is set free in the last fifteen minutes to crawl out of a television set to scare to death the unsuspecting ex-husband of the heroine, as well as others who might happen to play the cursed videocassette.

Horror films have always explored the real monsters under the delicate surface tension stretched over the water, and our fascination and repulsion when we stop floating and slip under. They play out the deepest of human fears—that some devil has broken from his chains and is now free to abuse the community which must desperately attempt to shackle him back up. Someone speaks the wrong words, plays the wrong tape, tests the wrong chemicals, gets in the tent with the wrong fortune teller, or, in the case of *What Lies Beneath*, sleeps with and kills the wrong undergraduate, and now hell has literally broken loose, and somebody else had better figure out how to exorcise the loosed demon or demons so that the world can putter on awhile longer. As valuable as Freudian and post-Freudian critics have proved film scholars in search of a critical sieve through which to refine these difficult texts,[1] their attempts to extract the simple essence of the horror film are mocked openly by many of the very films they attempt to unpack. The films

1. What Lies Beneath *the Horror Genre*

would tend to argue that no better explanation exists for our various embodied dreads than the old theological paradigm of Christus Victor advanced by the Church Fathers.[2] As that formula goes, the devil has roared and is taking captives, and implicitly—thanks be to God, the Christ alone triumphs over the Evil One.

Working against the grain of a scientific age that tends toward the denial of the possibility of not only a personal God, but a personal devil, the genre of horror insists that what lies beneath our dread of the mysterious and dangerous unknown that horror explores is Satan himself, his minions, and a grisly un-reality that if seen without the ghostly veils would make Milton's Pandemonium seem a rather familiar place. Zemeckis's opening sequence, whether he fully intended it or not, functions as an establishing metaphor that warns us to beware of underestimating the world underneath the familiar surfaces of the text, or of simple explanations. We might think we understand what we see and hear in the story, just as we may think we can wake from the darkness of the screening room to the cool and refreshing outdoor air, but to think such thoughts is to dismiss the obvious implications of what has drawn us to, and what we have seen in, the darkness, not to mention the cold finger just touching our spine. The camera journey of horror film makes plain that something is indeed down there waiting to come up and out, and that our curious and foolish assent to see it has awakened the attention and pleasure of this beast who loves the curious fool most of all. Claire cannot get out of the bath and assume all will be well, nor can we—especially three minutes into the film. In fact, her expression and demeanor after the "dream" say as much.

The most effective horror films command the viewer's attention like no other cinematic art. They tease at a fundamental metaphysic with their display of a damaged universe where lost creatures, to borrow an argument from a Pauline epistle, "suppress the truth in their unrighteousness."[3] That is to say, the fallen deny the desire to rebel against both heaven and the world's natural balances, and thus hide their secret longing to see and experience, if only momentarily, the anarchy behind the wall hiding the domain of the devil. In the horror genre, victim and viewer are compelled to admit these dark desires,[4] and spiritual and moral denials. Once the toll is paid to enter the theater, access is granted to brief glimpses of an unchecked will to evil; the victim-viewer is compelled to acknowledge evil's *personal* existence, as well as a self-deluded, secret love of its ways. No, it is not *only* a movie, as one tagline suggested. If it were, if horror were only a seek-and-reveal genre game,[5] the genre should have lost some measure of its popular power after nearly a century, and viewers wouldn't be found so often trembling in the corner of the wrong tent. The truly dreadful horror films compel the visitor to check all sophistries and denials, while at the same time offering a false promise that this innocent gesture of paying for a ticket to a teasing journey into the underworld will have no significant bearing on the naïve pilgrim.

When, with superficial earnestness and professional ease, the psychiatrist in *Psycho* convinces Marion Crane's sister and former boyfriend that Norman Bates can be understood simply as poor victim of a suf-

Norman Bates (Anthony Perkins) posing "real danger in the forest" as he considers his prey in Alfred Hitchcock's groundbreaking *Psycho*. 1960. Paramount Pictures.

1. What Lies Beneath *the Horror Genre*

focating mother love that eventually caused his repressed sexual desires to break out in murder, transvestitism, and fetishism, only Freud himself might be comforted. Nobody sitting on the disarrayed blankets of the bed at home or on the dark, musty cloth of the theater seat can really accept such a pseudo-scientific diagnosis, especially after the film's concluding shots of what in the old days would be readily acknowledged as a "demon-possessed" Norman sitting alone in a cell and then hovering superimposed over the site of one of his crimes. The psychiatrist character with his two-dimensional, formulaic explanations of the chaos played out on screen is the Dr. Watson of the genre, the dupe who holds the sleeve of the naïve reader. Meanwhile, the text itself whispers a contrary message, the ancient folk wisdom about real danger in the forest.

And so, the voices heard under the water in the opening sequence of *What Lies Beneath* warn us to beware what we cannot see and understand. They bring to mind the benevolent voices of wisdom which have taught pilgrims and children to dismiss naiveté and to keep away from the demons who secretly fascinate, whose sugary voices are so very seductive. Don't glance twice! Don't go into the woods at night! Don't speak those words and open that box! And certainly don't listen to any damned fool who tells you otherwise!

But curiosity draws its Pandoras who need to see what is under or over or inside there, just as surely as Eve was drawn in the biblical story. And the forbidden tree that had to be tried was, unfortunately, the epicenter of good *and* evil, as it is still for the viewer of the horror film. Little succor can be found in labeling the dangerous, curious impulse toward evil incarnate with jargon phrases like "the fascination of the uncanny,"[6] as if such labeling will function as fairy world incantation when a mysterious hand lifts us bolt upright in bed as the clock on the table touches 3 a.m. and our head is turned toward some real or imagined dark shape in the corner. The films that prompt these night terrors challenge philosophical materialists, as does the tradition of the church which still asserts that the real danger that makes clock hands run in reverse once spoke in impudent *personal* introduction, "Call me Legion."

The evil embodied in the horror film takes a body, and the body is the monster. The monstrous form, then, horrible though it may appear, is a phantasm, only a vestige of some *thing* so much worse. In *What Lies Beneath*, the monster appears as the ghost of a murdered young woman with staring eyes; yet, even when the film shows us that woman in the final scene and she is pushed back down into her watery prison, she still lives. She is only satisfied, not killed. The monster always lives again, for the monstrous form is accidental to the thing itself, and the demon cannot be destroyed by the hand of man. Ask the opinion of the child staying up past midnight to watch Saturday's *Creature Features*, for that child knows that when the Frankenstein monster is set ablaze in the windmill, it will somehow escape to haunt the sequel, and the sequel's sequel, and so on ad infinitum.

Those monstrous shapes might be considered moral grotesques, diabolical incarnations formed around a former virtue in mockery of, ultimately, the one true incarnation—putrid skin placed over the perverse demon who feeds, as Dante envisioned it, on a particular vice. The monster demon roams the landscape as avenger breathing pestilence and death, punishing the community constructed over unholy ground. So, in the older films of the genre, such as the Universal studio classics *Frankenstein* (1931) and *The Mummy* (1932), a clear moral transgression triggers the plot. In *Frankenstein*, the scientist Victor Frankenstein has allowed hubris to corrupt his work. He chooses artificial life over the natural life that would come were he to limit his intellectual pursuits and settle down to marry his fiancée. The monster, a wild and hideous child, thus becomes the demonic analog to what God might create were Victor to check his moral rebellion. In *The Mummy*, the sin is of larger scope as a team of archaeologists unearth the tomb of the ancient Egyptian priest Imhotep, and then one of the members unwittingly reads an incantation that brings the decrepit priest back to life; modern disrespect for the dead, once youthful human beings who had souls that longed for life and love, causes the demonic avenger to come back and disrespect the callous living—the ancient, resurrected Egyptian priest will attempt to sacrifice a living girl to call back the spirit of his dead princess.

The pattern carries through the entire genre. The cruelty of dropping a nuclear bomb over civilian strangers becomes the trigger to raise *Godzilla* (1954) and *The Beast from 20,000 Fathoms* (1953) and countless other mutations, which then in turn rain random fire and pestilence

1. What Lies Beneath *the Horror Genre*

upon those playing the part of the transgressors. National hubris driving science toward space exploration, especially during a post–World War era that proved we can build towers but not govern ourselves, brings on the avenging aliens of *Invasion of the Body Snatchers* (1956) who come in true imperialist fashion to remake humankind, of course, stripping us of our greatest attribute in the process: the ability to love. In the sixties and seventies, the sexual revolution which legitimized the old transgressions of fornication and adultery witnessed the rise of the avenging sexual predators—Michael and Jason and Freddie and others—who punish the teen population playing the part of transgressors engaged in backseat trysts. Bloody yet distant wars, coupled with domestic traumas involving students and minority groups, played nightly on television sets across America, transform into invasions of grotesque zombies feeding on the flesh of the living and dead in *Night of the Living Dead* (1968) and the subgenre that followed it. The transgressions differ and so do the beasts; the transgressions continue, and so the beasts refuse to die, for they are principally demonic spirit and not flesh. The body may melt like the Wicked Witch of the West, but when the stench of the earth becomes distracting and Pandora flips the lid again, the demon returns.

As for the spectator watching the horror film who, as the logic goes, suppresses by the rules of a conflicted human nature the real consequence of real transgression, be it private or communal, that soul is lured forward not by the mechanical expertise of costumers and set designers, cinematographers and editors, but by the opportunity to perhaps somehow witness *the calling up of the thing itself.* And that soul must mask the impulse by an obvious lie—that the enterprise is safe. There, on the puppet stage of the screen, walks an unholy monster born of sin to punish sin. Certainly that monster is contained by the screen, or so goes the logic of denial; it is a fantasy creature borrowed from the nightmares of an older age, medieval minds. And, although elusive, it can be observed objectively and then killed, or at least stopped for a while. The teenager who watched *Halloween* (1978) cuddled next to his frightened girlfriend would assume, of course, that the consequences of his own moral transgressions cannot really occur, and that his voyeuristic pleasures likewise invite no reprisals, for the massacre that he watches on the screen references only a troubling relic of an older era that was oppressed by unenlightened moral strictures, the hauntings of a decayed mythology that needed scapegoat rituals to dispel primal fears tied to some depressing primal curse. Besides, the film allows such a delightful, if forbidden or even pornographic, pleasure in the full-color display of real sadism at work. Pass the popcorn across her warm breast, and know all is well.

But it is not. The monsters mock the false assurance on the faces of the victims who parade in. The monster is not the thing either, not some made-up bogey. It comes through the text as demon playing that part, schooled under the prince of demons, and it wins in the end of these dark morality plays. The demon rises from film to film like a phoenix from its own ashes to bring more and worse mayhem. It always takes new flesh and kills again.

And it may just have reality *beyond* the screen. There is the rub. Like a moral virus, the thing behind "the thing seen" attaches itself to the victim. The narratives say as much. Orlok is carried back in a cloud of pestilence from his home in the Carpathians to distant Wismar, where the vampire will feed on the unsuspecting Ellen in *Nosferatu*. Larry carries the infection from the bite of a werewolf back with him into his ancestral home in Wales, where he will transform into a monster and terrify even his own girl Jenny in *The Wolfman* (1941). Miles leads his girl Becky to the cave where she will be infected by the pods in *Invasion of the Body Snatchers* (1956). The crew of the ship *Nostromo* investigates a foreign planet, only to have one member infected by a monstrous parasite in *Alien* (1979). And, of course, the deadly video with its images of chaos and pestilence provides the channel through which Sadako can enter the land of the living and kill her victims in *Ringu*. Once the curious move the peep-show curtain aside and meet the eyes of the demon, the infection gets passed. The demon has privilege now to walk among the living. Again, at the very least, that is what the film narratives tell us, and that is the one part of the fear and dread that the film spectator and scholar must suppress.

Yet, this unthinkable should be pondered beyond its play life in the plot of horror narratives. What if the film spectator does leave the theater with some dreaded incubus or succubus as companion, despite those

1. What Lies Beneath *the Horror Genre*

elaborate veils of self-denial? What if the risky *Ouija* board of the horror film does open some unknown portal? The narrative contained the demon and it was destroyed, nearly, or so goes the delusion the viewer tries to accept, but what a particularly mindless delusion especially in this era when the cinematic demons don't even show the courtesy of playing dead until the sequel. The viewer certainly gets to go home, perhaps purged of these dark nightmares, right? Or does something else occur? Is the narrative somehow inextricably tied to our immediate reality? Does the fly on the screen seep through into our own world, as it does in *The Ring*? Is the daylight now infected by the dark dreams of the night?

Perhaps the horror genre carries a warning that must be taken seriously, like the one accompanying Chris Van Allsburg's *Jumanji* game, but not within the context of a game. It would not be the first instance in which films played a prophetic role in the culture. Siegfried Kracauer argued in his landmark 1947 study of the films of Germany's Wiemar Republic, *From Caligari to Hitler*, that cultural fantasies and motivations expressed themselves in the popular film narratives that anticipated the rise of German fascism.[7] His controversial claim troubled many critics inclined to believe that movies are only movies, despite Kracauer's careful documentation and identification of the fascist tensions implicit in Germany's Weimar films. Still, to argue that films record past cultural tendencies and ideological paradigms is one thing; to suggest that films capture the evils currently bubbling under the surface and both indulge in and prophetically warn against them is quite another. Is it credible to take the leap with the horror genre—that where a great deal of criticism has been focused on these films as reflectors of past and current anxiety, it might also be entirely plausible and consistent to suggest that the films presage destructive spiritual forces on the horizon, which, in this case, happen to be demonic? Put more directly, taking Kracauer's model a step further could lead to the troubling conclusion that one of the dominant cultural fears of the late twentieth century was that the veil between the underworld and our perceived brick and mortar, cell phone and video-stream world had been torn.

This hypothesis seems entirely consistent with common experience. The curiosity that drives the typical viewer's attention through the narrative of a horror film travels beyond it to the dark fantasies carried

A Christian Response to Horror Cinema

The possessed wife Claire (Michelle Pfeiffer) invites her husband into a game of sexual violence and devilry in *What Lies Beneath*. 2000. 20th Century-Fox.

1. What Lies Beneath *the Horror Genre*

away from the film. Images and sounds linger on long after the movie, yet another alignment between horror and pornography. Fantasies about telekinetic powers as a means to vengeance linger in the mind after being indulged through spectacles like *Carrie* (1976) or *Scanners* (1981). Fears of the dark or of being caught in vulnerable places, such as the shower, become more palpable once they become iconic through the medium of film. The person who goes to the cinema to see *Jeepers Creepers II* or streams it at home is enticed not only by the play of the narrative, but by the kick that will occur afterward, the exhilaration of the new dread that gets carried away like an infection into the ordinary of a grey suburban day. And with such haunted dreams now alive in the daylight, the only recourse will be to revisit the source and seek some closure to the nightmare, or a temporary fix at least, which is exactly what happens. Horror film is addictive and predictive.

It is especially interesting, then, that central to the narrative convention of the genre is this one fact—that the hope for the last victim, the antihero who walks alone through the wasteland of demonic vengeance, is that an exorcism be performed. The demon must be finally assigned a name and placed back under contract to the higher power of a living god. It cannot be stopped otherwise.

The word "exorcism" itself derives from the Greek concept of being put "on oath." The demon once released by some transgression born of dark curiosity is brought back under the terms of original bondage through an exorcism, which is the invocation of higher authority. Satan is only allowed to trouble Job by permission in the prophet's account. His leash is stretched, but still connected; he is still only permitted, not rendered free, for "the Lord reigns over all the earth." The 1999 Roman Catholic Rite of Exorcism reads:

> I command you, unclean spirit, whoever you are, along with all your minions now attacking this servant of God, by the mysteries of the incarnation, passion, resurrection, and ascension of our Lord Jesus Christ, by the descent of the Holy Spirit, by the coming of our Lord for judgment, that you tell me by some sign your name, and the day and hour of your departure. I command you, moreover, to obey me to the letter, I who am a minister of God despite my unworthiness; nor shall you be emboldened to harm in any way this creature of God, or the bystanders, or any of their possessions.[8]

A Christian Response to Horror Cinema

The demon must be brought back under the authority of a larger binding contract. Such is the case in *What Lies Beneath*. Dr. Norman Spencer, a career-driven geneticist from Harvard on the verge of discovering a breakthrough drug, has murdered a young student, Madison Elizabeth Frank, with whom he has had a potentially career-ruining affair. His wife, Claire, who has given up her own brilliant career as a cellist to marry Norman, discovers that their house is being haunted by the murdered woman. Claire eventually conjures the ghost, at which point the film shifts from suspenseful mystery thriller into genuinely chilling Gothic horror, less dependent on jump scenes and clever Hitchcockian references than on the real presence and play of evil.

In the most unsettling scene of the film, a now demon-possessed "Claire" confronts Norman in the center of domestic security, the kitchen, by the refrigerator, offering him an apple, of all things. She lures him into a sexual embrace in which she dominates and hurts him. The iconography suggests sexual violence and devilry—the apple, a red dress, a vampiric bite of Norman's lip. The modality of the film likewise shifts in the sequence. Claire's eyes are green, like the dead girl's. The camera cranes up and over the couple, as if adopting the point of view of the now disembodied original Claire looking down upon the demon woman straddling her victim husband. When the demon Claire pulls off Norman's belt, the threat of castration seems imminent, especially given the dark logic of vengeance which would have the dead girl come back to castrate and kill the lover who ruined her. As the demon wife reaches for a letter opener to do her work, she herself is startled by another haunting as the real wife returns, first rustling leaves outside the house and then looking out of a dressing mirror in the room. The demon smiles at the real Claire and says to Norman, and covertly to the viewer, "I think she's starting to suspect something." When Norman asks who, the demon smiles and says, "Your wife." At this, Norman pushes her off. She falls and rises again as the original Claire, who suddenly and rather mysteriously remembers and understands the sequence of events that included Norman's murder of the girl.

Claire's return relaxes the action, since the demon has once more yielded the privilege of flesh. Yet curiosity forms the rules of the horror game, and the demon will certainly appear again to allow a closer view.

1. What Lies Beneath *the Horror Genre*

Regrettably, the next appearance grants little satisfaction of the real dread and glee which carries the viewer forward. Norman enters Claire's room to take a book of witchcraft from her while she sleeps. The camera pans from his exit back to the bed where the demon Claire is awake with alert green eyes. She walks from the bedroom outside to the end of a pier and looks back eerily at the house and the camera before plunging into the lake in which the dead girl was deposited and in which a clue to the dead girl's death lies in a box near the bottom. Later, the real Claire will plunge into the water to recover this box, a logical development of the narrative that will further serve to satisfy the viewer's desire to see the demon again.

The next transformation occurs in the place where Claire first saw the demon's face, in the waters of her tub. Norman has decided to kill his wife who has learned the full details of Madison's murder and threatened to expose Norman. He paralyzes her with a drug and then takes her to the bathtub to drown her and make it appear as suicide. As the waters rise in the tub, Norman looks down at Claire's face, the reverse camera point of view of the previous seduction sequence. Suddenly, as Norman examines a locket previously worn by Madison now around his wife's neck, Claire's face transforms into that of the murdered girl, ghastly and terrible. As the viewer has been made to adopt Norman's point of view, the shock of the scene punishes the transgression of our own curiosity as much as it does his, who falls back and cracks his skull on the porcelain sink. Thus, the viewer is scalded with the fear that the demon might appear as suddenly in our space as the story's villain. The viewer longs to know the demon's name so an exorcism can be performed even more than Claire's escape from the rising bath waters.

The longed-for, yet dreaded, further revelation of the ghost woman who haunts the wife in *What Lies Beneath* occurs at the end of the narrative, when the demon animates her former body and drags Norman to the bottom of a lake. Both Claire and the viewer watch with relief. Norman was the transgressor and he will pay. At least today he was the target. But we have transgressed as well. We wanted the forbidden tree with its forbidden fruit, too, and we have done things, not terrible things, but things. We wanted to see the avenger[9] in the hope that seeing it would give us strength against it when in fact the opposite proved true. Seeing it meant it saw us.

A Christian Response to Horror Cinema

We must beware the monsters of the horror genre, which are wild and cannot die; they may not just be extensions of our own repressed feelings and thoughts, monsters from the id,[10] that can be dismissed once recognized as phantoms. Scrooge foolishly taunted Marley, "You may be an undigested bit of beef, a blot of mustard, a crumb of cheese, a fragment of underdone potato." We attempt no such clever dismissals. There is no psychic pill which dismisses the haunting of the horror demon, no catharsis to make the story intellectually satisfying. The viewer feels all the worse for indulging in the experience, and totally incapable of shutting down the haunting nightmares that will follow. The restoration and balance of the social order within the narratives of even the earliest and tamest of horror films does not imply equilibrium in the world we inhabit.[11] The films suggest an exorcism is needed to return the beast and close the story. The spectator wonders, do I need one, too? The question leads to further probing into the source of the haunting. What brought all this on?

What the narratives of horror film reveal about cause is the violation of taboo, the problem being that those who violate the taboo rarely understand the full danger; some transgressions occur under the surface of the story. Especially troubling is that we who play voyeur in the game of horror with the same limited awareness likewise assent to the conditions of the game and so must admit our complicity in that transgression. Not only that, but we take pleasure in watching the massacre that follows; the films encourage such pleasure. We pay the ticket price to see not just Norman Bates, but the voluptuous Marion Crane posing in bullet bra in *Psycho*. We watch her undress. We watch her die. We secretly laugh at two young people of the sixties disrespecting the sacred ground of a cemetery in *Night of the Living Dead* (1968); the film invites complicity. We laugh as the brother mocks the need to remember the dead and dismisses the importance of church. We laugh as he teases his sister, and then we rather enjoy that the zombie chooses him first victim. Taboos are violated within and around the films.

It was James Frazer in *The Golden Bough* who fully articulated the function of taboos in society, taboos as "electrical insulators to preserve the spiritual force with which these persons are charged from suffering or inflicting harm by contact with the outer world."[12] For Frazer, cultures

1. What Lies Beneath *the Horror Genre*

instinctively acknowledge in one way or another that certain people in certain conditions or while practicing certain behaviors hold the key to the prison out of which demonic avengers push in their eagerness to escape confinement and enjoy the pleasures of mayhem in human society. Lines are drawn to protect the community from the demonic. These are taboos. The violator of the taboo must die, for the gods must be appeased. More than that, the demons must be kept at bay.

Christian doctrine explains the phenomenon more directly. The demon has a name. The taboo is moral and specific, non-arbitrary. The transgressors, whether intentionally committing the offense or not,[13] have somehow triggered a sequence of events whereby God allows Satan to play his chain and reach further with the arm of chaos. The priest must be called, the exorcism performed.

The task of identifying the transgression that unleashes the beast has been an ongoing task of film scholars over the past three or four decades, although few would agree with my assignment of the evil as demonic. Interestingly enough, the scholarship has been a mirror enterprise to the simpler pursuits played out in the movies themselves. Claire literally searches under the water for the box of secrets that tells how Madison was killed. She calls up the dead girl through a *Ouija* board and lock of the girl's hair and asks that the girl guide her to the truth. The demon girl will then expose Norman as villain and execute her vengeance on him.

But, just as there was more under the water than seaweed and a ghostly face in the opening scene, there is also more to the transaction of sin and punishment addressed by the film. What lies beneath Madison's haunting of Claire is the violation of a different taboo than the murder of a young woman. Murders happen every day, but very few tear the veil between the layers of reality in the universe. So, the film narrative calls us to play the role of the scholar and search for the deeper truth, one more fitting the chaos the viewer has experienced.

In *What Lies Beneath*, Madison, the murdered woman, is much younger than Claire, a seasoned mother who as the story begins is sending her own daughter off to college. Madison, therefore, is a closer double to Claire's daughter than she is to Claire herself. Madison is the school girl cut free from her parents' protection and sent into the seemingly tame world of the university who finds that the university is not tame but is a world of conflicted allegiances and violent obsessions. Norman, the professor, is not the noble humanist seeking the good of humanity through research. Rather he is a still willful child, obsessed with the task of overcoming his father's reputation and establishing his own name. He puts an end to Claire's career as a cellist by marrying her and locking her up like the maiden in the tower—a prop for his own respectability, the trophy bride. He murders the student he uses sexually once she threatens his prestige and likewise attempts to murder Claire when she discovers the truth.

In a scene early in the film, Norman sits upright in his bed, his bare chest suggesting sexuality (the casting of the still-virile Harrison Ford as Norman adds to the iconography of the sequence), with his, no doubt, university-issued laptop flipped up. Claire approaches him provocatively, offering the choice between dueling pleasures: his wife or his computer. He chooses Claire, but as they embrace, they hear the moans of a neighbor woman across the way in the throes of pleasure with her husband, also a university professor. He keeps the window open and pulls Claire in.

The university world of seeming equality, open access, and female empowerment is thus displayed instead as a world of authority, secrecy, and male pleasure. In the scene where Claire says goodbye to her daughter in her dorm room, the dorm is depicted as a den of promiscuity and free living. Claire seems unable to let go her embrace and allow her daughter into this predatory environment, but while Claire struggles, Norman stands in approval of this change of scenery from home. He responds to Claire's motherly concern in a patronizing fashion. This scene adds further to the dark equation, since Norman's attitude, coupled with what is revealed later of his behavior, suggests the university as a place of institutionally approved exploitation. Norman approves, allowing his stepdaughter into a world where she stands a good chance of being used, just as he has used Madison. Beyond that, a hint of incest wafts across the space, the modern variety whereby fathers allow their daughters to play a part in a pop culture porn ring, wherein Britney Spears might be the most recognizable recent icon.

Norman's laptop stands also as icon of a business world that feeds

1. What Lies Beneath *the Horror Genre*

upon the secret sins of pornography and incest. Computers double as the means to the market and the machine for the peep show. On screen is not only the daughter of caring but gullible and short-sighted parents like Claire, but also the daughters of the respectable moguls and entrepreneurs feeding a public addicted to greater and greater doses of what feminist critics have termed "visual pleasure."

So, the taboo violated in the narrative of *What Lies Beneath* is far more significant than the murder of one woman. Her death in the wider context suggests crimes greater than murder. The demon who takes residence in her body to exact vengeance on Norman is resident elsewhere on the cornices of hell where Lamia resides, the corrupt mythical daughter of Lybia and Belius. After Zeus seduced Lamia, Hera, Zeus's wife, condemned the victim girl to eat her own children, a feast that later gave the madwoman appetite to eat all children. Lamia, the prototype for all *femme fatales*, comes into Norman's world, a mock image of Eve in the garden, fruit in hand inviting Norman to eat with her so she might devour him. When the demon Claire offers Norman the apple, she subsequently presses it hard into his mouth to gag him.

In the film's resolution, satisfaction of the demon occurs through an underwater marriage between the corpse of Madison, animated for the purpose by the demon, and Norman, who is trying to drown Claire. Yet the cause of the transgression and the abusive world of the university, still exists. Claire's daughter continues to matriculate in this world the film depicts as dominated by male professors with self-serving agendas like Norman's and with male undergraduates following the lead of their mentors. That is the narrative logic. Further, the demon still exists. In a final sequence, Claire places a red rose on Madison's grave. As the camera pulls back a ghostly face appears in the snow of the graveyard, as if blessing the gesture and accepting her return to the underworld. In accepting this closure, the viewer must implicitly consent to the evocation of the demon as the means of resolving the social evil of the girl's murder. The demon acts as avenging angel. No exorcism needed, all is well. Send the priest home.

It is this final benediction that renders *What Lies Beneath* so telling in the evolution of the genre. Historically, the monster demon needed to be exorcised through some difficult process that had grievous conse-

A Christian Response to Horror Cinema

quence for the "exorcist"; this would be the case in Friedkin and Blatty's *The Exorcist* (1973) or Scott Derrickson's *The Exorcism of Emily Rose* (2005) or, in another form, Murnau's *Nosferatu* (1922). Satan is not so easily bound again. Some demons only come out with much prayer and fasting, the gospels record. The seed of the woman crushes the head of the serpent in the *protoevangelium*, but has his heel bruised. Here, in Zemeckis's film, the haunted woman Claire makes an unspoken pact with the demon girl, approving her act of vengeance against Norman, Claire's husband. In this, *What Lies Beneath* follows a trend in horror over the past thirty years to allow the demon to gain the upper hand by substituting exorcism with appeasement. And if we assume that the act of watching the film opens a crack in the underworld, then the film seems to carry a new level of foreboding. But this we will explore later.

For now, suffice it to say that to approach horror on its own terms the questions that need be asked must grow out of the basic paradigm of Christus Victor which governs the genre—the monster masks a demon let loose by some violation of taboo who threatens an array of screen victims, and also us. The demon can only be overcome through an exorcism. The questions that viewers and critics should ask are, then, perhaps the most obvious.

What is the monster? Frankenstein is an unwanted and corrupted child; Dracula is a venereal disease incarnate; the werewolf is a libidinous male predator; Godzilla is an angry mutation caused by bad science; Norman Bates is a disturbed pubescent killer; Madison Elizabeth Frank is the outraged mistress of a college professor. But all of these forms are not the evil itself, for the forms, like the shark in *Jaws* (1975), can be blown up. They are mocking, demonic, incarnate phantasms of the bastard children the irreverent sinners brought into the world. Identifying the monstrous form identifies the transgression that unleashes the evil. Underneath the smothered child turned psychotic murderer in Hitchcock's *Psycho* is a post–World War II youth culture of sexual repression, think Dr. Spock, and sexual display, Janet Leigh in the bullet bra. The taboo violated is the selling and corrupting of the virgin, legitimized and enhanced voyeurism, a practice central to commercial film.

The next question to ask is, *What inhabits the monster?* In the con-

1. What Lies Beneath *the Horror Genre*

text of exorcism, this might be phrased better as "What is the name of the demon"? Michael Myers has "doll's eyes" in *Halloween*, according to the psychiatrist/exorcist of the film. He has dead eyes behind which is an incomprehensively cruel entity, a thing not affected by modern medicine or guns even should the bullets be silver. He is the stunted evil child, an Ares who is numb to his own sadistic entertainments. In *What Lies Beneath*, under the ghost of the victimized female student is the image of the demon Lamia, the corrupted woman who eats children.

The third question addresses the machinery of the genre—*Why is this chaos unleashed on these people?* The world of horror recalls a Dantesque medieval world in which the punishment meted out is retributive. The gluttons lie in fetid slush, the violent are boiled in blood, the fortunetellers have their heads turned in reverse, and so goes the nightmare vision of this Inferno where punishments are grotesque reversals of the crimes committed. In the world of the horror film, a dark poetry aligns the manner of the massacre with the sin lurking in the shadows of the broken taboo.

The fourth question follows naturally from the third—*What is the broken taboo?* This is somewhat easier to answer once the demon has been identified and some sense made of the carnage. Many horror films, especially classics, stretch the plot around this violation. The young archaeologist of Karl Freund's *The Mummy* (1932) working late to translate the ancient hieroglyphic reads aloud the formula for unearthing the dead. He intends no harm, but is, nonetheless, motivated by pride and numb to his own hubris. So, when the mummy quietly drifts past, dragging his bandages, he goes mad—"He ... he ... he went for a little walk." But he was mad already, of course—mad in his conscienceless pursuit of new knowledge and glory for him and his team of scientists. He disrespected the dead and had no fear of the world of angels and demons. In *What Lies Beneath*, the mother sends her daughter off to the same institution that destroyed Madison Frank, despite the signs of danger. A mother should know better and work to protect her daughter and not give her over to the traders in flesh, but Claire has been compromised herself and given up her own unique gifts, her cello playing, to gain the protection of a powerful man. Norman may be the villain, but the haunted Claire has violated the age-old taboo and sold her daughter to the flesh traders after she has corrupted herself.

In 1486, Heinrich Kramer published his infamous manual for identifying and understanding the methods of witches, *Malleus Maleficarum*, or *The Hammer of Witches*, in which he turned existing church teaching against occult practice into a manual for the Inquisition's witch-hunters. The treatise asserts that three elements are necessary for witchcraft: the evil-intentioned witch, the help of the Devil, and the permission of God—a paradigm clearly drawn from the Book of Job. Horror films imply a fourth and that is one tied to the specific willful agency of man, this trigger of the broken taboo which functions as the *Ouija* board in the narratives.

The fifth and final question asks, *How the exorcism may be performed?* Christian exorcisms follow an ancient formula. Early church fathers put forward the power of exorcism as an apologetic that authenticates the truth of their faith. The rite was common and eventually became part of normal priestly duties, as all priests and other clerics were ordained exorcists. Centuries later, after the Reformation a significant increase in the frequency of exorcisms led to cautions issued by both Catholic and Protestant churches alike. The Roman Ritual, issued by Pope Paul V in 1614, gave instructions on how to differentiate true possession "as opposed to those suffering from melancholy or some disease."[14] Fewer exorcisms were performed; yet cases continued, even after 1917 when church law insisted a bishop approve of the procedure.

The rite of exorcism has retained a basic consistency through the centuries. In fact, there is a distinct pattern of sameness to cases of demon possession and methods of exorcism that argues against skeptics.[15] The demon is isolated, then God is evoked, and the demon is sent back to the abyss by the power of the Triune God:

> Do not think of despising my command because you know me to be a great sinner. It is God + Himself who commands you; the majestic Christ + who commands you. God the Father + commands you; God the Son + commands you; God the Holy + Spirit commands you. The mystery of the cross commands + you. The faith of the holy apostles Peter and Paul and of all the saints commands + you. The blood of the martyrs commands + you. The continence of the confessors commands + you. The devout prayers of all holy men and women command + you. The saving mysteries of our Christian faith command + you.[16]

1. What Lies Beneath *the Horror Genre*

In Christian exorcisms, the exorcist accompanies the speaking of the ritual formula with the use of physical objects relevant to the sacraments—salt for purity, bread and wine, crosses, rosaries, or relics. In the context of the horror narrative, these become the familiar stakes, special bullets, canes, secret chemicals and so on. In the context of *What Lies Beneath*, the underwater box and key are actually passed from the demon girl to Claire in an odd transaction enabling Claire to identify Norman as the killer. Once Norman dies, the demon retreats, as if in agreement, and returns to the world of the damned.

We are speaking of the mechanics of the genre here, and of the methodology by which types of horror film and individual films can be identified and assessed. Because horror film has so long and complex a history, however, these assertions can best be argued through a careful examinations of a series of illustrative and significant films from the century in question, which is what follows. For now, one observation seems most relevant for a conclusion, that what lies beneath and drives the terror inspired by the genre of horror is our innate dread of evil not as quality or behavior, but as presence, and our related desire to ward it off.

2

MONSTER AND MAN
Guillermo del Toro's *Pan's Labyrinth*

> *There is no more Vendée, Republican citizens. It died beneath our free sword, with its women and its children. I have just buried it in the swamps and the woods of Savenay. Following the orders that you gave to me, I crushed the children beneath the horses' hooves, massacred the women who, those at least, will bear no more brigands. I do not have a single prisoner to reproach myself with. I have exterminated them all.*—General Francois Joseph Westermann ("The Butcher"), letter to Committee of Public Safety, 1794

Under the banner of "Liberty, Equality, and Fraternity," roughly 40,000 citizens were killed during the Reign of Terror in France. During the ensuing Vendée Wars, tens of thousands of mostly Catholic citizens tasted the "free sword." This slaughter provided a foretaste of the new Enlightenment "progress," a genocidal course which has mapped its trajectory through a surreal litany of twentieth-century horrors punctuated by Hitler's murder of over 11 million, Stalin's 20 million, and Mao's 30 million. The University of Minnesota Center for Holocaust and Genocide Studies has concluded that in the twentieth century war casualties neared 35 million, while the victims of genocide and "genocide-like" campaigns numbered nearly 120 million.[1]

Utopian dreams with bright slogans like "youth must be led by youth" and "peace, land, and bread" defined the modern experiment. Those banners would now seem to broadcast across history the empty promises that fueled the bloodiest and most cruel of social programs, usually aimed at the poor and the faithful—barbarism instead of the promised fruits of Reason. François Mauriac described this catastrophe in memorable fashion in his Foreword to Elie Weisel's *Night*:

2. Monster and Man

> I confided to my young visitor that nothing I had witnessed during that dark period had marked me as deeply as the image of cattle cars filled with Jewish children at the Austerlitz train station.... I believe that on that day, I first became aware of the mystery of the iniquity whose exposure marked the end of an era and the beginning of another. The dream conceived by Western man in the eighteenth century, whose dawn he had thought he had glimpsed in 1789, and which until August 2, 1914, had become stronger with the advent of the Enlightenment and scientific discoveries—that dream finally vanished for me before those trainloads of small children.[2]

So it is that halfway through Guillermo del Toro's *Pan's Labyrinth* (*El laberinto del fauno*, 2006), when fascist soldiers under the demonic Captain Vidal offer food to poor local farmers, that familiar discordant note sounds through the words of utopian promise. The soldiers, holding out barely enough bread to make one submarine sandwich, proclaim over and over, "This is our daily bread...." "Receive our daily bread"—the slogan serves as diabolical communion anthem of the story. In *Pan's Labyrinth*, the soil is watered with the blood of those who want different than what the benevolent state chooses to offer. The intractable ones must be executed quickly, if fortune is on their side. What else can be done after all with those who resist and are blind to the benefits when the great man holds up the banner of the enlightened dream guaranteed to make life better for all? Who is so selfish as to stand in the way of a new and better world? "I want my son to be born in a new, clean Spain," Vidal asserts to a group of table guests.

Plans to improve the lot of all by managing the life of all have bequeathed to the world not only genocide but the evil supermen of the new age. These madmen, like Captain Vidal in del Toro's film, have risen again and again from the ashes of previous debacles with new visions and new disciples. Their slogans continue to be spoken with the tone of prophecy; all the while the knives for sacrifice get sharpened. A century and a half ago, when Leo Tolstoy depicted Napoleon presiding over the ruins of Moscow in *War and Peace* ordering death to any peasant found holding a torch, the greatest of historical novelists himself played the prophet and not mere chronicler of events. Perhaps Tolstoy had come to understand why Lear began his calamitous descent with the words, "Give me the map there." Here is the prophesy—behold the great man cometh and his children shall follow, the re-shaper of history, Zarathustra's Übermensh, an incarnate, enlightened demon with a map and a plan. Here stands the man who loves the earth so much that he torches its orchards when they fail to grow fruit to his liking. No doubt Tolstoy would have been surprised, however, at the speed by which the technological advances of the twentieth century allowed these great men to carry out their schemes. Who in 1869 could have imagined the extent of evil perpetrated by Himmler and Stalin? Historians such as Christopher Lasch have since noted the further terrible truth that the Enlightenment myth of progress, which should by all measures have died with the world wars, did not. The great "dark cloud of Mordor" has only spread, as Tolkien suggested.

To allow the new generation to emerge, the case has been made that the old order of faith has needed to be pushed aside—a good deal of literature suggests as much. Robert Hugh Benson feared such consequences of totalitarianism on religious life already in 1907 when he published *Lord of the World*, a compelling novel that plays out an easy transition from the exaltation of "man" to the destruction of man of faith. Recent popes of the Catholic Church, like John Paul II and Benedict XVI, have likewise warned of what they saw as inevitability, and been earnest in their attempts to halt it. Still, one hardly need evoke papal concern to recognize at the very least the alignment between the collapse of the old faith in the West as the dominant cultural force and a cancerous rash in human history; however the sequence of events is explained. Evidence enough might be the stream of dystopian nightmares in literature and film written over the past two centuries. A black cry of anguish over things lost or soon to be taken flows through Orwell, Huxley, Lewis, Golding and Bradbury, into and through an even larger pool of films—deep and thoughtful reflections like Kubrick's *A Clockwork Orange* (1971), Tarkovsky's *The Sacrifice* (1986) and John Hillcoat's 2009 rendering of Cormac McCarthy's novel *The Road;* and, especially relevant here, the popular genre of horror film.

To play this out, the new men, ripped free of the binding moral code given to the once chosen men made in the divine image, live now to devour the old and replicate only themselves, creating in the words of E. Michael Jones "a society populated by machine-like, amoral men whose thoughts about higher things were chimera but whose pleasures were very real."[3] Yeats would envision this horror as the era of the rough beast waiting to be born. Many Christian communions still holding fast to the old tradition under assault saw and see it as the revelation of the rule of Antichrist, the one whom the apostles identified as the coming man of sin. His era might be said to be curiously well-chronicled through the metaphors of films like *Dracula*, *The Night of the Living Dead*, and *Pan's Labyrinth*.

Here, then, is the context that explains the choice of *Pan's Labyrinth* as lamp post for the present study. Del Toro's film doesn't feel like a traditional horror film after all. It doesn't always act like one either. Yet, as horror is most clearly defined as that genre which allows a form of the beast to insinuate itself into a narrative, *Pan's Labyrinth* perfectly describes the operation of horror. The *tell* is in this depiction of the beast: the vicious, calculating captain who plays the father but kills his own children, and who is eventually banished childless, exorcised and eradicated. He carries a watch when he first enters because he purports to be the shaper of time, a great craftsman of history. His goal is to die heroically and break the watch at that very moment, thus punctuating his destiny. And his evil intentions and actions mimic those of the biblical father of all evil—he will drag down with him all who stand in the way. His is a "mind not to be chang'd by Place or Time," in Milton's words; he will make a "Heav'n of Hell." He stands in place of all who have shaken a fist at the one father of time, and he carries the upside down banner of the prince of the un-beings who choose night over day, rebellious pride over simplicity. In the end, he is brought down by simplicity itself in the form of a young child.

Captain Vidal is the monster of *Pan's Labyrinth*, and especially terrifying because he wears a human face. Del Toro has indicated in interviews that he prefers horror films where the monsters are wholly visible[4] and few are as wholly visible as the fascist Captain Vidal. He does not transform shape at night. He has no "doll's eyes" that give away the dark secret of his essence. He is evil fully and credibly in the form of a man, and a man first introduced in the narrative in the context of a loving family but who is made in truth of the same essence as the Golem or Count Orlock or Hannibal Lecter or Michael Myers. He is the incarnate image of the dark lord himself. The promised father, he reveals his true self quickly by breathing pestilence and death; he cannot be stopped by human agency but only by the deeper magic of divine intervention.

A Christian Response to Horror Cinema

The monstrous Captain Vidal (Sergi López) in his lair, evil fully and credibly in the form of a man. *Pan's Labyrinth*. 2006. Warner Brothers.

Something has happened to Captain Vidal long before the narrative of the film begins, but, this something is barely hinted. Was it the abuse of a father who demanded a perfection that cannot come in so fallen a world? This suggestion comes only with a gesture as Vidal tremors slightly at the mention of his father during a dinner conversation. In another scene, he feigns slashing his own mirror image, as if attacking the thing that has made him what he has become. Whatever the cause, the captain has lost his soul and become the mechanical demon that brutally and repeatedly stabs a peasant farmer in the face and later mocks and tortures a disabled man. His motions in the acts of cruelty suggest so great an emotional distance from his victims that calling him a sadist might even be a misnomer. When his servant Mercedes slashes open the side of his mouth and he is forced to stitch closed his own wound, he does so with minimal hesitation, as if the monster is mending a costume. She has revealed more of the real beast by disfiguring the outward form.

Vidal's dark social control has established an ordered world where

2. Monster and Man

masculine strength alone has value. Thus, he represents a monstrous gross parody of Spanish *machismo*, all force and no compassion. One might be tempted to follow this toward a different political intention in *Pan's Labyrinth* which ties the dark *machismo* of the captain to the oppression of women in the village where the events take place. Some critics hostile toward Franco and Catholicism have read into the film a social subtext antithetical to the film's more overt intentions:

> Forty years of dictatorship did more than halt the process of women's emancipation; the imposition of a traditionalist National-Catholicism and ultra-reactionary social norms set the clock back dramatically for Spanish women. Francoism cannot be understood without taking into account the fact that until 1975, the date of Franco's death, a married woman in Spain could not open a bank account, buy a car, apply for a passport, or even work without her husband's permission. And if she did work with her husband's approval, he had the right to claim her salary.[5]

However, as tidy an analysis as this is, such a view of Franco and his regime works through the film only when the critic is predisposed to see Catholicism as a religion antagonistic to the plight of women, a disposition which might puzzle a great many Catholic Spaniards for its topsy-turvy rendering of social history, and which does not particularly fit the overall system of the film. *Pan's Labyrinth* will, in fact, assert something far more in keeping with Catholic orthodoxy before its conclusion.

A better understanding would be that del Toro's film stands as warning to all modern regimes enamored with their own sense of possibility; so naive that they might allow as ruler not the true servant leader promoted by religious and political ideal, but the Enlightenment usurper who comes at a time of cultural weakness promising a balanced order of new law and justice, but who provides only the demonic exaggeration of the virtues perceived to be lacking. The Spanish setting of the film is more mythopoeic than historical, and the themes must be interpreted according to the rules set by the film itself, not specific historical biases. The real political point in *Pan's Labyrinth* promotes an old moral with its source in a Judeo-Christian root. In the biblical account, the Jewish people, tired of their judges, cried out to Samuel for a king without consulting Yahweh, and they were then given as judgment the very king they secretly coveted, Saul, who would eventually be possessed by an evil spirit and would pursue and attempt to kill Israel's true king David once divine favor shone in that different direction.

Following this logic, *Pan's Labyrinth* actually invites a straightforward anti–Marxist reading, especially as Marxism in many aspects represents the antithesis of Catholic social teaching. Social injustice has been met by Marxist dictators with programs that promise social equality but which historically have tended to produce greater inequality and injustice, for the plans depend upon the benevolent enforcers to remain pure while given absolute power. The church has viewed this as Marx's naiveté, a "fundamental error" grounded in a misunderstanding of how thoroughly original sin has corrupted the nature of women and men. Using the words of Benedict XVI:

> Together with the victory of the revolution, though, Marx's fundamental error also became evident. He showed precisely how to overthrow the existing order, but he did not say how matters should proceed thereafter. He simply presumed that with the expropriation of the ruling class, with the fall of political power and the socialization of means of production, the new Jerusalem would be realized. Then, indeed, all contradictions would be resolved, man and the world would finally sort themselves out. Then everything would be able to proceed by itself along the right path, because everything would belong to everyone and all would desire the best for one another. Thus, having accomplished the revolution, Lenin must have realized that the writings of the master gave no indication as to how to proceed. True, Marx had spoken of the interim phase of the dictatorship of the proletariat as a necessity which in time would automatically become redundant. This "intermediate phase" we know all too well, and we also know how it then developed, not ushering in a perfect world, but leaving behind a trail of appalling destruction. Marx not only omitted to work out how this new world would be organized—which should, of course, have been unnecessary. His silence on this matter follows logically from his chosen approach. His error lay deeper. He forgot that man always remains man. He forgot man and he forgot man's freedom. He forgot that freedom always remains also freedom for evil. He thought that once the economy had been put right, everything would automatically be put right. His real error is materialism: man, in fact, is not merely the product of economic conditions, and it is not possible to redeem him purely from the outside by creating a favourable economic environment.[6]

Vidal's little dictatorship is hardly "a favourable economic environment," unless families can grow content with "the daily bread in Franco's Spain," and women can be content in lives of marginal servitude, and the masses

2. Monster and Man

can close both eyes to the persecutions and imprisonments and murders of their kinsmen.

Still, any political reading of *Pan's Labyrinth* simply introduces the larger theme and purpose of the work, for political tyranny of this sort masks a moral problem which demands and must receive a moral solution. The suppression of women in the film resolves in their ultimate triumph, not alone by the means of the revolutionaries in the woods who storm the captain's mountain base in the end, but in the blood sacrifice of Ofelia, the child princess and hero of the story. The two forces work in tandem. Resistance blessed by holiness overturns the evil in the world, as is the case in the biblical records and in the older rendering of Western history. The film stands as warning of what the new era of enlightened man has produced; yet it perfectly aligns with traditional, orthodox conceptions of how all such evil can and will be overcome.

Put more directly, the fact that the captain is overcome in the story by Ofelia recalls the equilibrium of the lost society that respected the role of the Virgin in divine and human history. Ofelia's purity and humility exorcise the beast of the captain's oppressive masculine totalitarianism. Male rule gets tempered by female wisdom and goodness. Childhood recovers its joy through submission and protection within the context of a redeemed family. The land is restored by virtue of the benevolence of king and queen working together. All of this is made possible through the power of an atonement, as Ofelia's blood sacrament drips upon the enlivened under-kingdom of her true fatherland perpetually. The image of Ofelia lying beside the well in the final scene gets superimposed over the entire film narrative, and thus it remains perpetually curative and noble. The ending reflects the paradoxical logic of the Virgin's struggle and triumph in the biblical record. The Beast pursues the Woman in the twelfth chapter of John's Revelation who flees to the wilderness:

> And when the dragon saw that he was cast unto the earth, he persecuted the woman which brought forth the man child. And to the woman were given two wings of a great eagle, that she might fly into the wilderness, into her place, where she is nourished for a time, and times, and half a time, from the face of the serpent.

So, John sees Christ pursued while in the lap of Mary and then his followers pursued through the end of the age. But the persecution ends with the crushing of the dragon's head once and for all by the seed of the woman in the fulfillment of the *protoevangelium* of Genesis 3: 15 with Christ himself coming on a white horse with the sword of judgment in his mouth.

Bringing the discussion back to the primary terms of the horror genre, opposite the monstrous captain in this fantasy is the child deliverer, Ofelia. Her name is of Greek origin and means "helper," although her literary lineage passes through Shakespeare's heroine who provided little help to her doomed lover. Del Toro's Ofelia is a Christ-like redeemer, a princess of an underworld kingdom given the task of reversing a terrible curse and setting free captives on earth. She proves herself worthy through three rigorous moral tests, and ultimately faces the embodiment of evil and overcomes. In the final confrontation, as with Christ, her heel is bruised, but she still prevails and delivers the captives.

Ofelia's three tests are administered by the Faun in the story, who functions as messenger of the true father and lost king. In the first, she

The heroic Ofelia (Ivana Baquero) glances back toward home before journeying into the underworld of the Pale Man. *Pan's Labyrinth*. 2006. Warner Brothers.

2. Monster and Man

must go down under a blighted tree to confront a monstrous toad who feeds parasitically on its roots. Ofelia is to feed the toad three stones and recover the key it has eaten. She cleverly succeeds, of course, but not before a gruesome exchange with the slimy thing. The monsters of the fantasy world entered by the heroine Ofelia reveal the true character of the captain, here in another form. He feeds off and upon the people of the community and blights all he touches, including Ofelia's mother who will be poisoned and killed before the end. In the second test, Ofelia meets the Pale Man who sleeps a monstrous sleep before a table of sumptuous but cursed food which no one dare eat. The Faun warns Ofelia to go into his chamber to recover a dagger, and not to give in to hunger and eat from that table, but in true fairy tale fashion she breaks the injunction. The Pale Man awakens, bites the heads off two fairies assisting the girl, and then chases her with similar depraved intentions. She escapes through another bit of magic, but having suffered loss of the fairies and the temporary goodwill of the Faun. The Pale Man, like the Toad, is Vidal, the Übermensh in another form. The connections are obvious—the food, the all-seeing eyes, the viciousness, the symmetry of his demonic world.

The larger theme which emerges clearly in this second test might be best described in a dictum—do not taste the Pale Man's food. The warning echoes the "Ethics of Elfland," as G. K. Chesterton labeled the strange logic of fairy stories. The food looks good, but don't eat it. The paradox seems arbitrary unless understood in the larger context of that older fairy order with roots in the fantastic elements of the Old Testament. The Jews were told to avoid mixing the unclean with the clean, be it blemished sacrifices with pure, or shell fish with trout. Then, when they entered the Promised Land, they were told to destroy the Canaanite tribes completely, to the point where their failure to carry out the commission speedily enough led to their judgment in the era of the Judges and their eventual fall from grace. Evil is to be destroyed or, at minimum, completely avoided. Taste not. Touch not the unclean thing. So with *Pan's Labyrinth*: both Mercedes and Ofelia's mother are cursed and blighted by eating from the captain's table. Mercedes will break free but at a hefty price; Ofelia's mother will not.

This makes the story sound like pure romantic fairy tale. Ofelia asks Mercedes if she believes in fairies. Mercedes explains that she has not believed since she was a little girl. Ofelia's mother likewise chastens the girl in the opening scene to turn from fairy tales, just as she herself has given them up. In fact, her decision to marry the captain, seemingly for security and companionship (she was "alone too long"), puts her at odds with Ofelia, who asks in a telling moment how she thought herself alone when "I'm with you." However, the story goes beyond romanticism as the film reveals more and more of what Ofelia does "see." How can the girl doubt fairies when one flies her to the labyrinth? And finally, how can she not believe when her sacrifices ending in her own blood redeem the kingdom of her true father?

The major idea at work in *Pan's Labyrinth* is not political, nor something out of J.M. Barrie, but biblical. As the savior Ofelia's blood drips into the well in the final scene, the father's voice from fairyland commands, "Arise, my daughter." Ofelia's first word as she walks toward her father the king is "Padre." She is then suddenly robed in splendor and restored to her place of honor, having completed her pilgrimage on earth by defeating the enemy through blood atonement.

It should be noted here that Ofelia's sacrifice also mends the gender conflict suggested earlier in the plot. She restores the lost balance. Like Carroll's Alice, Ofelia descends a rabbit hole into a world amenable to female leadership. She finds a respect from Faun and fairies that does not exist in the household of the captain, where her mother has been relegated to breeder status and the other strong woman, Mercedes, a slave. Vidal's tyrannical patriarchy will be replaced in the end by the true, compassionate and humble patriarchy of her real father, who places her beside her mother likewise on a throne.

With this understanding the injunction to taste not the captain's food has further resonance as part of Ofelia's moral testing. Like Percival, she must retain her purity in a grail quest and so present an emblem to the remnant of the lost kingdom, a hope for life beyond their earthly lives. The challenges given to her by the Faun speak to her virtue, not her innocence or inexperience. They are challenges that the characters around her cannot fulfill. Captain Vidal has fed the people around him his own communion bread in exchange for their souls. One by one, they have tasted and they have died.

The first two of Ofelia's three challenges require her to turn from

2. Monster and Man

worldly concerns. In the first, where she must feed the destructive toad the stones that will destroy it in order to recover a lost key, she must first must remove a dress given her by her mother, the dress she was to wear when presented before the captain, and so a dress suggesting her mother's own bargain with the devil. When Ofelia leaves it on a tree branch at the start of this challenge, it is blown off by the wind and soiled in the mud where it belongs. In the second challenge, Ofelia must use the key to open a chamber in the Pale Man's room and recover a dagger. To do this, she must again resist, though she has not eaten for many hours. Here, notably, she shows herself human, not divine, by succumbing to the temptation to eat one grape.

Then there is the third and final challenge. Ofelia must take the dagger and use it as the Faun directs. Certainly the dagger should find the breast of her false father, but when the Faun indicates she is to use it to sacrifice her baby brother, she refuses choosing her own death instead. The lust of the eyes in the first challenge with the dress, the desires of the flesh in the second, the pride of life in the third—overcoming these temptations proves Ofelia's worthiness to stand against a world held sway by the darkness. To recover herself and her kingdom, she must separate herself: "Love not the world, neither the things that are in the world. If any man love the world, the love of the Father is not in him. For all that is in the world, *the lust of the flesh, and the lust of the eyes, and the pride of life, is not of the Father, but is of the world.*"[7]

Like the divinely appointed hero she is, the noble Ofelia is found worthy to stand against the devil disguised as her father. Her blood sacrifice at the well breaks the evil spell. Captain Vidal will walk away from the well to his own judgment. Mercedes and her brother, leader of the rebel forces, confront and kill him in the presence of those he has banished. But first, Mercedes speaks him into oblivion. His son shall never know his name. The watch shall be stopped not to signal his heroism, but his destruction. The captain is then shot in the face, judged in the biblical fashion of an eye for an eye. He is exorcised, left without breath or legacy.

One symbol in the film particularly underscores this redemptive pattern: a mandrake root which the Faun gives to Ofelia earlier in the story to save her mother, appropriately named Carmen. Fed by Ofelia's own blood and soaked in milk, the childlike mandrake lives as scapegoat for the mother. The consequence of Carmen's transgressions, her horrible crime of sleeping with the devil captain, is imputed to the mandrake. It takes in those sins and so Carmen gets better. When the mandrake is found and tossed into a fireplace, the disease falls back on the woman and she begins again to die. She does not deserve the health brought by the mandrake, this gift from the fairy world accessed by the love of her daughter. It is grace, but when that grace is rejected, the curse falls again. The mandrake also foreshadows Ofelia's final sacrifice at the well which will break the curse on her true mother once and for all.

Still, other symbols abound in the narrative and reinforce the redemptive themes of Ofelia's quest—the labyrinth itself, a magical book, a doctor's glasses and vials, Vidal's timepiece. Each in its own way suggests that the dark prison created in the captain's world by his corrupted, selfish new order can only be overcome by the deeper magic bubbling from the underworld spring that Ofelia has come from and must return to.

This becomes most apparent in a scene which functions as narrative turning point, when Ofelia's mother reveals her complicity with the captain and urges Ofelia to give up fairy tales. The scene follows the brutal torture sequence with Vidal and a poor, stammering rebel soldier, and introduces the climactic trajectory of death that will conclude the narrative in the typical fashion of the horror genre.

The scene takes place in the shadowy perpetual darkness of Carmen's bedroom with her ornate bed prominent in the background, along with a strong fire in the hearth. Both the bed and the hearth suggest the corruptions of the traditional securities in this home, a parody of the home Ofelia is trying to recover as her real self, Princess Moanna of the fairy world. In the captain's realm, the bed stands as reminder of the complicity of Carmen in the perverse cruelty around her, and the fire suggests corrupted passions worthy of Hamlet's mother. This is the one scene, curiously, in the whole narrative where the captain seems to defer authority—to Carmen.

Ofelia has climbed under the bed to tend to the mandrake root keeping her mother alive when the captain finds her and pulls her out. Rather than doing the expected, striking Ofelia and tossing the mandrake into the fire, he defers to his wife, "Look at this! Look what she was hiding under your bed!" Ofelia's terror is imaged from above to suggest her pow-

2. Monster and Man

erlessness against the captain in the beginning of the exchange, and when Carmen steps into the shot, Ofelia is likewise overpowered visually by her presence. Carmen takes over from the captain and commands complicity of the girl as well, "Ofelia, you have to listen to your father." The captain steps away from the two and apparently submits to the wife in the situation. So, when Carmen throws the mandrake into the fire and pronounces that "magic does not exist" and that "the world is a cruel place," she does so with dark authority. The captain has no power over the child until Carmen bestows it, which she inadvertently does, for the destruction of the mandrake spells Carmen's own doom. Without the mandrake, she immediately goes into a painful labor that will kill her. After that, the captain has complete authority and will strike Ofelia in the face later when she is captured with Mercedes, and then shoot her at the well, but, again, only after Carmen's death.

This scene cuts to the captain returning to the tortured prisoner, whom the doctor has mercifully euthanized. Unlike Carmen, the doctor rejects the captain's authority in this sequence and so saves his soul. After explaining to the captain that he will not simply obey orders, the doctor walks away and is shot in the back. Yet before he falls, he removes his glasses, a suggestion that he has recovered his true sight and rejected evil through martyrdom.

The underscoring of free will is noteworthy. As with all horror, a moral choice has unleashed the monster, and those who fall must in some fashion agree to the terms of the beast. Only the pure survive. Thus, a great villain in the morality play of *Pan's Labyrinth* is Carmen, Ofelia's mother. The captain is the monster, but Carmen is the Pandora who has opened the box. Like Claire in *What Lies Beneath*, she has sold her own child to the devil in exchange for material security. However, unlike the daughter in *What Lies Beneath*, who seems comfortable with the corrupt world of the college dorm, Ofelia's heart is "hidden with Christ in God," to use another Pauline phrase. She has come to relish her calling as Princess Moanna. She smiles in pleasure at the moon-shaped mark on her shoulder the Faun indicates to be a sign of her high calling. She removes the dress that will make her suitable for the captain's table. She chooses the magic of the Faun's book and follows it's tracing of history. She chooses death over betrayal of her brother.

A Christian Response to Horror Cinema

In this latter detail, Mercedes functions as foil for the girl. Although she, like Carmen, claims that she has put aside the fairy stories of her youth, she resists the captain's advances and stays loyal to her rebel leader brother, significantly named "Pedro," which suggests both St. Peter and the Spanish word for "Father," the word Ofelia speaks once risen, "Padre." Mercedes stands beside Pedro, her brother, when the captain is finally executed. She pronounces the judgment, that the baby will never know his father's name.

Mercedes, in addition, hums the mystical melody that interlaces the film, suggesting the spiritual realm of the under-kingdom. At the well, Mercedes holds Ofelia's body and hums the one lullaby she has earlier claimed to know, the Javier Navarrette melody that begins and ends the film. *Pan's Labyrinth* opens with a blank screen and with Navarette's haunting music. The plot runs in reverse as the first image is of Ofelia dying beside the well. A voice-over tells the legend of the exiled princess seeking the portal to return her to her father and homeland. So, in a sense, the film ends at the cross, then winds back to the journey leading there, and then passes back to and through the crucifixion to the empty tomb and ascension. Mercedes functions like the women in waiting, who weep that "they have taken him away." This is in keeping with the complex intertextual lacing of music in and around the narratives of the horror genre.[8] Alan Silvestri's soundtrack for *What Lies Beneath*, for example, sets the mood before any images appear in the water during the opening sequence. As also occurs with explicitly redemptive or sacramental films and musicals, music marks the formal shift in narrative mode that accompanies the entrance of God or, in this case, the Devil. Eerie music channels the evil presence into the dark sacramentalism of the horror narrative just as violins played in a minor key suggested, for example, that the Holy Spirit had moved through the camp to heal Ben-Hur's mother and sister of leprosy in that classic.

The mythopoeic world embraced through Ofelia's imagination and purity in *Pan's Labyrinth* is a world of healing and blessing. In the under-kingdom restored in the film's conclusion, righteousness flows like a river from the throne. The Princess Moanna rules "with justice and a kind heart," and her people love her. She has left behind traces of her time on Earth for those who have eyes to see. These final words are spoken over

2. Monster and Man

the image of a flower opening and a winged creature, the fairy from the initial sequence, landing upon a broken tree branch. The allusions to holiness and fidelity and the long narrative tradition of Christian romance are obvious. Ofelia's quest for purity concludes with all creation recognizing her worthiness. Her example has left the pattern for the pilgrims who follow the same quest of faith and holiness.

Thus, in *Pan's Labyrinth* the servant of heaven triumphs over the demon prince who holds earth captive for a time and times. The monster is man, and the hero is a child from another world. The horror of Antichrist is resolved then as prophesied in the final biblical struggle, with the reign of the redeemer in a bright new morning of righteousness and peace.

3

MODERN PARALYSIS AND ANCIENT FAITH
Carl Dreyer's *Vampyr*

> *And when the servant of the man of God was risen early, and gone forth, behold, an host compassed the city both with horses and chariots. And his servant said unto him, "Alas, my master! how shall we do?" And he answered, "Fear not: for they that be with us are more than they that be with them. "And Elisha prayed, and said, "LORD, I pray thee, open his eyes, that he may see." And the LORD opened the eyes of the young man; and he saw: and, behold, the mountain was full of horses and chariots of fire round about Elisha.*—2 Kings 6: 15–17

In the vivid conclusion to his famous 1941 sermon "The Weight of Glory," C.S. Lewis contended that "there are no *ordinary* people," and that we have "never talked to a mere mortal." Rather, "it is immortals whom we joke with, marry, snub, and exploit—immortal horrors or everlasting splendours."[1] And so must go the conclusion to any discussion of the presence of the demonic that takes as its base a theology not only of incarnation, but also one that affirms both redemption and damnation. The church has taught for centuries that men and women enter life, whether they accept it or not, as pilgrims with only one of two ultimate destinations, heaven or hell. Even the medieval doctrine of purgatory still embraced by the Roman communion adds only a footnote to that assertion, for those souls climbing over and around the ledges and cornices of Mt. Purgatory—blinded, prodded, and provoked though they be—have a fixed final destination once they ascend through the Earthly paradise purged of their inclinations toward sin. These pilgrims, too, post–Earth all attain heaven. So, viewed through any theological lens crafted by the guild that says God did become flesh to save creatures of flesh (be it those branches Catholic

3. Modern Paralysis and Ancient Faith

or Calvinist, Eastern or Western) souls enter this world with one of two dramatic destinies. There are no *ordinary* people.

Furthermore, both dogma and tradition have asserted that all of the extraordinary people who travel this pilgrimage are alternately encouraged or haunted by voices from one or the other place. Angels and demons stop pilgrims along the way in some guise with the intention of expanding their terrain, and the real proselytizers rarely hand out leaflets.

The question for the moment in this treatment of the horror genre is what keeps this unseen world of spirits separate from the world of extraordinary women and men, since the genre is defined by just this intermingling of worlds. How is it that they play so easily on some and not others, especially since the eternal stakes for all are so high? Is there an unseen curtain that moves mysteriously by some wind? Are there secret doors like those in George Nolfi's *The Adjustment Bureau* (2011), which open back and forth between the disparate realities once the right hand touches the knob? If so, what formulation makes the curtains move or the doors open?

The answer to these questions regards the violation of a spiritual or moral taboo, at least in the alchemy of the horror genre. Horror, like no other film genre, probes the metaphysics of spirit and body and poses answers to the secret questions. The best of these films explore what it means to be lost creatures questing for some means of redemption. In some, the quest reveals the collective dread of an entire culture or cultural group accelerating beyond control down a moral highway in the dark. In others, individual artists describe the terms of the quest according to very specific theological assumptions and drive the troika with a measure of disciplined control. A case in point to illustrate this more controlled type of horror journey would be Carl Dreyer's masterpiece *Vampyr* (1932).

For many years, available prints of Dreyer's film were faded, rendering critical readings difficult, especially as Dreyer preferred compositions that flattened the iconography and enshrouded his characters in darkness or light, a technique refined in his earlier masterpiece, *La Passion de Jeanne D'Arc* (1927). That technique applied to a film like *Vampyr*, which depends on far fewer close-ups than *Jeanne* and which uses techniques of superimposition and shadow projection, demands a clear print. Key moments in the plot of *Vampyr*, like the hero David Gray's dream sequence or the burying of the evil doctor in an avalanche of flour, lost so much clarity in many available prints up to and through the 1990s that simple narrative questions regarding cause and effect were often obscured. It might be safe to say that given this viewing challenge, especially in an era when art films were less accessible than now, many academic critics looked for an answer key. They found it in David Bordwell's meticulously detailed, neoformalist analysis of the shot sequences of the Dreyer film.[2] However, for ideological reasons unrelated to the crispness of the visual images in a celluloid print, Bordwell concluded his analysis with the assertion that issues of causality in *Vampyr* are intentionally unresolved and that the film only suggests the possibility of an interpretation *inclined* toward "Freudian or Christian allegory."[3] Since most viewers found the film simply difficult to watch, this conclusion satisfied. And so scholars have followed the herd and mistakenly tended to assume of the film a general "indeterminacy of meaning."[4] However, without intending to be contrary for its own sake, and despite *Vampyr*'s reputation as a difficult film and given that Dreyer does only offer minimal plot details, I think that once past the problem of viewing difficult visual images in a less than ideal viewing environment, *Vampyr*, albeit slow-moving, is remarkably straightforward in its plot and overall message. The accessibility of better prints of Dreyer's masterpiece, which now permit clear and multiple viewings, should *incline* even the most casual modern viewer to follow the story as a simple tale of possession and redemption structured around traditional theological understandings of those concepts. Plot questions like who fires the rifle to kill this specific character may not be directly answered, but neither are they in films praised for their narrative clarity (like *The Godfather*, for example).

The source material for *Vampyr* is Sheridan Le Fanu's neurotic vampire novella *Carmilla* (1872). In Le Fanu's story, Laura, a young virgin longing for companionship in a remote Austrian village, finds it in a lovely female vampress; the terrible fact is of course hidden from her. Carmilla, the vampress, takes on a catlike form at night, enters Laura's bedroom, and bites her repeatedly, thus beginning in her a transformation toward the dark and morbid:

> For some nights I slept profoundly; but still every morning I felt the same lassitude, and a languor weighed upon me all day. I felt myself a

3. Modern Paralysis and Ancient Faith

changed girl. A strange melancholy was stealing over me, a melancholy that I would not have interrupted. Dim thoughts of death began to open, and an idea that I was slowly sinking took gentle, and, somehow, not unwelcome, possession of me. If it was sad, the tone of mind which this induced was also sweet. Whatever it might be, my soul acquiesced in it.[5]

A series of providential circumstances reveal to the girl and her father that Carmilla, the seeming friend, is instead the evil form of the undead Countess Mircalla Karnsteins. At that revelation, the historical (and sexual) threads of the tale are brought together to Le Fanu's climax. Mircalla's tomb is found and opened, revealing "features, though a hundred and fifty years had passed since her funeral ... tinted with the warmth of life." Not only so, but "the leaden coffin floated with blood, in which to a depth of seven inches, the body lay immersed." Proof of vampirism thus evident, "the body, therefore, in accordance with the ancient practice, was raised, and a sharp stake driven through the heart of the vampire, who uttered a piercing shriek.... Then the head was struck off, and a torrent of blood flowed from the severed neck."[6]

Such macabre sensationalism might even be shocking to modern readers accustomed to the contemporary horror genre, and more so to those who may only know the story through the Dreyer film, which is austere even in its creepiest moments. Still, Dreyer was obviously drawn to the material for a reason—it being his first creative choice once given an opportunity with the large production company Tobis-Klangfilm. In interviews, he maintained that *Vampyr* represented a marked and somewhat needed change in direction from *Jeanne*. Given that, it is still more than reasonable to assert that Dreyer had not lost interest in the subject of ordinary people encountering the ineffable when he took up the Le Fanu material. And indeed, once the reader gets past the not-so-subtle hints of lesbianism and the lurid depiction of the bloody coffin, the story of *Carmilla* is perhaps only remarkable for the innocent point of view that the protagonist maintains throughout her ordeal. Laura's posture of guilelessness must have especially attracted the director's attention after he spent five years immersed in the story of St. Joan. He otherwise only took from the story the most basic details: the female vampress, the setting in a remote country town, a bitten girl sliding down toward black despair, and the ritual surrounding demonic possession and exorcism.

And, of course, Dreyer brought to *Carmilla* an entirely different aesthetic sensibility, a dreamlike exploration of *what is seen* versus *what is*. And he substituted a more active protagonist for the haunted girl—David Gray, the appointed protector and hero. Gray ultimately saves the Laura character, who gets split into two roles in *Vampyr*: the possessed girl fighting the vampiric possession nudging her toward suicide, and the noble sister who watches over the victim and is eventually herself rescued and spirited away.

This change of protagonist allowed Dreyer a better point of identification for the viewer, an objective character who observes firsthand the evil and participates in the destruction of it. Until the final sequence, most of the plot unfolds strictly through Gray's eyes as the viewer follows him in his transformation from frightened visitor to vampire slayer. This narrative trajectory serves to convert the Le Fanu material from Gothic thriller to psycho-religious drama designed apparently to nudge skeptics toward a reexamination of the older theological metaphysic assumed by the vampire tradition. As followed through Gray's point of view, the story of *Vampyr* actually bears some resemblance to Dreyer's 1954 apologetic to the power of faith, *Ordet*. Both employ unique camera devices that suggest metaphorically the dimensions beyond what is immediately seen, and both encourage intimate identification with characters drawn through a sequence of mysterious events toward a life-altering revelation of the miraculous.

Before proceeding further with this analysis of the context of *Vampyr*, one crucial assumption needs to be more directly addressed: namely, that the vampire genre is rooted in a theology of blood redemption, and so infused with ancient religious symbolism. With *Vampyr*, Dreyer is restoring the genre to its proper theological base, moving it away from the Gothic sensationalism that has ultimately driven its course toward the massive blood-lettings of late genre films like *Blade* (1998) or the adolescent sentimentalism of the more recent *Twilight* (2008–2012) series.

Note first that Le Fanu's *Carmilla*, which although certainly written to titillate, still draws upon the older theological assumptions in its conclusion. *Carmilla* is at its core a story of possession and exorcism, wherein the demonic presence is finally overcome through agents of faith who

3. Modern Paralysis and Ancient Faith

rely on spiritual means, "the ancient practice," to overcome and destroy the evil. One might even ascribe a certain measure of moral discretion to the rather clinical depiction of the "exorcism" offered by Le Fanu in the climactic scene. In a recent study, Susannah Clements argued a similar point regarding the orthodox, theological assumptions in Bram Stoker's archetypal 1897 novel *Dracula*, the most influential single work in the genre:

> It is by Christ's blood that the Christian is saved. And, in *Dracula*, the unnatural drinking of blood in an inversion of Holy Communion is a means of human damnation. When Lucy suffers physically from the loss of blood, Van Helsing knows that she needs a transfusion of blood to keep her alive. But this doesn't, of course, get to the root of the problem—a spiritual one, not a physical one—so the medical treatment only works temporarily. A religious ceremony is necessary. Spiritual warfare is the only way to save in the face of a spiritual threat.[7]

Although the form of the vampire genre transformed rapidly in the early twentieth century, as filmmakers discovered the voyeuristic possibilities of film technology, the origins of the genre emerged from deeper waters. The basic narrative elements of Stoker's classic must actually be traced back even further than Le Fanu to John Polidari's "The Vampyre," that other story which emerged from the celebrated literary game played by the Shelley circle staying at the Villa Diodati near Lake Geneva in 1816. The more famous outcome of that most famous gathering was, of course, Mary Shelley's *Frankenstein*, written by the pregnant nineteen-year-old paramour of Percy Shelley. But Polidari, the personal physician of poet and womanizing houseguest Byron, seemed to have understood on some level what the young mistress understood—specifically, the devilish effects the new Enlightenment philosophy would produce, particularly through the unholy means of libidinal men reading William Godwin and thinking their lawless expressions of personal indulgence to be evidence of high-mindedness. Both "The Vampyre" and *Frankenstein* offer a veiled prophesy about the evil conjured and let loose upon the world's stage through such self-aggrandizement. Despite the formal, personal allegiances of Polidari and Shelley, and their complicity in dabbling with the intersection of the new science and older occult practices, both grounded their moral fictions in the soil of folk myth from the Balkans that warned of a plague of demonic activity that would fall on those who stood unprotected by the blood of Christ and who foolishly challenged natural law. In short, the branches of the Gothic tradition that their stories birthed were dipped in orthodox, moral guilt over real transgression. The vampire tradition, traced through Polidari and Le Fanu and Stoker and Dreyer to its contemporary popularized forms, is formally haunted by characters exercising full, fig-leaf denial of the obvious—that human sin of a certain kind and degree has cracked open the portals of hell. The demons unleashed will have their way for a while since their victims are marked by moral slothfulness and the secondary characters by repressed complicity. Yet, though the demons remain focused and diabolically potent throughout and the mortals rather ineffectual, a merciful providence will ultimately find a hero bold enough to assert the power of God through the means of the crucifix and stake.

Whether through study or intuition, Dreyer seemed to understand the connection between the archetypes of the vampire genre and the new science that birthed them. This seems evident in the special place afforded to the "doctor" in *Vampyr*, an evil supporting character who has made a pact with the vampress Marguerite Chopin and who gives her access to the house in the country and the bed of her female victim. When the doctor is buried in flour in a climactic scene, we are reminded that the new science which has attempted to replace the old mysterious faith has no power to overcome evil, and will be ultimately judged and choked by it. Like a blank character in a medieval morality play, the doctor functions purely to spread the moral and spiritual pestilence by encouraging denial and repression. It is ironic that in the syntax of the horror genre, science encourages repression, while the old faith produces freedom.

The appointed champion of Dreyer's *Vampyr*, one cut more from Hamlet's cloth than Lancelot's, is David Gray. Dreyer's personality and career led him to envision himself in the character of Johannes in *Ordet*, holy yet driven somewhat mad from too much Kierkegaard, and he must have found a sympathetic figure in the character of David Gray, an ambivalent, timid traveler called by providence to rescue a pair of virgins and pious old people and revenge the murder of a poor father. Dreyer's films all tend to feature innocent women who need to be rescued, but few traditional champions. The addition of this David Gray character is essential to *Vampyr*. Unlike the original Le Fanu story, which places the spiritual

3. Modern Paralysis and Ancient Faith

conflict in the geographical and historical distance through an epistolary form, the character of David Gray provides the viewer a set of eyes through which to experience the forces of darkness and light more immediately. And Dreyer, ever the truth seeker, must have preferred this hesitant, modern hero.

Again, however, the plot of *Vampyr* is clear only when the religious context of the vampire genre is fully understood and accepted. The vampire story echoes the redemptive narrative of the Christian tradition—Christus Victor again, the devil has been unleashed and now the hero must step to battle as divine warrior using the simple means afforded by providence to overcome the terrible enemy and rescue the helpless and pure. The vampire is demonic, allowed entrance to the world for a time to punish the transgressors of divine and natural law, its punishment being in the form of possession and damnation. Identification with the character of David Gray pulls the viewer into a greater level of personal engagement with the metaphysical struggle, both in its presentation of damnation as a real possibility and its resolution in the salvation offered through the "ancient practice."

The opening title begins: "There exist certain predestined beings whose very lives seem bound by invisible threads to the supernatural world." Again, this might have been the opening to *La Passion de Jeanne D'Arc* or a description of Johannes in *Ordet*. In *Vampyr*, the introduction provides an immediate context for David Gray's character as spiritual quester. Gray has come, "lured as usual by fantasy toward the unknown," the cryptic title reads, to the remote village of Courtempierre, where evil is at play.

He arrives at night and obtains a room in an inn that exudes the supernatural. Outside an unidentified man walks past ominously with a sickle. Inside, curious shadows and odd portraits lead Gray to lock carefully his bedroom door. The setup is familiar in the horror genre. Also familiar is the narrative insistence that the odd occurrences of Courtempierre be seen exclusively from Gray's point of view. The hero of the story is as frightened of the unknown source of power as the viewer; when the key in his bedroom door turns slowly and the door opens, he is powerless to do anything beyond cower amidst the sheets and await his fate, somewhat reminiscent of the reaction of Jonathan Harker watching the shadow of Nosferatu enter his room in the famous Murnau film.

A Christian Response to Horror Cinema

What comes through the door is not some being from the other world, however, but instead a poor man in torment: the mortified father of two girls preyed upon in their chateau by the vampress. He appeals to Gray for help and leaves him a package to be opened should he suddenly die. This bizarre visitation inclines Gray to explore the surrounding area. What he finds is an old mill haunted by dancing shadows and presided over by the evil old woman and her accomplices, the doctor and a peg-legged soldier. Gray manages to escape this haunted mill but not before seeing the doctor and having the doctor see him. This meeting, although of no immediate consequence beyond reinforcing the mood of strangeness in the land, becomes important later when Gray fails to act on his intuition and prevent the doctor from his later evil mission when he is called to the chateau to help the bitten girl.

Gray finds the chateau but is not in time to prevent the murder of the father, committed presumably by the peg-legged soldier who fires a rifle through one of the windows in the place. An old servant opens the door for Gray and they tend to the father as he dies. This leaves defenseless the two daughters, Leone and Giselle. Leone is bedridden, tended by an

Death rings a warning as David Gray arrives in Courtempierre in this abstract composition from Carl Dreyer's long-misunderstood masterpiece *Vampyr*. 1932. Dreyer-Tobis-Klangfilm.

3. Modern Paralysis and Ancient Faith

old nun, convinced she will be damned. Giselle is the very definition of the maiden incapable of saving herself and so is drawn to Gray for help, although he suffers from the same malady. His immediate response is to open the package the father has given him, in which is a book about vampires.

While Gray reads of the unearthly events that have tormented the land, the doctor arrives. Giselle alerts him that it is strange the doctor only comes at night, but despite the caution and the words of the book and his previous viewing of the doctor's presence at the strange Walpurgis Night he witnessed at the mill, Gray allows the doctor to tend to the father and Leone. The doctor has been commissioned by the vampress to give Leone poison with which she can commit suicide, thus damning her soul. When Gray pieces together the rather obvious clues that something is ter-

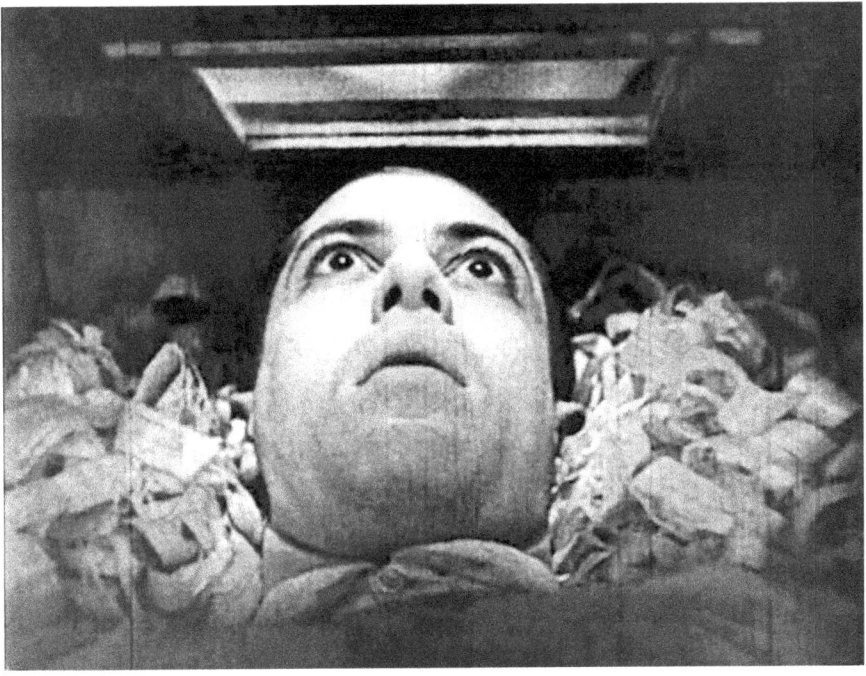

Weakened by blood loss, Gray (Julian West) longs for "death and damnation," envisioning himself looking out a coffin in the dream sequence. *Vampyr.* 1932. Dreyer-Tobis-Klangfilm.

ribly wrong in the area and the chateau, he confronts the doctor, but when he is told that Leone needs blood, he quickly agrees to a transfusion, something that anyone even remotely familiar with the vampire genre will recognize as a bad idea. In acquiescing, Gray renders himself unable to intercede while the doctor and vampress attempt to convince Leone to take her own life. Instead, he sleeps in a chair and dreams of the evil woman and death. This circumstance and what follows in his subsequent dream suggests that offering his blood for the doctor's use has begun the process wherein he has been tagged as the next victim, the process beginning with the longing for death and damnation.

Narrative providence intervenes in the form of the old house servant who has picked up the book of vampires and begun to read it himself. Unlike Gray, who seems only able to brood over the evil, the servant quickly determines a course of action. He awakens Gray and they go to Leone, who is about to drink the poison. They save her and leave her in the hands of the nun and then go after the doctor who has escaped with Giselle. Gray stumbles across the grounds in search of the girl, but weakened from blood loss he collapses on a stone bench. While asleep, he dreams that his spirit leaves his body, which perhaps it does, and he then continues on as spirit to the mill. There, he finds the villains preparing a coffin, inside which his own body lies. The point of view in the dream shifts, and Gray becomes the body looking up and out of the coffin. The coffin has a window through which he can watch the thing nailed shut and carried out past the church to the burial place.

Again, the old house servant intervenes, waking the corporeal Gray from where he sleeps on the bench and leading him to Marguerite Chopin's coffin in the church graveyard. They remove the stone and drive a stake through her heart, and her body turns to bones. Gray then returns to rescue Giselle who is tied up back at the mill. After this, he takes her away from the place, first leaving by boat and then walking with her into the morning light of a forest clearing hand in hand. Meanwhile, the old servant goes back to the mill. The peg-legged soldier haunted by the face of the dead vampress falls to his death trying to escape. The doctor runs into the heart of the mill and is closed in as the servant, presumably, turns on the machinery burying him alive in an avalanche of ground grain. Exorcism complete.

3. Modern Paralysis and Ancient Faith

The main curiosity in the film is in the enigmatic character of David Gray. Although identified as an agent of providence with sensitivity to the supernatural, he comes across as completely impotent in his role of knight, thus the earlier reference to him as more Hamlet than Lancelot; one might almost imagine Gray decrying the "cursed spite" that he was born to set right this haunted village of Courtempierre. That Dreyer was Danish makes this connection more than whimsical and speculative, and all the more so as Dreyer would later be asked to write the script for the short film *Shakespeare at Kronborg* (1950). More is expected of David Gray than he is able to accomplish; however, as *Vampyr* must end up as comedy not tragedy, Gray is allowed to walk off to a marriage with Giselle "hand in hand," like Bassanio and Portia in another Shakespeare play.

The real hero in the story of *Vampyr* is the old servant who knows to have the nun pray by the bedside of the afflicted Leone and who believes and acts immediately upon the words in the book. Unlike the father and Gray, he will not hesitate to drive a stake through the heart of Marguerite Chopin at the earliest opportunity. Thus, for Dreyer, the old peasantry with a simple faith rouses the new modern gentry plagued by spiritual paralysis unable to discern what is real and not, having read too much Kierkegaard and other post–Kantean philosophers.

That would be the message of *Vampyr*; yet, indeed, it is Gray's hesitation that Dreyer leaves the viewer to consider. We are, after all, introduced to the old servant and nun relatively late in the story and not given any significant context for them beyond their type. We are, on the other hand, urged to identify with Gray from the first title through the early sequences where the action is principally known through what he sees. Gray is the subject, the modern skeptic called to action in a world still haunted by demons but having lost the capacity to simply act. What he sees should be enough to get him roused to action in the chateau, but instead he chooses to be made victim, giving his arm freely to the dubious doctor and allowing his own blood to be corrupted by the vampire—thus causing his own morbid dreams. He is emasculated as hero, potent only in curiosity, hardly a knight at arms. He becomes by virtue of this impotence the complicit secondary servant to the doctor, the man of science, himself a lackey of the (very masculine) old woman vampress. Dreyer creates a challenging mirror game with character doubling throughout the story, both through plotting and through visual tricks, yet his bottom point remains clear: the modern world needs what the old world seemed to have—women and men with the capacity for faith and action. Modern knights may be curious and willing to explore the intersection of the natural and supernatural, but inquiry is all that they can finally manage. No conclusions are drawn with certainty and so no decisive action—Hamlet again.

Unfortunately, independent of what Gray can and cannot perform, and by extension what the modern "hollow" man paralyzed "between the emotion and the response" can and cannot believe enough to do, there still operate the potent forces of the demonic realm. Here will be, in fact, a prominent subtext of horror films from the 1960s on. Satan does not wait until the fight is fairer and the hero has recovered his weapon. The old woman is a vampress. The doctor has sold his soul to help her. Leone has been bitten and is becoming a vampress herself. Gray and Giselle are marked as next targets. The father is murdered. Something must be done.

Which brings up yet another curiosity embedded in the plot of the film. Why does the father not kill the vampress himself rather than handing the book off to David Gray with cryptic instructions to read it after his death? Or, given the *Hamlet* subtext, why doesn't the father go directly to the old servant for help, or to someone with more knowledge of the area and more resolve than the visiting stranger? The only reasonable response to these questions is to acknowledge the father as incapable of belief and action as is the protagonist. He, too, has gone to sleep spiritually and so goes to Gray as mirror of his own weakness. He cannot even find the energy to believe when his own daughters are in peril, which opens a further question about the absence of the matron of the house. What became of her? Did she fall victim in the past? Was the husband presiding over that death, too? The father's inaction makes a deep spiritual statement about how the curse of modern skepticism visits itself upon families, infecting whole generations and cultures. Dreyer would come back to this subject in *Ordet*, as the men of the Borgen home in that film cannot believe in the old miracles until shown one through the faith of the mad Johannes and a small child. Until that miracle occurs and pulls the men into the world of belief, the story follows a dark trajectory that would undoubtedly end poorly for the younger generations. As in *Vampyr*, the

3. Modern Paralysis and Ancient Faith

instinct of the skeptical males in the Borgen household in *Ordet*, including the new parson, is to seek help from those who suffer the same malady.

The visual cue used throughout *Vampyr* to suggest Dreyer's statement of the dilemma of the modern skeptic is the doorway. Most critics readily note that Gray is forever gazing at something in the film, from the curious weather vane over the inn to the man with the sickle to the shadow demons on the walls of the mill to the faces gazing back at him outside his dream coffin. By the end, this motif is put to rest when Gray and Giselle steal off, and we are offered the *Paradise Lost* departure of the couple guided by benevolent providence through the morning forest light. Gray's "look" and "looking" guides the narrative prior to that. But the doorway stands as an even more significant symbol of the film's larger theme. The doorway is what suggests the intersection of the two realities; it is in passing through literal and metaphoric doorways that final resolution is achieved.

The images of damnation and salvation juxtaposed in the film's climactic sequence illustrate the point. The vampress, who herself sleeps imprisoned in a coffin awaiting final judgment, attempts to trap her victims in similar encasement—rendering Leone bedridden and eager for the tomb, killing the father, arranging that Giselle be awkwardly bound, and sealing the dream spirit of Gray in a coffin. When judgment finally comes upon the doctor, he is entombed with flour. Salvation means motion. Leone must keep awake and fighting. Giselle must be unbound to walk away. Gray must awake and strike some blows on the stake penetrating the vampress' heart. To look at action through a window or hear it on the other side of a door, to acknowledge it as present but not rise to meet it, is not salvific. One must do something and pass into action, lest the rest indeed become silence.

So, in nearly every shot in the film, a character is placed prominently beside a passageway. The very first title alerts us that David Gray in one of his "aimless journeys" arrives at the village of Courtempierre in the late afternoon. A cut from him walking goes to the weather vane telling of the mysteries of the place and then back to Gray seen through the glass panel of the inn door. This sets the motif, especially since Gray finds that door locked and must step back and simply look at the outside of the place. The same pattern occurs once he is finally in his bedroom. The door becomes the primary object of inquiry, as he locks it to keep out whatever might be inside. Then, when he searches out the mill, the sequence begins with him at an open doorway. The pattern follows throughout, resolving for Gray when he wakes from his dream and opens his own coffin door and escapes with the peasant to open Marguerite Chopin's coffin door and kill her. The passageways suggest action between the two realms, the material and the spiritual. It is not enough to acknowledge or listen in to the voices of the other side; one must pass through in some fashion and engage them. The negative characters from that other world—here the peg-legged soldier, the doctor, and the vampress—do so without hesitation. Likewise the old peasant, but not Gray, and not the viewer, assuming Dreyer's intention is to address modern skeptics directly through all this.

Thomas Fleming has written that the problem with atheism is that atheists "have no religion to practice.... *Religion* is a precise word. It does not mean faith or belief so much as prescribed forms of behavior that we use to determine the will of god or gods and to act according to his or their will."[8] Skeptical characters can look through the glass and think they see or hear things on the other side. But they still cannot identify some specific thing and say it is such and needs a certain rendering. Gray is a philosophically and visually provocative character when just looking into other realities, but *Vampyr* is a provocative film because Gray is finally forced through the doorway with the viewer alongside. The film draws very traditional conclusions. It warns skeptical viewers to beware of demons and to guard their souls. It also says that the means to conquer the enemy of human souls is through the doctrines of the church and through her "ancient practices."

Carrying all of this back and then through the grid laid out in the opening chapter, it may be a useful exercise to examine *Vampyr* through means of the questions that drive the horror genre. What is the monster? What is its name? What is the chaos unleashed? What broken taboo led to this? How is the exorcism performed?

The answers come easily in this case. The monster of this metaphor is the corruption of blood, the incarnate shape of a moral contagion that spreads through intimacy and renders the victims morbid and ineffectual. It is the sickness of the soul that comes through sexual libertarianism and the consequent spread of that sickness through all the relationships

3. Modern Paralysis and Ancient Faith

affected—spouse, children, servants, subjects. It debases as it corrupts what is most sacred in all relationships—singularity, fidelity, purity, trust, discretion, grace. And after the debasement and eradication of virtue, doubt and paralysis are left.

The name of this beast is discordant sexual pleasure or lust, one of the seven deadly sins which Aquinas in the *Summa* (II.2. 153) identified as "a special kind of deformity whereby the venereal act is rendered unbecoming." The vampire genre, especially as evidenced in its more sensationalized renderings, depends on suggestions of "unbecoming" carnal relations.[9] Le Fanu's *Carmilla* floats on this tension as certainly as this vampire floats within a bloody coffin. Dreyer, although muting the display to serve his more philosophical intentions, still makes evident the nature, or un-nature, of the contagion. He does so in both a negative and positive way by splitting the character of Laura into the two sisters. The corrupted Leone looks with carnal hunger at her sister while in bed. Later, when Giselle is abducted, she is tied in a fashion suggesting sadomasochism. Leone's release will be back in peaceful sleep and restored maidenhood. When Giselle is set free, it will be to join David Gray in a traditional heterosexual union that one expects will head toward matrimony.

The chaos unleashed by the corrupted sexuality of vampirism is specifically here the destruction of family authority and male potency. The men in *Vampyr*, with the exception of the old peasant, are ineffectual lackeys to the corrupted women. This is true of the father and David Gray as certainly as it is the doctor and peg-legged soldier who dote on Marguerite Chopin. For the women to exercise this authority, however, they must be divested not only of virginity, but of what were once termed the ordinary female virtues of modesty and domesticity. Chopin is presented as sexless and passionless and altogether cruel. Leone and Giselle are marked for the same fate. Within the "home" of the demonic mill, shadows of men haunt the wall.

The taboo that has been broken in this rendition could be seen as the sin of lust, but that lower-level sin would not bring about so dramatic a shifting of the grounds of earth and hell, so something more must be involved. For lust to have so profound an effect, it must be wrapped in a certain idea, and that idea must be embraced by more than isolated individuals. Aquinas used the word "unbecoming" for a reason to describe

A Christian Response to Horror Cinema

The vampress Marguerite Chopin (Henriette Gérard), the antithesis of "modesty and domesticity," looks in upon the helpless David Gray. *Vampyr.* 1932. Dreyer-Tobis-Klangfilm.

carnal sins. Sexuality is to be an act "becoming"; that is, it is to be an act that produces life, which builds families and strengthens larger social orders. To separate the sexual act from its function in the creation of life and family and society is to make it an "unbecoming" act. So, one could argue that underneath the vampire genre, both in its birthing in nineteenth-century enlightenment rationalism and in all of its more modern permutations, glows the ember of a hidden cultural guilt over the wholesale promotion of a sin against the very order of human society. The initial command that the man and woman become one and leave mother and father to build new life in submission to the Creator has been collectively progressively dismissed since the rationalists of the eighteenth century published their work. And so in the logic of horror, using again the words of St. Paul, "since they did not think it worthwhile to retain the knowledge of God, he gave them over to a depraved mind, to do what ought not to

3. Modern Paralysis and Ancient Faith

be done."[10] Vampirism stands as the fictional curse upon the degraded family. In the stories the violation of the old order of things is played out via dark metaphors of sexual obsession, victimization, disease, despair, and suicide.

As for the exorcism that concludes all horror films (of this older sort at least), this has already been discussed here as a return to the old ways. It is interesting that *Vampyr* is decidedly Catholic in its overtones. Dreyer's *Ordet* suggests the Lutheran theology of its characters, the story resolving with the pronouncement of "the Word" and Johannes' childlike belief in that Word. *Vampyr* resolves with no word but the thrust of the stake. The killing of the vampire is as action-based as the sacrament of the mass. Vampires do not respond to formulas, but they shy from crucifixes and die in the morning light or from a pierced heart.

When Hamlet confronts his father's ghost and asks why its "canonized bones have burst their cerements," he follows that query with a more pointed question, "Wherefore? What shall we do?" I.4.27–38). Dreyer answers that question in plain enough fashion in *Vampyr*. Return to the old ways. Act. Then live and love. More like a morality tale than a horror story, *Vampyr* in a most *determinate* way presents not an allegory suggesting redemptive themes, but an orthodox response to deeply felt metaphysical and moral questions. We are lost in the dark. Our children have grown distant and cold. A stench of corruption rises in the land. What must we do before all is reversed and the darkness becomes the light? Repent and rise and slay the dragon in the Holy One's name and the land will be healed and the laughter of your children will again fill your houses and fields. Or so the film seems to encourage us to conclude.

ns.

4

CARNIVAL PLEASURES
Karl Freund's *The Mummy*

... one blinked before them as one blinks before a man with his face shot away. —H. L. Mencken, "The Libido for the Ugly"

In the early years of American horror, actor Lon Chaney made a name for himself as the "Man of a Thousand Faces," an apt title for the master of makeup, the star of ten Tod Browning films who specialized in grotesque characters like the Phantom of the Opera and Quasimodo. The peculiar ground that Chaney broke led to the success of a now more familiar name, Boris Karloff, Chaney's successor in the role of incarnate horror devil, the unlikely B-actor with the awkward frame and slight lisp who became a star after his sympathetic and unforgettable rendition of Frankenstein in the 1931 James Whale film and then through numerous other dark incarnations of the thirties and forties. Chaney and Karloff captured something essential in the development of the horror genre, as well as the psyche of early twentieth-century Americans, and that was the seemingly infinite possibility and interest of imaging "demonic" incarnations. Audiences were drawn to the dark, morbid, and deformed visages that monster movies displayed on the big screen.

Since most of the early characterizations (including Karloff's) invited a measure of sympathy for these dark creatures victimized by fate or a villain with a bottle of acid, the films borrowed their methods from carnival freak shows, as both forms depended on the voyeuristic pleasure of viewing the obscene and then saying what a terrible thing it was after all. It is noteworthy that Tod Browning, who would direct several Universal horror classics in the thirties, traveled with a carnival in his early years, and a year after directing *Dracula*, directed a film called *Freaks* (1932), a pre–Code tale of a troupe of circus performers who exact a terrible

4. Carnival Pleasures

vengeance on a trapeze artist who abuses them. The carnival freak show, especially popular during the late nineteenth century, eventually fell out of public favor by the middle of the twentieth century with some state legislation even written to make such shows illegal[1]; yet the horror producers sidestepped the censors and continued the tradition of peeping behind the curtain at the hidden thing, and benefited from the familiar and popular context. The creatures that populated these films, alien in nature and dripping with goo though they were, typically mimicked the movements and general aspects of humanity. The narratives built toward the gasp in revulsion at the full, screen-sized grotesque image, but then tempered that display with Lear's philosophical assessment of Poor Tom— "Is man no more than this?" Much of horror's effect today still depends on this strange allure of the grotesque.

Early horror film was thus quickly formed around a pattern of tease and reveal. The viewer was shown parts in shadow and then slowly more and more until the complete unveiling of *the thing*. And, in fact, as implied in the earlier analysis of *What Lies Beneath*, the full-frontal display of the incarnate demon still typically occurs at the high point in the narrative arc. For this reason, many critics have aligned the horror genre with pornography,[2] for horror, too, allows a taboo-violating glimpse of the human body in obscene aspect that develops an actual physical response. Although horror is far different in content than pornography, the analogy may be usefully drawn out, for the plastic display of the grotesque form on the large screen of a theater, gimmicked and transformed and moving with reasoned intention, has continued to produce some of the best "money shots" of the film industry—consider perhaps the familiar images of Hannibal Lecter peering out of his mask or Leatherface holding up his chain saw. The images of horror are sequenced and shot in fact with many of the same techniques used in the blue industry. Also, judging from the continuing popularity of the genre over the past century, the allure of the horrific image shares pornography's addictive potential, and thus it crosses a moral line that other film types do not.

This rather troubling phenomenon leads directly to a representative classic, Karl Freund's *The Mummy* (1932). The most memorable sequence in *The Mummy*—in fact, arguably the only memorable sequence of the film—is the four minutes of silent footage during which the mummy, the ancient priest Imhotep played by Boris Karloff, comes to life and walks out of his sarcophagus. The sequence is so good and so original in its awful, obscene beauty that in the judgment of many critics, it alone qualifies *The Mummy* for designation as one of the best movies of its particular kind, and certainly among the best of the early Universal films.

The power of one brilliant, revelatory sequence drives an entire movie, rather illustrative of the essential voyeuristic allure of the genre. Younger viewers will quickly agree that many horror films might well be pared down to ten minutes or fewer should the plot teases and silly *denouements* be eliminated. Certainly the early Universal studio classics tended to bog down terribly once the initial creations or transformations were achieved. *Frankenstein* (1931), for example, has moments of great poignancy, such as the dramatic scene with the small child, but the film drags overall and entirely depends on the promise of more scenes like that of Colin Clive quickening his creation amidst the thunderclaps and wildly yelling, "It's alive." Likewise, *The Wolf Man* (1941) succeeds as film principally by virtue of the initial gauzy transformation of Lon Chaney, Jr., into the werewolf. The other transformations and the plot, even with the memorable Maria Ouspenskaya, gypsy-tent scene, depend entirely on the success of the first dark incarnation and the hope of more like it. The same might be said about key moments from later films, from the birth of the alien in the original Ridley Scott film (*Alien*, 1979) to the half-formed, drooling beasts in John Carpenter's remake of *The Thing* (1982).

The actual transformation

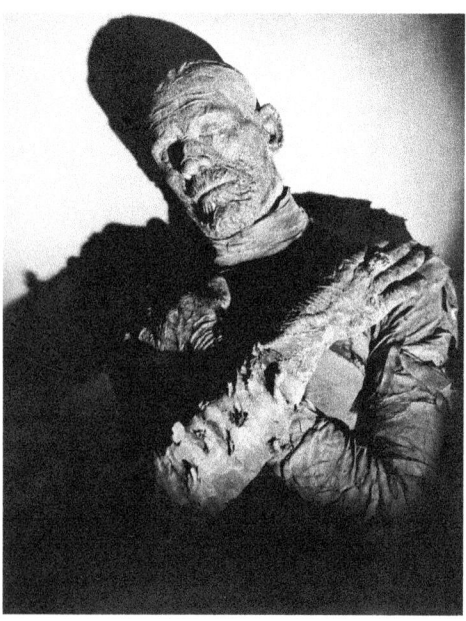

Boris Karloff mummified and ready for life in the opening sequence of the horror classic. *The Mummy*. 1932. Universal Pictures.

4. Carnival Pleasures

of the actor Karloff into the 2,000-year-old thing in *The Mummy* is matter of Hollywood legend. Karloff apparently spent a day in the makeup chair being molded into the ancient relic, followed by two hours of shooting to get just the right angle and lighting effects for the resurrection sequence. Karl Freund, directing his first film after a successful career as cinematographer, and apparently aware of how good a shot sequence he had in hand, kept the actor on set for retakes until 2 a.m. by some accounts, apparently oblivious to the discomfort of his victim and difficult task removing the layers of compound would be. Karloff was not released until near dawn,[3] calling it his "most trying ordeal."[4]

Still, despite the efforts made to accomplish verisimilitude of image, the real genius of the money scene in *The Mummy* shows more in photographic craft and editing. The quickening of the mummy comes via synecdoche and metaphor. In this, Freund's technique might well be compared to that often used in religious films. When Nicholas Ray meant to depict Jesus' miracles of healing in *King of Kings* (1961), he did so by shot-reverse shot—Jesus looks at the blind man, shot of blind man, shot of Jesus' eyes, shot of blind man now seeing. Pasolini who strove for authenticity above all else, used similar metonymic techniques in *The Gospel According to St. Matthew* (1964) to portray Jesus' miracles. Artful cinematography and editing play more on the imagination and are thus better methods of displaying the sublime than gimmicks and plastic casts. Freund chose to show less and suggest more through some clever editing. Later in the film, when Imhotep meets his end through the intercession of the goddess Isis, Freund gives in to visual gimmickry and the emotions fall somewhat flat.

This metaphoric style makes the mummy-come-to-life scene quite eerie, especially when added to the genuinely creepy visage of Karloff wrapped in layers of decayed bandage. The better horror films take the horrible image beyond the aesthetics of the peep show. While the grotesque creates revulsion and morbid curiosity, the real fear generated must transcend these immediate responses. Horror moves the incarnated demon toward the "victim" who haplessly tries to escape possession and conquest, but most victims typically either go mad or are massacred, and the fear of those fates evokes what might be termed a chilling, *spiritual* response. There is no physical danger involved for the viewer really, no pain and pleasure, just a profound dread of impending *lostness*, interestingly enough, the very same spiritual condition suffered by the victims of vampire bites in *Carmilla* and *Vampyr*.

Thus, horror shows us the subjects of hell and damnation and invites the viewer into an older spiritual conversation. The maiden is transformed back to devouring hag and comes toward the camera with arms outstretched. The mask is off the beast, and we are appalled and turned to stone. Or, using the original metaphor, horror lures us through the carnival curtain and reveals more than nature deformed. Nature has been replaced; a manifestation of otherworldly evil has taken shape. And, in this temporary yet terrible form, the incarnate thing will haunt the viewer's imagination, at the very least.

Rather than inspiring pity and compassion, horror chills us with the truth that evil runs deeper than any individual understands or believes. We experience momentary incarnations of evil in our daily encounters with people or events, but these are only brief manifestations of this thing which is altogether separate. Yet, every once in a while, even the most sheltered person has a close encounter, a chilling realization that the person who has taken the adjacent seat on the bus lacks an essential humanity and should be avoided at all costs. In the summer of 2011, a little boy was abducted in New York City by a man from whom he had asked directions. The boy was taken to the man's apartment, tied to a chair, tortured in unspeakable ways, then suffocated. The predator dismembered the boy and refrigerated the parts. How a human being can descend so low wonders the average reader, folding closed the newspaper. Has such a being retained any humanity or lost all along the way? Most readers would sense that the truth resides in the latter; such a man has debased that which makes him distinctly human, what theologians refer to as the "divine nature," and been given over to something else, something hideous, something confounding, something that transcends recognizable categories of violence or perversion—some *thing* purely evil in essence, no virtue, only corruption. We cannot fully picture that thing beyond its human manifestation, so we are compelled through the play of imagination to shape an idol that will afford us the closer look, the look that chills the spine.

What happens in the four minutes of silence in the opening sequence of Freund's *The Mummy*? A demonic avenger enters the world through

4. Carnival Pleasures

a cultic portal, and we are allowed to watch. The scene is a pure, pared down version of every transformation sequence in every horror film. Most of the film's remaining window dressing can be summarized briefly.

The plot of *The Mummy* derived from popular interest in the 1922 discovery of King Tutankhamen's tomb in Egypt. Carl Laemmle, Jr., wanting to capitalize on this event, commissioned a treatment and then screenplay around common fears regarding tampering with the ancient and foreign dead. He hired playwright John Balderston, who had created Universal's 1931 *Dracula*, and who seemed to have a knack for the genre. Balderston reconstituted the basic plot structure of *Dracula*, redefined the characters in the Egyptian setting, and wove them into a simple three-act script called *Imhotep* that became the basis for the shooting script of *The Mummy*.

The ancient high priest of Egypt, Imhotep, falls in love with a vestal virgin who tragically dies. He then uses forbidden magic from the cultic Scroll of Thoth to raise her again but is caught and mummified alive with the scroll. That mummy is then unearthed by archaeologists thousands of years later, a mimicking of the King Tut expedition. An overly curious and foolish young archaeologist from the expedition reads from the scroll while his companions are away, and Imhotep comes to life and embarks on a mission to find his lost love, the princess Anck-es-en-Amon.[5] Imhotep finds the princess's current incarnation in the beautiful Helen Grosvenor, conveniently in town as the daughter of an archaeologist. He captures Helen with the intention of killing her and then raising her again through means of the scroll, but the goddess Isis intervenes on the girl's behalf and Imhotep is struck down at the last moment, literally *deus ex machina*. Leslie Halliwell once made the comment that all good horror films have "a fine sense of comedy,"[6] and this conclusion supports the point.

Many of the gimmicks of the plot not borrowed from the Tod Browning film of the previous year came from Robert Wiene's now familiar classic from a decade earlier, *The Cabinet of Dr. Caligari* (1922). These include the potent male beast pursuing the uber-woman, the use of somnambulism as a means to control, the ineffectual men surrounding the victims, the mix of inordinate desire and blood lust, and the final conquest thwarted only by a plot contrivance. All of these make rather obvious that

A Christian Response to Horror Cinema

Balderston viewed the story as built around the notion of a perverse sex crime[7]—the monster as serial rapist-murderer who cannot be stopped because he is superior to the other men in town, a theme that, in fact, carries through the entire horror genre, particularly the post–*Halloween* (1978) slasher films and particularly those following the success of *Silence of the Lambs* (1991). The Hays Office of censorship recognized this set of allusions in the early Universal films and communicated frequently with studio executives to convey what they felt to be of public concern, but the censors were able to do little to curtail the sub-codes and suggestions of horror's world of "monsters, doppelgangers, or pieced-together people." Still, this moral pressure may explain why the most unsavory elements have been pushed so deeply and firmly into the thicker materials under the surface fabric of the developing genre.[8]

To return to the money sequence of *The Mummy*—Freund had just come off his greatest success as cinematographer, the memorable ending of Lewis Milestone's *All Quiet on the Western Front* (1930), wherein the young, disillusioned soldier, Paul, dies on the battlefield while reaching toward a butterfly. It was this tour-de-force as cinematography, which gave Laemmle confidence to hand Freund directorial duties for *The Mummy*. Freund came to the work with the firm attitude that "the most important thing is to catch the mood of the scene in a single shot."[9] In *The Mummy*, that single shot became the image of the revivified Karloff opening his eyes and peering out of the bandages.

The sequence is set up from the film's opening images. Just after the credits and title card, a revolving model of the sphinx and pyramids, is the unrolled Scroll of Thoth, which an ornate text reveals to contain "the magic words by which Isis raised Osiris from the dead." The Egyptian myth is actually a perfect metaphor for the horror genre as it contains many of the standard motifs—incest, murder, a revenge plot, and an attempt at resurrection. Isis and Osiris were brother and sister who ruled wisely over Egypt but were hated by their dark brother, Set. Set tricked Osiris into stepping into a glorious casket which his men then slapped shut and nailed and pitched with Osiris into the Nile. Isis then began a long and sad adventure to recover the casket in the hope of restoring her lover. So, from its opening moment Freund's film charts the course of unholy and doomed love.

4. Carnival Pleasures

The subsequent text on screen furthers the back story as it contains a prayer to the god Amon-Ra to allow the dead loved one to take shape in another form—"Oh! Amon-Rah—Oh! God of Gods—Death is but the doorway to new life." The camera moves in on this text drawing the viewer into the transgression implied, for although the film is set in Egypt, it is made for a largely Judeo-Christian audience which would know that such prayers are unholy in themselves as they make appeal to gods other than Jehovah and imply a denial of the one resurrection that is to follow the judgment. Thus, the viewer is led through the curtains of the carnival tent in violation of better judgment, and accepted religious principle. To watch the film is to sin already perhaps, to consent in the violation of taboo.

The next establishing images further the point. First comes a distant shot of the ruins being excavated. Then follows a close image of a marble pillar which the camera pans down, a movement that doesn't require a Freudian critic to explain. The pillar gets superimposed over a courtyard where the scientists have gathered their findings. The pillar, symbol of cultic male vitality, visually dominates the cargo of the scientists, which although orderly appears distant, lumpy, and lifeless in the frame. Then follows a rudely drawn banner announcing the "Field Expedition Season 1921 British Museum." The banner not only lacks sophistication in its lettering, but its imagination; it is the labeling of a soulless scientific culture dabbling with relics which it cannot understand. The image dissolves into a shot of a table on which fragments of a tablet are being assembled by a pair of hands, another reinforcement of the theme. The hands alone are seen, no faces; the camera tracks back several feet before a face is revealed.[10] It is of the lead scientist, Sir Joseph Whemple. As he moves the pieces, another set of hands types mechanically on a small machine. That typist is then abruptly revealed to be the young archaeologist, Ralph Norton, who will later haplessly read the scroll of Thoth and bring Imhotep to life. Norton moves carelessly and thoughtlessly and in a rapid, high voice tells Whemple that "that box" they uncovered, containing the scroll, would be the only thing bringing the expedition medals from the British Museum. Although Whemple will correct him and gently encourage patience and a more humble approach, the end of the scene has been foreshadowed.

The problem with science, the sequence suggests, is twofold. First, it lacks the ability to see beyond the material realm to forces of an entirely different kind than those readily observed. Second, it is useful when managed by the tempered hands of wisdom, but incredibly dangerous when in the hands of a fool, and science is incapable in itself of filtering out the fools who may use its equipment and apply its discoveries. In the specific context of the opening images, what science will not be able to contain in *The Mummy* will be the force of an erotic passion that will not submit to the discretions of polite society. Neither Whemple with his scholarly reserve nor Norton with his brash boyishness are any match for Imhotep contemplating the object of his desire for centuries and then set free from his bandages.

Dr. Muller, another archaeologist studying the sarcophagus, tells Whemple and Norton that the bandages reveal that the mummy died unnaturally, that he was, in fact, buried alive. Norton is intrigued by this, and while he and Muller talk, Freund cuts briefly to the image of the dead priest shrouded in a shadowy haze, an image much more evocative than any thus far in the film. This is the only glimpse offered of the mummy and it is offered as a tease. The camera is positioned behind the archaeologists so the contents of the sarcophagus are mostly blocked from view or hidden in shadow. No score accompanies the images. The scene is a classic example of what Hitchcock would call "pure cinema," especially appropriate here since the silence heightens anticipation of seeing what the movie promises to show.

At this point in the sequence, Freund builds in a short delay. Having shown the face of the mummy briefly and toying with the eager viewer who came just for this, he pulls away as the scientists decide to examine the chest that accompanied the sarcophagus. The chest contains the mysterious Scroll of Thoth with its incantation to raise the dead. The scroll is important as a plot device but a McGuffin for the person who came to the theater to see a mummy walk. What is interesting in this sequence is the way the camera remains focused on the three men studying the chest rather than the chest itself. However, Freund thought the editing through, the compositional subject that emerges is "men looking without really seeing." While the scientists look in vain, the viewer is drawn to concentrate on them looking while being told indirectly that it is the viewer who will be privileged to see. This setup is borrowed from old stage practices

4. Carnival Pleasures

in which the main action of a scene is in the background behind the actors in the foreground—the house falling over Buster Keaton in the well-known bit from *Steamboat Bill, Jr.* Frustrating for the viewer is that while the men labor to lift the chest from a packing crate and peer into its contents, Karloff remains on the edge of animation just behind them in the shadows.

The men move the "casket" onto a table and read its warning of death to anyone who opens it, and in doing so allow the viewer an even better view of the wrapped mummy in the background. Of course, the hieroglyphics that the men read, only briefly shown through a cut, have no meaning to the viewer and no interest. They further the distance established at the beginning between the modern scientific world and the cultic world Imhotep dwelt in. The scientists are as children reciting formulas off a blackboard.

What follows is more tease. Whemple declares the curse terrible, although it seems fairly normal for a story like this one, while Norton reaches eagerly to open the casket and see what's inside. Of course, by now the viewer has complete understanding of what will come of all this meddling and is eager for the undressing. But there must be a further delay, so Muller stops Norton and insists that he and Whemple go outside and talk matters over, a convenient maneuver in that it will leave Norton alone with the scroll and mummy, which by now the viewer finds a happy circumstance—and more so, for Muller's last words to Norton are "Do not touch that casket," virtually assuring that he will.

The two older men leave and the camera lingers a moment on the empty doorway, then moving in on Norton, who has taken a seat at his work table, the casket just beside him, the mummy behind. This closer shot pushes the wrapped Karloff out of the frame, a frustrating but clever device as it both enhances the suspense of the inevitable and allows Freund the use of alternate cuts from Norton to the mummy. As Norton reaches for more bits of stone to assemble, a cross cut takes the viewer outside to where Whemple and Muller are discussing the significance and danger of the scroll, the necessary "scientific consultation" before they will go back in to open the casket. Beyond the obvious serviceability of this setting to further delay the great moment, it allows an evocative image of the two scientists conspiring in the moonlight, and it allows another subtle furthering of the real plot of the story, for Muller is inexplicably holding the top of a cane positioned vertically in the center of the image while the two men sit and talk. The cane was nowhere present in the interior scene, during which Muller seemed quite spry, so it is intended no doubt as a graphic match to the pillar in the opening sequence and so references the real story, which is Imhotep's obsession with Anck-es-en-Amon and pursuit of her.

Given this context, the cut back to Norton at his desk takes on an erotic quality, albeit of the adolescent variety, as Norton looks up from his work with the broken stones to the forbidden casket, and then back to the door as if to see whether the "adults" have returned. Norton's body language and breathlessness, coupled with the absolute silence of the sequence, fit perfectly the suggestion of voyeurism evident throughout. He takes up the lamp and leans over the casket to get a closer look, places his face right up against it, then thinks better and pulls away. But his broken pieces of rock do not beckon him like the casket, so with a quick glance at the door in the resolve of passion, he rises and lovingly takes hold of the lid and lifts. The camera focuses on him, not the contents. He cannot resist. He reaches out his hands, then pauses to wipe them on his shirt, and then takes the scroll. It is tied by a ribbon, which he easily and delicately removes and lays gently on the casket lid. He slowly unrolls the scroll, his face close to it in eagerness, but it is all in hieroglyphics, except for an image of Isis and Osiris holding hands, which functions both as a reminder to the viewer of the cultic back story, and as wry humor for anyone who may be following the rather sordid visual allusions.[11]

The scene is again delayed as Muller attempts to encourage Whemple to put back the casket and its contents, but Whemple insists that the "interest of science" makes this impossible. The two men leave to rejoin Norton, who is translating the hieroglyphics on a paper. As he does, the camera sweeps back to Karloff in the sarcophagus, still motionless. Then a quick sweep back to Norton who has lifted the paper and is reading his transcription with a glazed look in his eyes. Then a cut and for the first time the viewer is allowed a full and prolonged look at Karloff's mummified face. As Norton reads, the left eye opens slightly, an absolutely riveting and chilling gesture, the very moment of resurrection in the silence of an archaeologist's lab—the money shot that hundreds of subsequent films

4. Carnival Pleasures

would try to replicate. Unlike the subtle motion of the raised Frankenstein monster's hand in the Whale film, here the viewer gets a lingering look at the window to the demon Imhotep's soul, the eye. Then the camera tilts down to the decrepit forearm slowly falling through the rotten bandages; all the while, Norton is oblivious and the audience hushed in anticipation. At this point, Freund does not fall into the trap of many other directors by continuing to allow the privilege of seeing the thing move through the room. Rather, as Norton continues to read, the camera moves to the scroll on which Imhotep's fingers slowly move. Norton looks over, screams, rises, and begins to laugh hysterically as the camera follows the stream of bandages dragging through the doorway. The viewer sees only this. When Whemple and Muller return, they find the hysterical younger man who points and offers the memorable line, "He went for a little walk. You should have seen his face." Of course, the viewer does not get that privileged view until later, when Imhotep, now Ardeth Bey, stands in the doorway to meet another set of archaeologists following up on the work of this first crew. But this view of the gaunt Karloff in the garb of a gaunt, resuscitated Egyptian priest has no power like the first peep at the mummy in its moments of animation.

All of which furthers the point that the genre of horror at its onset mixed the technique of the striptease with the dread of the evil undead. And the mechanics used to achieve this depended and still depend on a metaphoric suggestion that things physical always mask things spiritual, and things damned in many cases. Horror depends on the belief in a reality beyond the flesh, a supernatural reality which can only be seen in glimpses, and usually in the dark. The viewer is teased toward this reality as in the burlesque show, although the payoff is of a vastly different kind.

Of particular interest here is the aforementioned development of sympathy for the monster, mentioned at the start as a way of connecting the genre to its carnival roots. Because Norton and Whemple seem so crassly oblivious to the decencies of the ancient world they have unearthed, the viewer's natural sympathies are toward the monster and toward Muller, who advocates for leaving the mess alone but is impotent himself to stop the inevitable. Considered in this way, Freund's directorial choice of placing the image of Karloff in bandages slightly off screen for much of the sequence seems both a moral and artistic choice. One is compelled to avert

A Christian Response to Horror Cinema

the eyes when in the presence of physical calamity. Curiosity draws the attention, but decency averts the eyes.

Moral decency. Any viewer familiar with the great sweep of the genre will readily note a difference between some of the older horror films like *The Mummy* and those that followed, especially those of the second half of the twentieth century. In older burlesque shows, the chorus girl was allowed to escape off stage before the audience could grab hold of her, as depicted in, for example, the famous smoker scene of Ellison's *Invisible Man*. Not so much in the blue industry that would follow. Similarly, in the Universal horror films and many of the earlier science fiction films built with similar components, the audience is to a measured degree encouraged to sympathize with the beast and thus understand its mayhem. This manufactured sympathy allows for some measure of catharsis then when the beast is rather easily turned away in the end, typically through a *deus ex machina* contrivance. Not so the films that would follow some generations later. Later horror films, perhaps in response to the dreadful horrors of the twentieth century, have lost interest in this moral component and moved toward more blatant voyeurism and nihilistic violence.

Still, I'm not sure that one form has merit over the other since both derive ultimately from the same source and lead to the same end. Despite the closure of the older films, the monster did always tend to come back in a sequel like a bad political bill. It might be argued that the chaos of the twentieth century steered the world of horror away from its own built-in hypocrisy. Victorian moralism could no longer guide a the brave new world of mustard gas, atomic weaponry, space exploration, mass brainwashing, and widespread sex-trafficking. Be that as it may, even in *The Mummy* the sympathy directed toward Imhotep is eventually undermined late in the story when he threatens to kill Helen Grosvenor on an altar to resurrect his former love. The sudden "divine" intervention of Isis suggests as much: Imhotep is to be rejected when his motives are revealed as purely selfish, the main characteristic of all who reside in the lower circles of hell. At the very best, his motives are revealed as a corrupted version of the dark romantic pursuit of the blue flower. He would disembowel half the world to achieve his ineffable.

The genre of horror would not have its staying power were it not for two revelations: first, that the beast cannot be bound in the end to play

4. Carnival Pleasures

by rules of respectability, despite our momentary sympathies, and second, that the monster on screen stands for something far worse than even the monstrous form it inhabits. And this uncomfortable second realization places us in front of the final question that Freund's *Mummy* proposes. What is the demonic threat behind Imhotep's incarnate visage?

The answer seems obvious given the visual symbols of the film's initial sequence, as well as the eventual trajectory of the genre. If a film like Dreyer's *Vampyr* suggests the decay of the family order after Enlightenment rationality replaced older Western understandings, a film like *The Mummy* suggests something even more specific; namely, the birthing of the predatory male out of that dysfunctional family. More specifically, the film suggests the birthing of a predatory antichrist. Later films like *Rosemary's Baby* (1968) and *The Omen* (1976) make this suggestion more explicitly *the story*, but *The Mummy* gets at it already. Imhotep comes from the grave to find his beloved Anck-es-en-Amon, but his desire ultimately moves in the direction of breeding a better race, a restored cultic Egypt where people with chests, to borrow a polite phrase from C.S. Lewis, can live. The science-fiction genre which branched from horror in the 1950s drew out the motif. Films like *Invasion of the Body Snatchers* (1956), *The Blob* (1958), and *The Planet of the Apes* (1968) were all built on the premise of the demise of humankind and rise of a new order. The new order is demonic precisely because humankind must be annihilated for it to succeed. The initial success requires an antichrist come as agent of this change. The films all tend to begin with the birthing of the new order through one agent who then breeds, a story that parodies the Christian stories of the creation and the incarnation.

If this conclusion seems to jump too many steps, at least it should be acknowledged that the Mummy films, following *Dracula*, feature an incubus as main character, a predatory fertile male demon who seduces women in their sleep. That ugly reality cannot be denied. What seems to have brought this fear to the surface for late nineteenth- and early twentieth-century Westerners? Perhaps it was the sense that actual men were losing their potency in the family and larger culture; rogue males seemed to be a growing breed, at least as sensationalized news accounts of killers like Jack the Ripper would circulate and find their way into the popular imagination. Edgar Alan Poe's 1841 stories "The Murders in the

A Christian Response to Horror Cinema

Rue Morgue" and "Mystery of Marie Rogêt" had paved the way for this growing interest in the macabre that played its way through the sordid news accounts and the evolving genre of the detective story popularized by Arthur Conan Doyle for the late Victorians. However, the fictional stories typically featured a superior male (C. Auguste Dupin in the original Poe stories) who could outwit the uber-criminal. This potent male hero found his way into American dime novels and comics in the twentieth century as a more potent American version of Doyle's sexless Sherlock Holmes, but somehow that hero did not find his way into the evolving genre of horror. All the early horror films could offer was an eccentric Van Helsing character borrowed from the Stoker novel, the Dr. Muller of Freund's *The Mummy*, who seems to always arrive a few steps too late to do anything beyond interpret the obvious. And they offered the victim's impotent would-be lovers, who get mesmerized, slashed, eaten or otherwise disposed of in the unfortunate course of events.

Despite these impotent saviors, the theological paradigm behind the horror genre insists that the films conclude with an exorcism, and *The Mummy* follows that formula. The exorcism of Imhotep, before he can sacrifice Helen Grosvenor and raise her as his old love, will affirm a moral force in the universe which does adjust the direction of events to protect the weak and punish the cruel. Helen prays for the protection of Isis and receives it, the genre's youthful nod to the older Victorian need for closure.

But what happens when the culture and the genre move past such polite respectabilities, when there is no longer any need for prayer nor belief in Isis or any other deity? Michael Myers is shot but not killed, Freddy Krueger retreats to his dream world, Hannibal Lector saunters his way toward another lunch engagement.

It is noteworthy that despite this seeming closure of *The Mummy*, the film displays its own fundamental hypocrisy once its polite ending gets undressed. After all, how can one be saved from the forbidden thing when it is still secretly desired? If the appeal of *The Mummy* is largely the peep show view of the forbidden, and if the trigger which opens Pandora's Box of evils is impious science coupled with the allure of the forbidden, wouldn't a form of repentance be required to return the world's moral equilibrium? Wouldn't the scientific community at the center of

4. Carnival Pleasures

the drama need to acknowledge and turn from meddling into areas that should be taboo? Wouldn't a traditional marriage be required as a conclusion with its implication of family, as in Dreyer's *Vampyr*? Yes on all counts—but instead the film skirts its own moralism in the final moments and offers instead a concluding scene of even grander voyeuristic excess than anything that precedes it.

Helen, as Egyptian prisoner in the fetishized silky garb of an Oriental courtesan, is beckoned to the museum at night by Imhotep. A large, shirtless Nubian slave stirs some cauldron of boiling liquid that will apparently be used to mummify her after the Egyptian priest kills her with a large knife that he displays prominently. She screams and runs from the men but is caught by the slave, at whose feet she falls and pleads for mercy. The Nubian shows signs of pity, but Imhotep lifts his ring and the man cowers and backs away. Imhotep aims his ring at Helen who approaches

Imhotep (Karloff) prepares to do with Helen (Zita Johann) what he will. 1932. Universal Pictures.

mesmerized and says, "Do with me what you will." The camera captures this from behind Helen (Hungarian-born Broadway actress Zita Johann) whose curvaceous figure in silk matches nicely with an image of a lithe goddess over the sarcophagus bed which divides the "lovers." Helen is laid upon the stone and Imhotep prays for her resurrection to his former love while toying with the knife that will penetrate her. No repentance or moral seriousness, but rather another peep show, hard to watch without either snickering or leaning toward the screen to get a closer look at the not so subtle display of the woman in silks.

This territory of moral hypocrisy and exploitation in early cinema has been well covered by film historians and critics, especially as government censors wrestled openly with the film industry over these matters. The important fact here regards the potency of the evolving monster/hero in the genre of horror. The endings in which these runaway uber-men are stopped tend to be sham endings. The *thing* brought to life comes from a deeper place with spiritual principles that override moralism, sentimentality, and lukewarm faith. And it will breed; note that zombie films, a subgenre of considerable popularity, evolved out of the success of *The Mummy* and its sequels.

All of this leads to a conclusion that reaches far beyond a film like *The Mummy*. The popular literature of horror even in its earliest expressions seemed to be projecting the idea that the world had somehow turned an epochal corner. Some form of apocalypse was at hand and the rough beast about to be born; a crack had occurred in the retaining wall and the barrier that kept the demonic from us had lost its basic integrity. Over time, as the crack has opened more, the projected outcome would seem to be that either the beasts will break altogether free to take over or a true messiah will return and push the evil back once and for all. Older horror was constructed according to the assumptions of the latter, but the trajectory of the genre has moved in a contrary direction toward the former fear. Meanwhile, the Christian community continued to advance prophetic messages of impending doom that marked out the twentieth century as a hinge toward an apocalypse; witness the visions at Fatima or at Garabandal.

> The Blessed Virgin told me on the first of January that a warning would be given before the miracle so that the world might amend itself. This

4. Carnival Pleasures

warning, like the chastisement, is a very fearful thing for the good as well as for the wicked. It will draw the good closer to God and it will warn the wicked that the end of time is coming and that these are the last warnings. There is more to it than this, but it can't be said by letter. No one can stop it from happening. It is certain, although I know nothing concerning the day or the date.[12]

5

LAWLESS MEN AND BEASTS
Jacques Tourneur's *Night of the Demon*

> *That unmistakable mood or note that I hear from Hanwell, I hear also from half the chairs of science and seats of learning today; and most of the mad doctors are mad doctors in more senses than one. They all have exactly that combination we have noted: the combination of an expansive and exhaustive reason with a contracted common sense. They are universal only in the sense that they take one thin explanation and carry it very far. But a pattern can stretch for ever and still be a small pattern. They see a chess-board white on black, and if the universe is paved with it, it is still white on black. Like the lunatic, they cannot alter their standpoint; they cannot make a mental effort and suddenly see it black on white.* —G.K. Chesterton, *Orthodoxy*

The anecdote unfolds as follows. An astronomy teacher is offering a telescope session to a small community group. The teacher asks as a four-year-old boy in attendance if he believes in alien spaceships. "Of course," says the boy. When the teacher follows up with why he believes in them, the boy replies, "How else would the aliens get here?"

The story illustrates the logical fallacy of *petitio principia*, more commonly known as "begging the question." In a formal debate, one side may ask the other side to concede certain points in order to facilitate the proceedings. To "beg" the question is to ask that an idea central to the very point at issue be conceded, which is, of course, logically invalid.

Creedal religions like Christianity have long been accused of this fallacy when they insist that moral and spiritual principles be followed because they are written in scripture, while simultaneously insisting that the authority of scripture comes from God. Thus, for example, when the layman is asked how he knows the Bible lesson is true, he answers that the Bible says so. The Christian church will also point to the witness of the apostles, saints, and martyrs, and to two thousand years of tradition,

5. Lawless Men and Beasts

and, of course, the various testimonies regarding the historical Jesus Christ. But underneath all those arguments rings the foundational assertion that certain truth is certain because it is written in scripture; and, of course, many outside the fold claim this assertion begs the question.

Still, it is safe to say that whereas religious communities wear their paradoxes proudly, many a modern thinker hides his fallacies and leaps of faith. No scientific experiment, for example, has ever shown the evolution of one species into the next; yet, evolution as a system of thought is taught regularly in public and private schools as the universal conclusion of credible science. *It must be true*, the average boy thinks while climbing the steps of the school bus, textbook in hand, *or why would I be tested on it this Friday*? A similar point may be made regarding the more recent, politically charged topic of climate change. Although the data supporting such a theory has not been gathered over a long enough stretch of time to make any convincing case that the planet is warming due to carbon emissions, the advocates of climate control insist its conclusions be enforced upon a large segment of the populace. The impractical logic implied by the scientists and lobbyists, filtered down to the average shopping homemaker, might be expressed this way—if global warming were not true, why would so many new household cleaners on the market be green?

One classic work of short fiction from the late nineteenth century plays with the consequences of such fallacious reasoning as it falls upon specific individuals. In Charlotte Perkins Gilman's autobiographical "The Yellow Wallpaper," a nervous woman is given a rest cure at her husband and doctor's insistence; however, the cure involves keeping her in a room gaudily decorated that just makes her worse, a fact that the husband and doctor insist is a matter of her fancy. They keep her in the room; she complains; they dismiss her objections; and she goes mad. *Petitio principia* is best expressed perhaps by the neighborhood bully as, "It's so 'cause I say it is, see."

All of which is to introduce the thesis of one of the truly great small films in the horror genre, Jacques Tourneur's *Night of the Demon* (1957). Tourneur's film follows the trail of an American psychologist, John Holden, who insists that his medical training has convinced him that all paranormal phenomena can be explained naturally. Holden is in England for a conference to promulgate this notion when he is drawn into contact with a satanic cult and has a curse placed upon him. The result is that Holden comes face to face with a supernatural entity and has his materialistic assumptions challenged and transformed. So, Holden plays the prototype character who assumes a conclusion and then must be shaken from it—the impossibility of a supernatural, angelic or demonic realm. That pattern outlined, the film becomes a near morality tale after the order of Stevenson and Wilde, although the subject isn't the more familiar Gothic plot regarding the overreacher who tampers with matters beyond the scope of human concern; the subject of *Night of the Demon* would seem to be the obstinacy and folly of the Baconian, modern scientific intellectual, who, in freeing himself from the idols of the tribe, den, marketplace, and theater, has also freed himself from man's innate knowledge of the divine. Thus, he is the man freed not from superstition, as he fancies, but from metaphysics and from metaphysical encounter himself. And unfortunately, this seeming freedom makes him, according to the logic pursued in these pages, the plaything of the devil and (in the Tourneur film) a rather repulsive demon, the type which for generations has made little boys and girls climb under the bed on stormy nights.

The film's narrative arc follows the nineteenth-century tradition of the "night in the haunted house story," which writers of no less stature than Charles Dickens and Ambrose Bierce popularized. Dickens' "A Christmas Carol" (1843) and "The Haunted House" (1859) involve skeptics given a long night dose of the reality of the other world. Bierce teased his readers with similar, albeit darker, stories like "The Night Doings at 'Deadman's'" (1893) and "The Secret of Macarger's Gulch" (1893). The haunted house story was quite effective with audiences due to its alignment with late Victorian popular interest in the occult. In the haunted house stories more immediately related to the Tourneur film, we do not just have the presence of the lurking ghost as in Dickens, Bierce, or perhaps Henry James' *Turn of the Screw*; we have someone compelled to stay in the house with the ghost to fulfill a wager, combining the haunted house motif with a story of human arrogance like Anton Chekhov's "The Bet" (1889). By 1924, this specific storyline had already found its way into international film with Abel Gance's *Au Secours!*, which takes the story in a comic direction, a genre twist that would provide story material for Buster

5. Lawless Men and Beasts

Keaton, Laurel and Hardy, Abbott and Costello and many other American comics in the twentieth century.

Jacques Tourneur, a believer in the dark dream kingdom of ghosts and shadows,[1] follows this pattern by placing the psychologist Holden in the haunted place and then watching him sweat through his denials. That's the simplest overview of *Night of the Demon*. Once Holden cries for mercy, he is allowed access to the secret word that sends the wicked thing back to its corner and chains. Of course, as common with films of the horror genre, this one has an overt religious undercurrent, especially in its invocation of the story element closest to the core of the Western religious tradition—Holden is granted saving mercy through the mediation of a beautiful young woman, Beatrice, in the guise of Joanna, the niece of one of the demon's victims. She will lead him through the passages that reveal the nature of the universe below the universe, and then join him on his new journey toward the light, which is where the film ends—a conclusion not unlike the final images of Dreyer's *Vampyr*.

Viewed this way, Tourneur's horror classic is both redemptive and evangelical. The unbeliever Holden is saved. At the awakening end of his journey, he sees the beast with clear eyes and runs from it into the arms of the messenger of salvation. In fact, his last impulse before the credits roll is a chivalric gesture, to offer his manly protection to the sweet-faced woman. Since the viewer has been drawn to witness the universe from his point of view, the film offers not just a warning but something of a sacramental experience toward this better way of seeing, very much in the fashion of specifically religious films. A fair cross-reference might be Robert Bresson's *Pickpocket* (1959), in which a bitter student turned toward a life of crime is snapped into repentance and the hope of a new life by the persistent love of a pure, young woman; the film is Bresson's variation on Dostoyevsky's *Crime and Punishment*.

Beyond his personal interest in the subject of metaphysical reality, Tourneur was drawn professionally to the horror genre by the economics of the Hollywood B-film industry in the forties, and had the good fortune to team up with producer Val Lewton to direct successful lower-budget horror films at RKO, most notably the small masterpiece *Cat People* in 1942 and the poetic, if horribly titled, *I Walked with a Zombie* in 1943. By the 1950s, Tourneur had earned the right to pick his own projects. Hal

A Christian Response to Horror Cinema

Chester of Columbia held his work in high regard and signed him on to *Night of the Demon* after Tourneur had successfully completed *Nightfall*, a small suspense film full of evocative compositions that derived from a *noir* novel of the same title by David Goodis. The project Chester offered Tourneur was also an adaptation. The script for *Night of the Demon* derived from a minor yet intriguing and urbane Montague James story called "Casting the Runes."

The plot of "Casting the Ruins" contains most of the elements central to the Tourneur film, but with a much different tone. An Alistair Crowley–like occultist named Karswell has purchased a local abbey for a home and begun spreading pernicious ideas, causing trouble for local residents including children whom he terrifies by conjuring dark beasts at a magic show. Karswell doesn't like the children as they trespass on his property. He doesn't like anyone who crosses him, in fact, for he is described as a man who is "easily offended and never forgave anyone." When Karswell seeks to have his occult manifesto published, it is summarily rejected by the publisher on recommendation of a reader named Harrington. Three months later, Harrington is found dead under bizarre circumstances. The book is submitted again and rejected again, this time by a reader named Dunning, and when Dunning begins to experience odd hauntings and learns of Harrington's strange death, he starts piecing the story together. It turns out that Karswell killed Harrington by "passing the runes," a slip of paper with occult symbols on it. Once the paper is passed, the recipient has three months to live, unless he is able to return it to the giver. With help from Harrington's brother, Dunning manages to pass the rune back to Karswell through a clever maneuver at a train station. Three months later, Karswell is killed by a stone dropped mysteriously from atop a building.

Two key changes were made to this story by Hal Chester, Tourneur, and the writers at RKO. First, all humor was stripped out. The Montague James story begins with the publisher's wife reading a series of three rejection letters directed to Karswell. Given how irritating such letters are to any grown person with a measure of pride remaining, the plot is thus launched from a somewhat comic premise: the spurned writer seeking revenge on the callous publisher, a premise rendered all the more sympathetic as the three, callous rejection letters are printed without comment

5. Lawless Men and Beasts

at the start of the story. Any ordinary reader will be initially inclined to root for the wizard Karswell and perhaps follow the story as a dark fantasy, perhaps akin to Melville's "Bartleby, the Scrivener." But the film is no fantasy, dark nor light; it begins in the hazy gray stone of Stonehenge and ends in the black metal night of a railway yard. The second key change to James' story adds further weight by way of the addition of the character of John Holden. His character is pure invention, brought to the screenplay to create viewer identification, and then infused with various traits of the horror tradition mingled with elements of the American hard-boiled story. It is as if Tourneur has speculated that the Byronic American antihero so iconic in films from the forties is brooding over the loss of imagination and faith, rather than the loss of his ideal woman. Holden's presence converts the light Gothic tale of "Casting the Runes" into something far more philosophically compelling. The main conflict shifts from how to thwart Karswell's curse to how to believe enough in the threat to thwart it.

The adaptation is one of those great illustrations of studio production at its best, for it is remarkable how the modest source story was transformed into this compelling screen version. Beyond that, however, the adaptation underscores once again how easily the genre of horror shapes its materials into rich philosophical and theological explorations. Tourneur's *Night of the Demon* offers its share of visual pleasure, with its suspenseful plot and evocative settings, but it also articulates matters fit for a Sunday homily regarding the existence of the demonic, the essential faultiness of science stripped of moral sensitivity and metaphysics, the need for personal redemption through faith, and the overarching goodness and grace of the creator. Holden is shown mercy in the end, after all. And Tourneur's film manages this without once directly evoking the old faith or any of its associated icons. That is one of its more interesting features, its affirmation of faith without the usual means.

On the other side of the equation, the film does likewise pose evil in an orthodox, incarnational way. Holden really is haunted by a demon once the rune gets passed to him by Karswell. That demon appears in the opening sequence and murders the Harrington character. It appears again, although ambiguously, midway through the film when Holden attempts to break into Karswell's house to steal the occult volume that explains the strange goings on. And later, it appears at a remote train station to tear apart Karswell, who has had the rune passed back to him by Holden. In addition, the viewer is teased by a demonic cat which turns into a panther, a hatful of magical puppies, and a violent rain storm conjured out of a clear day by the dark magic of the wizard Karswell.

Night of the Demon owes its greatest debt, then, to the established logic of horror we have outlined in this book. It traces the story of a man who violates a taboo which allows a satanic presence to enter the narrative space. The haunted man must acknowledge the source of the evil and bow before the supernatural means toward its destruction. Then the presence is exorcised, almost—the beast is not killed or even sent into a herd of pigs by virtue of the exorcism, but only temporarily satisfied in the fashion of pagan ritual. It will certainly reappear the next time the secret words are spoken and the rune passed. This is a logical conclusion since the specific source of the taboo violation is never fully repudiated, that again being the early twentieth-century science which discounts metaphysics while drawing conclusions. Because there is no specific acknowledgment and repudiation of the source of the narrative problem, the formula for exorcism is likewise tempered. Harrington's daughter saves Holden by forcing him to consider and eventually embrace the possibility that he has been cursed. And she provides welcoming arms for him to embrace once free from the curse. But she does not lead him specifically to the church or to the means the literature of Christendom has provided to deal with such hauntings—stakes through the heart, prayers, rosaries, sunlight, or what have you. Regarding the name of the beast, one of the keys to understanding the particulars of the formula, the narrative of *Night of the Demon* suggests something large, Apollyon, the destroyer who is the embodiment of Satan himself. So, something large and very evil comes and goes, and will almost certainly come again.

This dark conclusion might seem a minor generic twist were it not so common in many more recent horror films; *Halloween* and *Ringu* come first to mind. It becomes quite explicit in various films that deal with demonic oppression and possession directly, like *Rosemary's Baby* and the more recent *Paranormal Activity* (2007). Either the efficacy of the divine community and her means of grace are diminished or altogether ignored in these more recent renderings of this genre. In some, the authority of the older faith is even subjected to mockery.

5. Lawless Men and Beasts

It is tempting to steer the conversation toward the subject of the gradual erosion of that old faith as a legitimate force in America's popular discourse after the First World War. So much has been written about the shift in cultural hegemony that no documentation would even be required to establish the point. Films which treat matters of faith seriously have become rarer over the past several decades. And it follows that producers and distributors have wanted to tune down certain elements of the older horror formula when possible. However, all this said, *Night of the Demon* dates to 1957 not 1997, so the suggestion of this cultural unorthodoxy might be somewhat anachronistic.

A better explanation perhaps exists without excluding the efficacy of the sacraments as a central matter in the narrative; as said, *Night of the Demon* does align with orthodox doctrine. A studio might posit a world where God is somewhat hidden as a gesture toward scientific materialism. A believer, on the other hand, might posit it as a judgment. The silence of God can just as well be understood as a mirror response to the silence of an unbelieving world that has forgotten how to pray.

Such a reading works well with the internal logic of *Night of the Demon*, from the opening credit sequence when a voiceover reminds the viewer that ancient runic symbols, like Stonehenge, that is imaged behind the rolling script, can call forth the powers of darkness. This introduction functions as warning. The "rune" which is Stonehenge will be mimicked by the mysterious characters who appear and disappear on a personal card Karswell will pass to Holden, and then on the actual cursed paper, the rune that is passed. The suggestion is that if positive religious belief is to be dismissed by the modern world, then the long history of the occult must also be dismissed, a history that has marked the world with monuments every bit as substantial as basilicas. But will it? That implied question echoes the familiar critique of modernity found in nearly all horror film. Science has a rather short history compared to that of both the light and dark arts, and the structures of science in many ways lack the substance of those older ones. If the sacred elements should be pushed aside, what will guard the world from the powers of the occult forces?

A set of symbols that punctuate the plot confirms this reading. Each major sequence in the film is associated with some large icon of modernity. At the start, Harrington races through a dark forest toward Karswell's

A Christian Response to Horror Cinema

Holden (Dana Andrews) appears sure of himself while facing away from an interior space that seems anything but reassuring in Jacques Tourneur's *Night of the Demon*. 1957. Columbia Pictures.

home in his automobile. Yet the camera view into the vehicle shows him contained and diminished by fear, hardly able to withstand the evil of the dark forest seen through the windshield. In the second sequence, Holden leans back awkwardly in his airplane seat while flying to London for his conference appearance. He can't get comfortable enough in the seat to sleep and asks the stewardess for a blinder to cover his eyes—another symbol that recurs in the narrative, but the dominant one in the sequence is the airplane tossed in the capricious hands of the clouds and wind. A third symbol regards the false security of interior spaces. Tourneur has the camera linger on secure interior spaces—the study area in the British museum; the lobby, halls and individual rooms of a newer hotel, the interior of Karswell's study—but then subverts that security. Holden will be haunted in each place. In one memorable shot, a hand is seen on a stair rail above Holden where no one is known to be standing. In a related scene, Holden tells friends that he hears a strange tune in his head, one he never learned and that has occult origins, suggesting that even the interior space of his mind offers no protection. The fourth symbol is the sci-

5. Lawless Men and Beasts

ence lab where Holden and two other scientists attempt to hypnotize one of Karswell's devotees who has been haunted by the demon. Rather than the lab providing protection, the man breaks free and runs through a window and falls to his death. The fifth and final symbol is the train and railway station in the film's concluding sequence. Even Karswell can find no protection here. The screeching train whistle and a speeding passenger train only mute the horrible sound of the demon brutally killing the wizard.

Related to these symbolic modern icons are direct assertions made in the film dialogue. For instance, Karswell's first words, given to Harrington who comes the night of his death to plead for Karswell to call off the demon, are "Some things are more easily started than stopped." Once the engines of technology turn, progress drives them inexorably toward conclusions far beyond human reach and control. Holden, in his opening scene on the plane, complains to the stewardess, "I must get some sleep and that light keeps shining in my eyes." Holden's preconceptions have rendered him allergic to the truth. When Karswell asks Holden just how much he knows about the occult book he is after, Holden admits, "Not very much." At the conclusion, Holden thanks Karswell for "convincing him of a world I never thought possible." Then, when Joanna and Holden look down the train tracks where Karswell has been killed by the demon, she tries to stop him from going to see the body by saying, "Maybe it's better not to know." He goes, nonetheless, and sees the mutilated body destroyed not by the train but by the thing and returns to Joanna with the concluding words, "You're right. Maybe it's better not to know." This conclusion restores the equilibrium of the film as Holden the symbolic cause of it all has been willing to admit humbly his spiritual blindness. Some mysteries are better kept mysteries.

The restoration of Holden punctuates the story arc in a fashion very familiar to certain biblical narratives. In the book of Daniel, Nebuchadnezzar, the great king of the Babylonian empire, has a troubling dream that his court advisors cannot unpack. What has been told the reader about Nebuchadnezzar in previous chapters is that he is a man of enormous power and equally enormous ego. The reason Daniel was thrown to the lions was his unwillingness to pray before the great statue the king had erected for himself. Daniel, of course, was miraculously spared so he is still around to interpret the king's troubling dream, and he tells the king that he will be humbled and made to live for a time like a beast. One night, as Nebuchadnezzar surveys his realm from his palace and extols his own virtues, God strikes him down. He is rendered insane and cast out to the beasts. When he is eventually restored, he acknowledges that the universe is ruled by one sovereign lord alone who is exalted above any man and "who does as he pleases with the powers of heaven and the peoples of the earth." This older story is echoed later by Jesus in his parable of the rich man who decides to build even bigger barns so he can eat, drink and be merry. God calls him a fool from heaven and decrees that his soul will be taken that night. Jesus' conclusion is that it will go as such with all who are rich toward themselves but not toward God. The application of this biblical pattern to the narrative of the Tourneur film, as well as other similar stories in the horror genre, is that the new science and technology of the modern world has made humankind rich in self-assessment but poor in spiritual discernment.

That pattern is not unfamiliar to the Western literary tradition. One can hear echoes of it in works as disparate as "A Christmas Carol," *Silas Marner*, *Wuthering Heights*, and even Shakespeare's *King Lear*. In fact, it is quite distinctive in *Lear*. The purgative trial of the castoff king on the heath, paralleled by the trial of the blinded Gloucester, enables him to regain a fundamental humanity and humility. He goes from arrogant tyrant moving people and nations along the outlines of a map to beggar stripping his coat to cover Poor Tom in the storm. When he is reconciled to daughter Cordelia, he has been restored to grace through the door of humility. She pronounces a final benediction on him which directly echoes Christ's words of "Peace" to his troubled followers after his death and resurrection.

So, *Night of the Demon* functions as an apology for a traditional articulation of religious faith without ever invoking the language of a specific faith—a further similarity to Shakespeare's *Lear*, which expresses a distinctively Catholic worldview in a fictional universe set in pre–Christian England. Holden and Harrington and Joanna ultimately acknowledge the forces of providence which can ultimately curse or damn.

Before pursuing the plot further, one technical matter needs to be addressed related to the way the film works upon the viewer. Scholars and

5. Lawless Men and Beasts

lovers of horror have made much of the fact that the scenes with the demon were actually shot without Tourneur on set. The model used for the "thing" apparently came from a drawing in a book on demonology, but Tourneur wanted it revealed to the audience subtly, as was done in his 1942 classic *Cat People*:

> I wanted, at the very end, when the train goes by, to include only four frames of the monster coming up with the guy and throwing him down. Boom, boom—did I see it or didn't I? People would have to sit through it a second time to be sure of what they saw. But after I had finished and returned to the United States, the English producer made this horrible thing, cheapened it. It was like a different film.[2]

That unfortunate artistic change did indeed weaken the film. The demon, especially in the concluding sequence, appears on screen too long and looks awkwardly artificial, recalling the worst moments of the original *King Kong*. And this glimpse of the machinery behind the curtain does serve to diminish some of the film's genuinely creepy effects. Still, *Night of the Demon*'s virtues allow viewers to sigh over these technical faults rather than reject the film outright. And the film's narrative circuits func-

The awkward demon approaches to take Karswell in an otherwise haunting composition from the conclusion of *Night of the Demon*. 1957. Columbia Pictures.

tion independent of this bit of producer overreach. Ironically, the age of the film has turned the flaw into something of a moral message since the mechanics of visual representation have dated almost all films that depend heavily on technical flare. Science-fiction and horror, especially from the 1950s period, heavily dependent on plastic devices, bore a double-edged sword. The films inevitably have lost verisimilitude as time has progressed; yet the losses have further validated the argument against the dangerous elixir of technologically-based utopian dreams. The awkwardness of the man in beast costume that lingers too long in front of the camera at the beginning and end of the action displays the hubris of the age. *Night of the Demon* actually makes this point directly in several not so brief scenes shot inside airplanes, automobiles, and secure modern spaces. André Bazin rightly articulated the maxim that film evolves always in the direction of greater verisimilitude, but he underplayed the reverse corollary, that time will naturally diminish and winnow the accomplishments of film art. Tourneur's film was shot in black and white and featured a poor representation of an ancient demon incarnate and some typically stiff studio representations of settings; but these shortcomings actually further the premise of the film, which decries the blindness of a tech-heavy age which undermines natural reason and instinct.

One key scene which makes the point with the forehand, not the backhand, is an exterior location scene depicting Holden's first arrival at Karswell's home, Lufford Hall. The sequence is established through a long shot of Holden and Joanna driving along an entrance road toward the estate, images that graphically match the opening images of Harrington's trip to Lufford the night of his murder. Whereas the Harrington sequence is shot from a vantage allowing a view into the car, here the camera is set back to emphasize the smallness of the car, which barely reaches the top of a fence lining the road. At one point, the car disappears behind a large tree and is lost from sight for a few moments. Again, when the car enters through the gate of the estate, the camera remains behind and at enough distance to emphasize the enormity of the surroundings and smallness of Holden and Joanna. Once through the gate the car passes under a long and imposing tree branch stretched horizontally across the screen space, which quite obviously suggests nature swallowing up the scientist and his inquiries. As the car arrives at the house, the camera remains at a distance,

5. Lawless Men and Beasts

making the car diminish even further into the shadow of the great building, especially as Joanna parks it beside several other vehicles. The shot of Holden getting out is taken from a very low angle, again emphasizing the size of Karswell's building. As he exits with Joanna, children can be heard screaming, and Holden flippantly says, "Sounds like a human sacrifice." It isn't, but the sequence that follows suggests that such an event would not be out of the question, and Holden would be ill-equipped to offer help.

The couple stops at a stone barrier and watches the scene below on the green as Karswell with clown nose and makeup performs magic for a group of children. Intriguing in the shot is the camera perspective which prioritizes Holden's position as viewer while the things viewed challenge his authority to interpret them. While Holden confidently suggests to Joanna that Karswell's skill as a magician answers why letters appeared and then disappeared on his business card, Karswell pulls three puppies from a hat and distributes them to the children. What Holden misses in his assessment is the extraordinary nature of the trick—lively puppies, not docile rabbits. Likewise, the scientist misses how genuinely creepy the sorcerer looks in his make-up. A few moments later, when Karswell greets the couple and discovers that Joanna was Harrington's niece, the wizard's posture and attitude change dramatically. The viewer sees this plainly and readily interprets the acknowledgment of guilt, especially as the viewer has been privileged to witness the demon's attack on the uncle in the opening sequence. However, Holden is oblivious to what is being offered. Moments later when Karswell introduces Holden and Joanna to his mother and offers them her homemade ice cream, the viewer again is led to shiver at the creepy courtesies of this real warlock, while Holden remains oblivious to the real danger. Everything Karswell will tell Holden in the ensuing conversation underscores the scientist's dullness. The viewer is thus led to conclude that even if a man were raised from the dead, to borrow from the gospels, the man of science would dismiss the event as a hallucination or medical misdiagnosis. So, when Karswell actually calls up a storm to convince Holden of the powers inherent in the formulas of his occult book, the viewer is not surprised that Holden brushes off the phenomenon. Nor does Holden seem aware that Karswell is literally walking him downhill as they talk, a movement highlighted by a long tracking shot.

A very similar scene thematically will occur later when Joanna convinces Holden to attend a séance with a Mr. Meek, a medium whom Karswell's mother knows. The house where the event takes place is entered through a ground-floor door draped in shadows. The scene takes place at night in a deathly still corner of the city. Joanna wears gloves and coat suggesting the cold, which has been marked earlier in the story as sign of demonic presence. And Holden admits while going in that "there are some things" he doesn't know. When the séance begins, all turns extraordinarily strange, from the medium's overall demeanor to the odd song the women present around the table sing to welcome the spirit to a series of voices that emanate from Meek while in a trance. The voices really couldn't come from the man, especially the last, which is Harrington's. Joanna acknowledges it, while Holden becomes more and more dismissive despite the evidence. When Meek warns Holden of the demon and provides him the key that its appearance and disappearance depend on a formula translated from Karswell's book of magic, Holden gets up and leaves the séance, despite the women warning that it is dangerous to the medium to break a trance abruptly.

Holden's obstinacy puts others around him at risk, but he doesn't seem greatly concerned, and his callous attitude cannot be taken lightly in a film made in 1950, only a few years after the Nuremberg Trials and the dropping of the nuclear bombs and during the early stages of the Cold War, an era that would trigger a series of similar filmic warnings via the science-fiction genre. Holden's obstinacy will grow even more acute in the penultimate scene when he and his associates conduct a demonstration of the power of hypnosis to "exorcise" the psychological demons troubling mental patients. On a rather crude medical table, Rand Hobard, one of Karswell's former disciples, is stretched out on display for a roomful of scientists and students. It's a familiar scene which recalls those Mary Shelley had Victor Frankenstein observe as he formed his ideas for the animation of the dead. The shadows and hazy lights and lines of tubes and wires make for an unpleasant viewing experience and naturally create certain sympathy for the victim, Hobard, who has been rendered catatonic from fear of the demon himself. Not much needs be said about the sequence beyond the obvious disparity, as Hobard is terrified and virtually tortured in this public display by the coldly benevolent doctors who seem genuinely surprised when he breaks free and commits suicide.

5. Lawless Men and Beasts

Were the film not so grounded in the sanctified ground of the horror genre, Holden's damnation would be complete with this shocking conclusion to his demonstration; and until this point Tourneur has offered little cause to sympathize with the scientist, beyond the inexplicable affection shown him by Joanna. He has been arrogant, blind, and obstinate from the opening scenes. And he has shown little sympathy for Harrington, Meek, Hobard, or any of the characters who wander in and out of the action. However, immediately after Hobard's death, Holden asks of Karswell's whereabouts as he has decided to pass the rune back to him. Apparently, the blow to the head has restored some vision and the formerly hard-hearted scientist has come to his Damascus road. Holden comes to like a man given smelling salts, and the film moves through the final sequence on the train with a remade hero.

The logic of this change, as stated earlier, is the power of generic convention more than anything explicit in the narrative, beyond the symbolic redeeming presence of the golden-haired woman who has set her affections on him. The genre moves by the force of its own nature toward exorcism and restoration. At least, this is where the genre was in its evolution in 1950. By the mid-sixties and seventies, it would be more likely that the appropriate end of the film would be the death of Holden, not Karswell. Karswell, like Jonathan Demme's Hannibal Lector or Cormac McCarthy's Anton Chigurh, should walk away at the end as the divine avenger allowed to pillage the earth by a providence that has decreed silence as the best response to widespread cultural decay and blasphemy. Perhaps an even better cross-reference to *Night of the Demon* would be *Ringu*. Although that story follows a curious and open-minded investigative reporter, not a skeptical scientist, it does involve a kind of passing of the rune and does pose a similar conclusion that the demon has won the day and will be allowed to continue to kill in a world void of faith and true prayer.

To turn all this toward a single conclusion, a highly evocative passage in the Pauline epistles might be brought to the discussion. In response to questions from first-century converts about the specific events preceding the second coming, the apostle wrote,

> Don't let anyone deceive you in any way, for that day will not come until the rebellion occurs and the man of lawlessness is revealed, the man doomed to destruction. He will oppose and will exalt himself over

everything that is called God or worshipped, so that he sets himself up in God's temple, proclaiming himself to be God.... And now you know what is holding him back, so that he may be revealed at the proper time. For the secret power of lawlessness is already at work; but the one who now holds it back will continue to do so till he is taken out of the way. And then the lawless one will be revealed...

Who or what the "man of lawlessness" might be has been much debated by biblical scholars and commentators over the centuries, with renderings largely dependent on how the church interprets various moments in its history. The papacy was this anti-Christian force for the reformers. Some single uber-villain has been posited by late twentieth-century fundamentalists. If one follows the evolution of the horror genre, an intriguing new interpretation of "antichrist" suggests itself; that the incarnation of a particularly modern, Baconian mindset like Tourneur offers in the character of Holden perfectly fits the description given in the epistle of the "lawless" man to come. The man of science divorced from conscience and belief is, by some definition, a lawless man. And that such a character has sat and is sitting in positions of authority not only in universities and town halls, but in modern religious institutions is seemingly incontrovertible. If we play through this line of speculation, an obvious conclusion would be to recognize that the incarnation of this lawless man in the modern world, seen thus as the coming of the Beast, has triggered many of the artistic, and here filmic, productions of the collective conscience driving the genre. It also seems plausible to suggest that the marauding demons whose initial assaults met with a restraining hand have more recently been allowed free rein, as the hand of providence has pulled back in judgment.

Whether or not a student of either biblical eschatology or film history embraces such a speculation about both scripture and the arc of Western civilization, Tourneur's film does offer a compelling critique of modernity and the demons it has awakened. In a vision not far removed from the troubling dystopias imaged by Orwell, Huxley and Golding, *Night of the Demon* suggests a world in which the future will not be troubled by a soulless technocracy, but by a pandemonium come to earth, a haunting judgment upon those whose spiritual pacifism has blunted their swords into briefcase clasps and laser pointers.

6

KILL THINE ENEMY
Howard Hawks' *The Thing*

> *But now, when by the grace and power of the Most High he was beginning to think of holy and useful things, while he was still clad in secular garments, he met a leper one day and, made stronger than himself, he kissed him. From then on he began to despise himself more and more, until, by the mercy of the Redeemer, he came to perfect victory over himself.*—Thomas Celano on St. Francis of Assisi

Once you have dropped a bomb on an entire urban population and incinerated nearly every living thing for miles, the conscience demands its due. The terrible war was over but at a hideous cost. The transformation from cultural psyche built around the notion of shining city on a hill, the people of the divine covenant, the "model of Christian charity" (in John Winthrop's words), nurturing mother to the immigrant and poor, to global police officer and executioner left the generation living in the 1950s morally traumatized, as one might expect. Film scholars have long recognized and described this condition as it played loudly across several genres from maternal melodrama to the emerging darker Western to horror. That trauma manifested itself in stories of characters paralyzed by neurosis and chronic anxiety who broke into criminal or violent activity when pressed to conform to a corrupted elder culture, the stories that produced troubled icons like Marlon Brando, James Dean, Montgomery Clift, as well as Vivien Leigh, Betty Davis, Joan Crawford and Elizabeth Taylor. But the trauma also manifested itself through stories with larger-scale narrative outbursts that played out like childish tantrums, sudden eruptions of hysteria and petulance and then punishment. Many of these came through the forms of overwrought melodrama, but an equal number were of the science-fiction horror genre, where plagues and monsters were let loose to spread chaos only so angry men with clubs could bludgeon them to silence, or at least so it would seem given the extreme logic of many of the story lines. Howard Hawks' 1951 production, *The Thing from Another World,* represents this latter narrative form in our present study.

Though on the surface Hawks' film is underplayed and straight as an arrow in plot, something contradictory and deeply troubling rumbles under the surface. As one of hundreds of productions concerned with alien invasion of one form or another and the need to quash the invaders, the events roll predictably from infection to attack to eradication. This is not a film like *Night of the Demon*, which haunts and surprises because it depicts a haunting. It is a predictable story that confounds and lingers in the imagination in spite of itself. Auteurists might attribute this to the dominating presence of Hawks' creative mind behind every sequence, but that is a rather controversial contention in this case since the film actually credits Christian Nyby as director. Nyby had worked with Hawks as film editor on *Red River* (1948) and other projects, and collaborated with him to a significant degree on the set of *The Thing*. Something is at work in the deep structures of the film besides the force of a single creative personality, something which connects more immediately to the genre of horror and its interest in demonic presence and exorcism.

To get at this "something," it might be momentarily useful to consider that phenomenon of certain disordered personalities that Sigmund Freud labeled "narcissism" from the Greek myth of Narcissus, who drowned reaching toward his own flowery reflection in a pool. Once you peel back all the wrappings that have shrouded Freud's diagnosis over the past hundred years from the pop, pseudo-psychological descriptions of aberrant sexual behavior to Christopher Lasch's re-application of the term to the modern post-prosperity culture in America, there remains in Freud's observation about a certain kind of diseased ego something essentially true regarding the individual or collective human consciousness bent inward. In other words, Freud's identification of an acute psychological condition has a common application. Narcissism is a familiar condition; at least it is in its early progressions. Unfortunately, it develops into a potentially untreatable disease. Once the roots of this internal disorder are down, pulling them up requires figuratively or literally a divine act.

6. Kill Thine Enemy

The condition of the narcissistic personality involves the self as a whole. The narcissistic "self" is fragile, empty, and fragmented. It lacks coherent structure and so flees or attacks all real or perceived challenges to its existence. Where the threat poses annihilation and shame, the narcissist responds with various forms of self-idealization. Because these challenges and responses are structured around perceptions of reality rather than reality, once the self falls into the condition of narcissism, all attempts to restore it are perceived as threats, which circle back to feed and further the condition.

Depictions of the narcissistic illness in film tend to involve some dangerous cloud of hysteria emanating from the disordered consciousness of that personality. The narcissist is not a nuisance and social bore, but rather a palpable social threat capable of anything since she or he functions from perceptions of grandeur detached from ordinary social convention, decency, or morality. The prototypical tale of narcissism is the Gothic story with its thick haze of paranoia, repressed sexuality, and death. The narcissist is the perfect killer in such a context for she or he has already murdered all beyond the self, including God in many cases.

This connection to the Gothic is telling in the larger evolution of horror, for it leads back to one of the most singularly narcissistic characters in all British and American literature, Mary Shelley's antihero Victor Frankenstein, arguably the father of all of horror's antiheroes. Shelley's main character was a man completely blind to the consequences of his own actions. Victor pursues the source of life by defiling the dead. He destroys his own family in the course of constructing a single monstrous progeny. He creates artificial life twice, but abandons the first upon sight of it and tears apart the second. Victor cannot be called in any sense a good man, except as he projects his hubris outward to make better creatures than the creator himself made. And except by his author, who projects that construction upon him, despite all the evidence handed the reader. Shelley needed for Victor to be a good man, one might argue, because he was in fact based on her own husband, Percy, whose child she carried while writing the novel, a logic Mary would continue through legacy building after the poet's drowning, seemingly oblivious to the suffering he had caused so many throughout his short life. But that is another story for another analysis. The point here is that the modern horror genre began with a prototypically narcissistic main character, the mad scientist whose love for the mind, and ultimately his own mind, trumped all other human decencies.

So, out of Shelley's troubled vision came the doomed sub-creator whose crime isn't in what he does, but in what he negated by what he did. Like the adolescent with the Ouija board who shuts the main doors of reason and grace but leaves the rear open, the narcissistic protagonist stares at his own reflection while evil enters the kitchen quietly and removes the carving knives. This character of Dante-esque disordered reason typically creates the beast that kills all others, and then he will kill himself in a morbid and twisted murder-suicide arc.

Every one of the main characters studied in the films already discussed in this book suffer from or struggles against this condition—Norman from *What Lies Beneath*, General Vidal from *Pan's Labyrinth*, Alan Gray from *Vampyr*, the British scientists in Egypt in *The Mummy*, Karswell and Holden in *Night of The Demon*, and the entire exploratory team in the Arctic in *The Thing*. Each has lost essential grip on the realities and entered some stage of denial and paranoia. Each has become dangerous because of these denials. Even the meek Alan Gray in *Vampyr* threatens the most vulnerable women in the house by allowing the doctor into the house and then allowing himself to be transfused. Apart from the intrusion of grace in the form of the peasant servant, Gray would have become the next vampire feeding on the blood of young women.

This characterization plays itself out in Hawks' *The Thing from Another World*. The film does indeed foreground a narcissistic scientist who "creates" the killing beast and thus offers an image of this kind of disordered modern personality; the story suggests it is something more than just another "alien-from-space" 1950s thriller. That point needs to be established early because unlike many of the sci-fi horror films of the period, such as Don Siegel's more famous *Invasion of the Body Snatchers*, *The Thing* lacks the evocative *mise-en-scène* that suggests a large haze of mental disorder, the signature of the older horror productions. It likewise lacks the type of bloody carnage which now seems necessary for the horror film to horrify.

A distinction should be made between horror and pure science-fiction. Horror film deals in the demonic. Science-fiction may, but does

6. Kill Thine Enemy

not need to. A film like M. Night Shyamalan's *Signs* is a science-fiction thriller that has frightening moments and that develops a religious theme, but it is not a horror film. The threat really is a big green alien who is finally killed. The theme doesn't revolve around transgression, guilt, and retribution, but mercy and redemption. Science-fiction develops fanciful projections, some good and some not, of a world fundamentally threatened and transformed by emerging and potential science. Horror, on the other hand, plays out a nightmare where incarnate evil wages war on the guilty. Bad science is secondary to the point.

The Thing initially seems more aligned with science-fiction, and it might have been initially intended as science-fiction, but it transformed into something else. There will be good reason years later for John Carpenter having the children threatened by the demonic Michael Myers in *Halloween* watch Hawks' film on the night of their haunting.

Several details should alert the viewer to the horror context of *The Thing*. The first is obvious on a single viewing, and that is the cross-referencing of the film to James Whale's *Frankenstein*. This is achieved by the simple physical resemblance of the monsters in both works. When the Thing enters the mess hall midway through the action and is trapped and set on fire by the scientists and military men in the Arctic base, the reference to the Karloff character batting flames in the old mill is unmistakable. Likewise, when the monster moves along a metal ramp toward the remaining soldiers and scientists in the climactic scene, it lumbers like the monster of Whale's film. It should be noted that Shelley's original creature was rather nimble, bounding through the Alps in pursuit of his maker.

In addition to Whale's *Frankenstein*, *The Thing* also cross-references Freund's *The Mummy*. Some of this emerges from the physical allusions to Karloff, but it also shows up in some of the central suspense moments in Hawks' film. First, when the scientists carry the frozen Thing into their base for observation, they wax confident that their subsequent and most necessary observations and analyses will benefit mankind. Then, of course, the monster wakes to life terrifying the young soldier with the unfortunate task of guarding it. Finally, when the military men and scientists open a storage case in the base's greenhouse to find a dead dog the monster has been feeding on, the visual reference points back to the "don't-open-that-case" moment early in the Freund film.

A Christian Response to Horror Cinema

Add to this that Hawks' beast is thirsty for blood, literally. Granted, its vicious deeds are all done off-screen, unlike the John Carpenter 1982 remake, but they are the deeds of a bloodthirsty entity nonetheless. The viewer is informed that a couple of the victims hang from the rafters of the greenhouse with their throats slit for easy feeding. The monster's thirst is an overt reference back to the Dracula tradition and its many offshoots.

And the monster is associated with lowering temperatures, a phenomenon in fact and fiction which is typically associated with demonic presence. It comes in from outside the base and brings a chill wind with it, then attacks the scientists by cutting off their heat supply, their generator, threatening to kill the men and women by hypothermia before feasting on them.

These more superficial details, possibly explained away by the natural cross-pollination of one genre to the next, are reinforced by something more substantial still: the solid bedrock of what might be called generic modality. The horror genre, like the Hollywood musical, functions as genre not only by virtue of narrative structure, theme, and characteristic symbol; it is most clearly defined by the way the cinematic elements engage the audience. Horror anticipates dread the way that the musical anticipates pleasure and escape. When the music plays for Fred Astaire, the narrative world is placed on pause and the audience is directly engaged by theatrical performance. In this way, the pause is redemptive. The analogy could be a sacramental liturgy where the narrative logic of the worship service is interrupted and transformed by the sacramental liturgy of the Eucharist in which the real presence of the living Christ is believed to become the physical elements lifted up. This is different than, say, a conventional thriller where a well-paced and yet extreme plot, the meat of all suspense stories, pulls the viewer toward the screen. In horror, the narrative is infected, so to speak, by the real entrance of a living dreadful and damned presence, with all lost unless an equal and greater intrusion of some agency of divine grace enters and halts the dark possession and its consequent evil trajectory. This presence engages the viewer directly, and the redemption or release offered at its expulsion is deeply personal.

The modality of *The Thing*, while not challenging the security of the viewer as quickly and powerfully as a film like *Night of the Demon* or *Vampyr*, still functions according to the terms of immediate spiritual

6. Kill Thine Enemy

engagement. The best way to illustrate this is by examining the way the visual elements of the film speak against the simple propositions of the text and thus suggest a higher order evil at work in the story than just the lumbering monster named in the title.

Setting plays a prominent role in this equation. The film is set around a desolate air force base north of Alaska. Whereas the opening scene is labeled by the visual cue of a sign for the "Officers' Club" in Anchorage, Alaska, the action will require that the key characters fly further, beyond the securities of men playing cards and sharing stories of romantic exploits. The most visually striking moments of the film occur during the plane flight as the large craft is dwarfed by the unknown, vast, white landscape of the Arctic around the base. This is not a flight into the domain of science so much as it is a flight out of the known into the uncanny. The motif, which will be repeated in later science-fiction-turned-horror films like *Event Horizon* (1997), suggests a Faustian approach to science— science that points to alchemy and opens the door for the entrance of Mephistopheles. Interestingly enough, such a view of science is what teased Victor Frankenstein into his alchemical act of sparking life into the sewed parts from various cadavers, as it no doubt teased Shelley, Byron and Polidari in their private readings.

That the players are domesticated in the opening scene is significant as well. Just as the film carries the notion of science toward something much more threatening, so it places at the center of the story a potential marriage that will be threatened by the entrance of the Beast. One might think of Coleridge's "Rime of the Ancient Mariner" here, as Coleridge, haunted by his own demons, framed his story of demonic incarnation as a tale told with "glittering eye" to a wedding guest. Hawks' film references domestication throughout. The main character, Captain Hendry, is the typical American hero-type, brash and manly, and free-roaming. Upon his plane reaching the site of the science base where the action will occur, he is quickly reunited with an old flame, Nikki, a pinup type that one would expect came from the pen of Gillette Elvgren rather than a real casting office. She will quickly remind him of the liberties he took on a previous meeting after he had too much to drink, and so she sets a traditional marriage snare before Hendry. All the men around the couple recognize the inevitability of their captain becoming husband and father and

Captain Patrick Hendry (Kenneth Tobey), with pinup girlfriend Nikki (Margaret Sheridan), banter about their former fling in Howard Hawks' *The Thing from Another World*. 1951. RKO Radio Pictures.

so being lost to the Officers' Club family of men—such male fellowships are always challenged by the prospect of marriage stealing their members. But here the threat to the domestic stability of the club provides little more than a green screen metaphor for the real threat that will come once the Thing is released into the community around the base. It will literally kill and eat a husband and wife and all potential children in its way.

One must remember here that horror displays the logic of the diabolic through imitation—grotesque families marked by perverse sexual fetishization, incestuous marriage, and corrupted and dangerous children. For a while, only people in the industry and academics uncovered these elements, but now they have become overt and so quite familiar within the genre, especially in its more exploitive forms—a child zombie eating its mother in *Night of the Living Dead* or a savage family in a perverse table arrangement in *The Texas Chainsaw Massacre* or demon women

6. Kill Thine Enemy

curling around the Jonathan Harker character in Coppola's 1992 version of *Dracula*. This is what incarnate demonism does; it replicates in vicious and filthy parody the most precious and sacramental of human relationships.

This diabolical context for the story of *The Thing* as fundamental challenge to what might be termed sacred family order becomes unmistakable when the devilish Thing is birthed from the block of ice under a warm incubating blanket. It is a mix of imagery worthy of medieval imaginations or perhaps young boys reading the latest edition of *Weird Science*. Such contradictory terms of hot and cold, death and birth, marriage and rape hold the center of the horror genre.

In *The Thing*, the elements were drawn from the earlier Universal films blended with the older cultural tradition that informed those films, and, of course, its immediate source material, John W. Campbell's evocative novella *Who Goes There*. The Campbell novella begins by underscoring setting and symbol over story. An odor of decay and corruption in *Who Goes There* surrounds the scientists who wait for an evil birth from the melting block of ice in which is trapped the alien they have discovered:

> The place stank. A queer, mingled stench that only the ice buried cabins of an Antarctic camp know, compounded of reeking human sweat, and the heavy, fish oil stench of melted seal blubber. An overtone of liniment combated the musty smell of sweat-and-snow-drenched furs. The acrid odor of burnt cooking fat, and the animal, not-unpleasant smell of dogs, diluted by time, hung in the air.

The smell of death permeates the chamber of life in the language opening the source story. Scientists wait on a discovery purportedly to further human life, which will rather devour life and spread like cancer the logic of corruption and the grave.

So in Hawks' film, the greenhouse on the base in which vegetables are grown to feed the researchers becomes the place where the monster will grow new Things by dripping blood from its murder victims onto fragments of its vegetable-like self. It is all rather a curious mix. The lead scientist on the base, Carrington, the main "mad scientist" of the story, believes he has a new discovery, a creature with massive regenerative powers that will certainly advance the cause of humanity, and, of course, prove to the world his own genius. So, he encourages the growth of the Thing in the greenhouse and then creates his own macabre flower garden of little pod Things incubated by a lamp and nourished by the plasma that should be used to help the wounded men in the base. Death from life. Corruption from birth. Sexual reproduction apart from love. Action without feeling. The terms from Eliot's haunted "Hollow Men" come to mind. All natural and divinely ordained categories of life and virtue are not just challenged and dismissed, but inverted in the fashion of a Black Mass. And the agency of this inversion is not some psychic conjuror or occultist like Karswell in the Tourneur film, but a respectable scientist and his associates speaking and acting on behalf of science itself—science as religion with a brain in a bottle as the divine image. It is all rather grisly and morbid and dreadful in the purest definitions of those words.

This aligns with the previous discussion of narcissism in the horror genre. The inability to see reality for what it is, but to filter all through the disturbed, dangerous self, is the end of enlightened inquiry as played out in the films. Here, science exists to advance machine men without emotion, men unable to love. Science pronounces reason in unreasonable terms; in the older medieval view, reason led to humility and prayer. Aquinas cast sins as disordered reason, or reason run to foul, and that is what we get. In *The Thing*, rather than running from a corrupt monstrosity safely encased in ice, the narcissistic mind insists on cracking it open, and for no good reason other than the pure pleasure of asserting the self, the authoritative will to be and do contrary to all better sense, and certainly contrary to any demands of cautious charity. The compulsion to do the irrational—so essential within the horror genre, so inexplicable to the viewer watching with knuckles tight around the chair rest—emerges from the narcissistic pool. The self reaches out to death and discards life. It cannot see life. It creates an artificial form to walk about in and murders all who threaten the artifice.

An immediate visual cue to this way of understanding the film comes early as Hendry and his men fly to the base in the key scene already referenced. There is no logic to the trip. The base was warm, while the plane is not. Within the Officers' Club, the camera's field of vision is wide, the men moving easily across and within the frame. They leave this space and fly in the metal tube of an airplane to the unknown expanse described

6. Kill Thine Enemy

above, and for no compelling reason. The film marks this contradiction with metaphoric matches. Several shots of the plane seem to celebrate the machine as a modern marvel. The metal tube fills the screen. Its skis gracefully glide across the ice. The men are laughing inside. Yet the visuals also address the contradiction. As with the plane in the Tourneur film, the machine is really only imposing and celebratory because the viewer is told to see it that way. It offers no beauty of its own. It suggests claustrophobia and death, a metal coffin-tube with bodies buried alive. It shrinks the men to ants as they exit, which is what the technical innovations from the nineteenth century on tended to do. Evoking the biblical language of Proverbs, like a prostitute it lures the living with sweet words but then turns those made for real life into loaves of bread.

A similar and more shocking contradiction will come later, after the scientists and soldiers have discovered the skid marks of a crashed rocket in the snow. Although the men who go to investigate appear calm and sane, their actions are thoroughly irrational. After standing around the edges of the buried shape and determining it to be perfectly round and thus exotic and dangerous, they decide to resurrect the ship by thermal explosion. In other words, they respond to the challenge of fresh knowledge by an act of consummate destruction. The explosion destroys the ship, leaving only the frozen alien pilot alive in the block of ice. One would have expected the alien to be destroyed and the ship spared, but in the reverse logic of black horror, the good is overcome by the aberrant, the evil allowed to grow and prosper.

Another aspect of this scene is striking. What the men see in the snow before pushing the detonator is a lone fin sticking up like the dorsal of a shark. The Geiger counter they use detects radiation. So, two cues—one visual and one auditory—tell of threat and danger. Its foreignness is the threat which must be destroyed, so they kill the shark-like thing, or at least try. And they do so by a nuclear-style blast, which to them poses no threat.

What we have then from the start is the pattern of irrational inversion and destruction. Pseudo-science exists to kill the foreign, including angels one might assume should they show up—a concept developed in another film of the period, *The Day the Earth Stood Still* (1951). Here again, much has been written about the way the horror and science-fiction films of the

A Christian Response to Horror Cinema

fifties tended this way because of various cultural phobias that needed fictional purging. For example, fear of nuclear explosions post–Hiroshima and Nagasaki led to Godzilla and all sorts of other mutant creatures from under the sea to punish the non-liberal oppressors. Scholars have made careers describing how xenophobia led to films like *The Invasion of the Body Snatchers* with its foreign pods replicating people; how fears of women set free from pre–World War domestic tensions led to the *Fifty-Foot Woman* and *Cat People*; and how fears of racial blending led to films about mutant man-flies and fish men. These readings follow the logic of marketplace productions. Films are commercial products designed and sold by an industry with one eye in the newspaper after all. The concluding scene of *The Thing* has a newspaperman named Scottie, who has followed the drama and provided some comic relief, speaking into a microphone wired back home warning that people should search the skies and beware the coming invasions.

The relevant point is that deeper forces are also at work in these stories in addition to the cathartic displays of cultural anxieties. These deeper forces came bursting out of some of these safer story patterns like the Alien in the Ridley Scott film. In the decades following the fifties came films like *Rosemary's Baby*, *The Exorcist*, *The Omen* and a host of others where the alien had become Satan himself. The culture did not suddenly become more religious; nor did the generic form simply need some new innovation to survive another generation's changing interests. Rather the deeper waters under these genre stories bubbled up. These demonic allusions were always there, just mostly unspoken apart from the more overt horror films being made by the more eccentric Hammer Studios or Roger Corman at American International Pictures. What seems to have happened is that the further cultural shock of the emerging American youth culture, a generation that rejected the authority of the father and the church, brought to the surface cultural demons waiting to be unleashed to punish older transgressions crusted over by guilt. The surface narratives about xenophobia and postwar trauma hid a deeper narrative about universal transgression played out through particular moral choices in a particular moment.

To put it more explicitly, bubbling up from under Hawks' film is a story about a demonic apocalypse. The film is precursor to the zombie subgenre birthed in the 1960s with *The Night of the Living Dead*. Science

6. Kill Thine Enemy

is proposed as the new religion, but it is impotent to stop the onslaught of demonic avengers it opened the door to after first shooing away the guardian angels and then dismissing the protective authority of the church. One of the more memorable lines from *The Thing* has the captain looking at the self-regenerating arm of the monster and saying, "an intellectual carrot, the mind boggles." The comment is so thoroughly silly that it draws attention to itself and other bits of forced interpretation sprinkled throughout the film, like Scottie's concluding remarks or the mad scientist Carrington commenting that the demeanor of the soldiers trying to kill the Thing look "like a lynching" or Captain Hendry listening to an overly technical scientist at some sort of radar control telling the scientist, "You lost me, but I'll take your word for it." Characters with such a bent, limited understanding of the mysteries of life deserve to be eaten by zombies. They are zombies themselves, after all, men who have lost hold of the function of reason and science and the overall purpose of life. They are men without chests, to borrow again the memorable description of C.S. Lewis, occupants of useless and unvigilant cities that get overrun by the real machine men, the orcs in Tolkien's epic. The dead men of science have become so subhuman in their basic understanding, so stupid and infectiously so, that they are the perfect food for the intellectual, carnivorous carrot, the Thing in the story.

As we have seen, the basic structure of the horror film follows a pattern of transgression, then chaos, then exorcism. Each component speaks to a very specific type of sin that opens the door to the dark incarnation. In *The Thing*, the sin is murder. The social critics who see the genre as response to the traumas of the nuclear age are correct in part. America did work out her postwar anxieties in the nightmare worlds of science fiction and horror. However, what these cultural critics overlook is the real effect of real transgression. The films suggest that scientific materialism is a moral transgression that leads to barbarism and genocide, the very cause of the horror, not its solution.

The Thing is fundamentally a film about cold-bloodedness. The scientists and soldiers put on the mask of human advancement and cultural expansion but their actions suggest they just want the foreign thing in order to explode it. After the initial attempt fails they melt the beast and then set two traps, one to light it on fire and the other to electrocute and incinerate it. That's the one picture we get. Meanwhile, the lead scientist, Carrington, a reshaping of the character of Renfield, has fallen in love with the rampaging Thing and works to aid its survival since to his enlightened mind an intellectual carrot represents something higher than old fleshy, messy humankind. That's the other. Either way, the modern experiment has at its heart a fundamental hatred of the human condition.

The film is certainly responding to cultural anxiety in a nuclear age, but it is speaking even more to the resulting apocalypse that comes when man loses the spark of divine love and goes the way of Cain, murdering his brother. That's where the guilt comes in, and it is real blood guilt, not mere psychic trauma. The RAF and USAF did firebomb Dresden in 1945. U.S. planes did drop bombs that incinerated not two armies, but two civilian-filled Japanese cities populated by real people with families and pets and vegetable gardens in the back. Justify a war, use even the terms laid out by the Vatican for a just war, and it is still hard to swallow such large-scale demonstrations of violence. It might be noted that since the Second World War, the door has opened wider in America and western Europe to the practices of abortion and euthanasia, so something has certainly happened to devalue the worth of the individual in the lands where church spires still mark the towns and cities. Once some lines are crossed it is impossible to go back; after the first transgression, the second and third produce far less remorse.

A deep sense of blood guilt triggers narratives like *The Thing*. The demonic avenger of blood is the zombie, the possessed corpse, a step even further toward the infernal heart of evil than the possessed woman or man. What is especially interesting of the beast in Hawks' film is its anonymity; the zombie hordes have this characteristic, counter to older beasts like Frankenstein or Dracula or the Mummy. Even Godzilla developed a personality. But the Thing has no personality. Typical of the elaborate seduction tease of horror, the full revelation of the thing delays the viewer through half the film. First, the monster is seen in shadowy haze frozen in ice, and then it is seen through darkness and snow throwing off a pack of sled dogs. Then it is seen growling for a brief moment in the greenhouse doorway once Hendry opens it. Then it walks into the trap in the mess hall and is seen in darkness and shadow before the men throw kerosene on it and set it ablaze. Finally, it emerges in the darkness on the

6. Kill Thine Enemy

walkway wired with an electrical trap, but even there it is seen from a distance at the side where the men huddle waiting to throw the switch. Its electrocution becomes a kind of weird crucifixion as the giant carrot beast turns to ash with arms outstretched. The faceless enemy is destroyed from a distance. Even the reporting of events is with face slightly turned; the viewer is informed that the greenhouse and Carrington's lab have likewise been incinerated, but not provided with any images or sounds.

Still, these are shallow assurances, and the savvy viewer realizes that the last words of warning function not to dispel the horror but to further it. If one lone intellectual vegetable can wreak such havoc, what of a team of pods—which, of course, will become the plot device in the later Don Siegel classic. Demons come back. As in the memorable parable of Jesus, once the house is swept clean of one demon, seven more return to take its place, which is precisely what the genre will go on to document over the next several decades.

All of this leads to the film's exorcism sequence. Somehow it seems significant that the natural element of fire is replaced by electricity created by a generator. First, the use of electricity hardly seems a higher order principle, given that the Thing knew enough to shut down the generator in an earlier sequence. Fire spreads and is easily produced. Electricity, unless lightning bolts come hurtling from the sky, requires maintenance just to be kept at sufficient level to do its work. Second, however, electricity in the genre of horror hearkens back to those impulses Victor Frankenstein used to give birth to the scourge that would kill his family and wife, and ultimately himself. It was the occult energy that enabled the uberman to achieve his goal of fulfilling the wish of Milton's Satan, overthrowing heaven itself. Of course, that attempt didn't quite go as planned. To find satisfaction in an ending where soldiers electrocute the demon on a platform using a generator requires a massive suspension of disbelief, not to mention some literary memory loss.

There can be no true exorcism in this soulless world. In the Tourneur film, a real demon haunting a real man, skeptic though he is, prompts his fear toward a very simple faith. He does what he is told and follows the spiritual logic presented to him, even though it does seem extraordinarily like Chesterton's ethics. He passes the parchment to the wizard Karswell and steps back into the arms of the girl who loves him for no good reason

The electrocution of the beast (James Arness) in the climax of *The Thing*. 1951. RKO Radio Pictures.

beyond those elfland powers of fairy love. She has her heart set on him, although he is indirectly complicit in the death of her uncle; she bears with his stubborn resistance to her attempts to steer him from the dark wood; and she receives him a broken but better man and soon to be husband in the end. In the Hawks film, the pinup girl in love with Hendry bears no resemblance to the Madonna or to the traditional American girl next door. She is the fetishized projection of a materialist society that has reformed femininity around the notion of sexual allure rather than domesticity and motherhood. She is the *femme fatale* of another film who took a wrong turn in the back lot and wandered onto a different set. Likewise, Hendry and the scientists at the base show no understanding of the limitations and potential evils of science and military force. They fail to see that the madman Carrington is the amalgam of two images, the jackboot who also wants to do experiments toward the development of a master race. They do by impulse the very things they aim to protect the world from. They operate in a void where there is no sin and guilt, no God nor Satan, no sacraments, no blessed hearth and home. All that exists is force and greater force, smart and smarter.

6. Kill Thine Enemy

This swings this entire analysis back to where it began, with what the condition of narcissism implies for an individual and for a culture. By definition, a narcissist cannot be cured through human means. Any attempt to address and treat the condition or at least control it will be perceived as a threat and will trigger a greater response of self-glorification and delusion. This applies to institutions and cultures as well. Looking at this from the theological point of view adopted here, one might align narcissism with demonic possession, and it very well might lead to that very thing. The self emptied of divine coherence attracts like a magnet a coherent presence that unites those fragments. It is paradoxical that the entities which embody chaos and disorder would become those which order the disordered self, yet that seems to be the case. The amulets and Ouija boards and séances that allow the emptying of the self and openness to outer presence find an analogue in the pool into which the narcissist fixes his or her gaze. It might very well be said that the horror genre is mostly about fear of possession.

But can there be protection when the common means of exorcism, the traditional rites of the church, have been stripped of power and dismissed? The simple answer would be no. Christian theology will insist that a return to grace is required. The power to repel the evil presence must come from outside the disordered and empty self. It must be called upon and received according to other terms evoking other special privileges.

Transformation of the narcissistic character requires an intentional, sacramental act, which may begin with an exorcism but which, as the church has taught for centuries, must proceed with consistent application of the means of grace and a life of self-abnegation and discipline. Such transformations are miraculous on the rare occasions when they occur. However, it might be helpful to recall the fact that ecclesiastical history abounds with such examples of the camel going through the eye of the needle. It is said that St. Francis, to use one of the more prominent examples, intentionally reversed the trajectory of his own narcissistic tendencies by serving the outcasts of the world. He kissed the leper and preached to the poor:

> ... in the kenosis of Christ, Francis saw God's infinite love for men and women in the condescension of the Word in becoming human and lay-

ing down His life in Calvary. This coming down, this humbling, this stooping to become small, this humility and poverty, this minority was appropriated by Francis when he gradually stripped himself of all signs of power and status in order to identify with the poorest, the lepers.[1]

That an entire culture would be jolted into such a reformation would seem to require an even greater miracle than that a single individual be transformed in such a way. A culture devolved toward the celebration of murder from afar through the movement of machines would seem to be a culture far from grace. Although, as the older films in particular show, no culture far from grace is ever entirely apart from grace.

7

THE RETURN OF MOLECH
Robin Hardy's *The Wicker Man*

Sometimes one is bound to ask: "What is left when everything else is gone?" When something happens which seems to make life no longer worth living, when we feel that we neither want nor can go on, what is left then? The answer to that is very simple—when everything else is gone, a sense of duty remains.—William Barclay

Theorists of horror have readily grasped that the genre has dark stories to tell us about ourselves. This would be the main point of Robin Wood's seminal collection *American Nightmare*,[1] which cemented in the mind of seemingly every film critic since its publication the Freudian model of "the return of the repressed" as the best tool to use in analyzing individual horror films, generic threads, and the whole moral landscape implied in both. As the thinking goes, horror uncovers what the political and cultural powers that be will not face about the oppressions that make possible their power.

Although Wood's primary concern by his own admission was his commitment to radical Marxism and specifically the confluence of Marx and Freud,[2] his view of horror has become conventional in academic discussion, for many scholars tend to measure theories on functionality and not credibility, and this one works, most likely because the monsters in horror all trace their ancestry to or through Mary Shelley's repressed nightmares. That is, in suppressing the truth of the Godwinian enterprise she and husband Percy had undertaken, Mary projected onto the fictional landscape the nightmare version of the cursed birth she feared, paradoxically what David Skal called the "most potent creation myth of modern times."[3] And so, because of the built-in psychosis of the genre and the neatness of the critical tool, the monsters in horror have been variously identified with whatever critics have determined the culture has pushed to the side, from the primal id to immigrants and homosexuals and abandoned children. So, tell me, Michael Myers, what do *you* think your father did to you on those weekends you cannot remember? The horror theorists have gotten to choose what to designate as being repressed, largely based on their ideological predispositions, and which films to use for illustration, largely based on which work best with the adopted theoretical apparatus. Because the horror genre has proven so fertile a field for film producers, the couch sessions have been ample.

What scholars inclined toward Wood's methodology might object to in this present study is, therefore, not the use of the repressed-other model, but that it seems here to serve a specifically theological, and not a political or ideological, end. I agree that horror does chronicle the works of the demons we had rather not face. But my contention is that the fear that drives horror is that the repressed demons may be real, not mere fictional devices, and that the genre depends on the paradigms of Christianity and especially those quirky salvific elements like bread and wine and the prayers of priests and the faith of children. It just seems cleaner and simpler to say that what tormented Shelley, for example, was a sense of old-fashioned moral guilt and its sister fear of the judgments that would come as result of the transgressions that brought it on. After all, at the end of *Frankenstein* the monster and maker both repent and grieve after their own fashion, which seems odd in a story so married to enlightened moral principles. One can see the same in Bram Stoker's famous novel, where the vampire is killed finally by an act of sacrificial and redemptive love.

Let me just state directly that the genre of horror appears to drip less with blood than with guilt over transgressions committed and their consequences. And secondarily, the development of the film genre from the atmospheric thrillers of the teens and twenties to the grisly carnage films of the present day has followed the dark trajectory of what seems to occur inevitably when lines are crossed; that is, its heart has grown harder and its behaviors more excessive and defiant.

Few films support these conclusions as convincingly and memorably as Robin Hardy's cult classic *The Wicker Man* (1973). Hardy's film suggests that the horror genre tells a larger story than the oppression of certain groups. It suggests that the horror genre has evolved to a stage where it describes the battle of good and evil played out on a large scale, as the old, patriarchal Christian faith has been besieged by an emerging matriarchal

7. The Return of Molech

neopaganism. As Hardy said in interviews, the film "is a cautionary tale," a tale about what seemed to be happening and where it might logically lead.

The Wicker Man proposes that the "Woodstock" youth culture of the 1960s in Britain and the United States marked a significant cultural challenge and regression. In the film, the established patriarchy, that which unfolded from the biblical revelation of God as Father, gets embodied, then bound and burned and expelled from the camp by the representatives of the new age. One critic called the film's final movement where this message is made plain one of "the most unexpected (but logical) climaxes in horror history."[4] Unfortunately, that same critic, like many of the pop-cult followers of the film, completely missed its "cautionary" nature, arguing inadvertently on behalf of the film's monsters that "they don't have churches, or ministries, and yes, their rites feature nudity and fertility, but that just makes so-called 'paganism' different from Christianity, not necessarily wrong."[5] The logic is that which Joseph Campbell popularized several decades ago: that a Mass which reenacts Christ's substitution on the cross in a quiet cathedral is roughly equivalent to the giving of an innocent child to the god of the sea or sun. The extremity of the logic suggests a post-orthodox age looking to retain the vestiges of its lost faith.

To miss the warning of Hardy's film is a naiveté that the film itself condemns. It brings to mind a memorable scene from Bruce Beresford's masterful *Black Robe*. In that film, a younger priest novitiate falls in love with an Indian girl and begins to side with the Algonquians he is called to evangelize over the more civilized French Jesuit missionaries he represents. Later, when he and his older mentor are forced to run a torturous gauntlet when captured by a brutal tribe of Sioux, he asks forgiveness for romanticizing the tribe and its friendlier customs. At the end he must stay with his Indian bride as a form of penance.

The Wicker Man has no such salvific conclusion and thus is deeply troubling. Curiously, it is a film with a troubled production history as well. Few cult films have a talent pool of its caliber. Although Hardy gets credit for direction, the screenplay came from Anthony Schaffer, who with his brother Peter, had, remarkable credentials for theatrical writing. The lead roles went to a very mature Christopher Lee, seasoned from years of work in the Hammer Studios horror mill, and Edward Woodward, who was starring in the popular British spy series *Callan* and had a highly successful theatrical career before that. Musical compositions used were skillfully researched by Paul Giovanni who used both folk tunes and a setting of a Robert Burns song. The art direction, which included finding the correct locale in rural Scotland and the artifacts of old Celtic paganism, was done by Seamus Flannery who went on to a productive film and television career in Canada. The film's problems were not from a lack of talent, but derived from the difficulties of locale and staging in the cold Hebrides about fifteen miles off the Scottish mainland, and the uniqueness of the film within a genre that had specific marketing criteria. When British Lion changed management and the original producer, Peter Snell, was replaced, the film was cut considerably to accommodate a low-expectation marketing campaign. When the film later developed a following, it was discovered that the original negatives were somehow lost by British Lion, and the original cut lost with them. Most people to this day are only familiar with a shortened version of the original.

But these are just curiosities. The real trouble with *The Wicker* Man comes from its success, in depicting a weirdly plausible neopagan culture on a remote Scottish island that blends both Shaffer's research into Sir James Frazer's *Golden Bough* with the dreamy elements of the 1960s hippie movement. One could almost imagine the film's epigraph as the famous Joni Mitchell line from "Woodstock," "We are stardust, we are golden, and we've got to get ourselves back to the garden." The story features what folklorist Mikel Koven calls disparagingly an "indiscriminate inclusion of any and all forms of 'folklore' into the film's diegetic mix,"[6] everything from the ritual jumping of maidens through the fire to the use of toads to cure sore throats to the climactic wicker man sacrifice. Hardy himself made plain his patchwork intentions:

> As to the pagan culture, everything you see in the film is absolutely authentic. The whole series of ceremonies and details that we show have happened at different times and places in Britain and Western Europe. What we did was to bring them all together in one particular place and time.[7]

Thus, with a studied nod to civilization's pagan past in various forms, the film shapes its mimicry toward the mythic past that was being romanticized by youth culture in that eclectic, yet telling cultural moment, right down to the '60s celebration of glamorized free sexuality, featuring, in

7. The Return of Molech

fact, one of the icons of the period, Britt Eckland, for visual pleasure as a promiscuous tavern keeper's daughter. Youth sexuality, which at the real Woodstock was a muddy, messy and finally dreary business, gets filtered through the golden lens of naïve romanticism in *The Wicker Man*, as it did in so many pop ballads of the era. Meanwhile, waiting on the other end of the story is all the brutality of Druidic sacrifice that even the more civilized Julius Caesar brushed aside with disdain in his history of the Gallic Wars, specifically the burning alive of an innocent victim in a gigantic wicker statue to appease the gods of the harvest.

The human sacrifice that concludes the film is what startles the viewer out of the fanciful daydream into the reality of Hardy and Shaffer. When all is revealed at the end, the lovely maidens appear more like witches after all, and the islanders like demented ghouls. It is a conclusion hard to miss and hard to take. Still, as might be predicted, the wicker man sacrifice depicted in the conclusion has been contested by some as more brutal than what the old Celts really did, but that just seems another bit of question begging by proponents of the enlightenment notion that humans are kinder and gentler than history tends to show.

Many Roman writers such as Tacitus and Cicero wrote of Celtic human sacrifice, but it was Caesar, a rather sober observer, who in Book VI of *The Gallic War* described the wicker man ritual:

> The nation of all the Gauls is extremely devoted to superstitious rites; and on that account they who are troubled with unusually severe diseases, and they who are engaged in battles and dangers, either sacrifice men as victims, or vow that they will sacrifice them, and employ the Druids as the performers of those sacrifices; because they think that unless the life of a man be offered for the life of a man, the mind of the immortal gods cannot be rendered propitious, and they have sacrifices of that kind ordained for national purposes. Others have figures of vast size, the limbs of which formed of osiers they fill with living men, which being set on fire, the men perish enveloped in the flames. They consider that the oblation of such as have been taken in theft, or in robbery, or any other offense, is more acceptable to the immortal gods; but when a supply of that class is wanting, they have resource to the oblation of even the innocent.[8]

The last line of the account implies more than it says. Caesar was not that far removed from what Old Testament prophets condemned as the worship of Molech, and he saw it for what it was.

A Christian Response to Horror Cinema

Anyone prone to question the frequency and barbarity of human sacrifice in the ancient world will run into a challenge not only with accounts like that of the Roman general, but also with the Hebrew scriptures. The writer of II Kings, composing sometime after the Jewish exile to Babylon in 587 BC, indicated that one of King Josiah's reforms was to prohibit the sacrificing of Jewish children to the Ammonite deity Molech. The ritual included the children passing between two lines of fire and then being killed. The practice was likewise frequently condemned by the prophets:

> For the sons of Judah have done evil in my sight, declares the Lord. They have set their detestable things in the house that is called by my name, to defile it. And they have built the high places of Topheth, which is in the Valley of the Son of Hinnom, to burn their sons and their daughters in the fire, which I did not command, nor did it come into my mind [Jeremiah 7: 30–31 ESV].

And,

> Moreover, I gave them statutes that were not good and rules by which they could not have life, and I defiled them through their very gifts in their offering up all their firstborn, that I might devastate them. I did it that they might know that I am the Lord [Ezekiel 20: 25–26].

The Wicker Man takes this type of ritual sacrifice as a given and uses it as an irrefutable argument against paganism of whatever form, but particularly the paganism that was being advanced in the '60s as a better road than the one that led to Rome. Ritual sacrifices to the earth gods that allow fertility of land and womb seemed to always culminate in some degree of two practices, sexual commerce and human sacrifice. This is because all such religions blended the need for generative life force, symbolized by the phallus, with the need to propitiate the gods to make this happen. After all, droughts always come and some women cannot bear children. Those two harsh realities are explicit in the Hardy movie, for the whole purpose of the ruse that leads to the final horrific scene is to render the island's apple orchards once again fertile, and by extension, to ensure that all the young maidens continue to be fruitful as well.

It should be interjected here that orthodox Christian theology does likewise turn on themes of propitiation and fertility. However, it doesn't require the killing of other men's children. Rather the doctrine is that

7. The Return of Molech

God the Son was given by the Father as the sole propitiation for the sins of the world to turn away His righteous wrath, so that not only apples but all creation might be restored to the fruitfulness of Eden. That the pagan world understood this by an intuition and practiced a perverse foreshadowing of what would occur in Jerusalem at the turn of human history is not evidence of some common mythic root to all religions, but might be taken as better evidence of the fulfillment in the coming of the Jewish messiah of the best desires of all religious systems. As G. K. Chesterton would memorably put it in the *Blatchford Controversies*, "If we are so made that a Son of God must deliver us, is it odd that Patagonians should dream of a Son of God?" And to finish the thought, apologists will ask, is it shocking that rebels to that truth should develop systems that attempt to replicate in human terms what God alone accomplished, and that these replicas would go bad in time? Chesterton also made plain that all religion is revelation, a vision, "a vision received by faith, but it is a vision of reality."[9] And he consistently argued that the old faith poses a vision of reality that both fully explains the human experience and provides the means through which human life can be made as beautiful and harmonious as a cursed world will allow, its vision grounded in reports of a historical fact, every bit verified and more by many credible witnesses.

That a culture should turn from this more upbeat vision and practice toward a revived paganism with its cultish and at times diabolical vision and practice should cause even the most hardened skeptic to pause since modernity poses religion as an evolutionary process whereby humankind develops more sympathetic and enlightened coping mechanisms. *The Wicker Man* does not pose a vision of evolutionary progress. It warns against the opposite, cultural collapse and regression into something teasingly lighter but really far, far darker. The film is the cinematic analogue to what Shirley Jackson had troublingly proposed in the late '40s with her memorable short story "The Lottery": a world fallen backward into time and blind to the consequences of that fall.

The story of *Wicker Man* runs as follows. Neil Howie, a devout police sergeant, is informed of a missing child on the island of Summerisle off the west coast of Scotland. He flies to the island and begins his search for the child, a girl named Rowan Morrison, but to his chagrin all the islanders claim they have never met nor seen the girl in the picture Howie shows.

Determined to find the truth, he checks a room at the local Green Man Inn, where he is given a display of shocking promiscuity by the revelers inside. After he retires to his room, the tavern keeper's daughter Willow attempts to seduce him, but he resists.

The following day Howie searches the island for the girl but learns instead of the pagan sexuality that dominates all local practices, especially as the locales are preparing for the coming May Day celebrations. There is no sign of Rowan Morrison but plenty of young maidens exposing themselves or inviting local boys and men to play. After a frustrating search, Howie gains an audience with Lord Summerisle, the local laird, who explains that the island was converted back to paganism by his father and grandfather who imported a strain of apples that brought prosperity to the people. Paganism seemed the best way to keep the islanders on task tending the new orchards.

Howie comes to believe that Rowan is being held captive as an innocent sacrifice for the May Day celebration, the crops having failed the previous year. He restrains the innkeeper who is to play Punch in the pageant and takes that role himself so he might save Rowan before she can be executed. After a harrowing experience playing the fool in the dance, Howie indeed finds Rowan, who, it turns out, has been used as a decoy to bring him to the final event of the celebration. He is to be the perfect sacrifice, as representing law, a virgin, coming with free will, and as fool, king for a day. Summerisle has the islanders restrain Howie. He is then cleaned and anointed and burned alive as a sacrifice to the sun goddess Nuada. As he awaits the flames in the wicker man pyre, Howie calls on Jesus for justice and prepares himself for a martyr's death using the form of a prayer Walter Raleigh used before his death—"Do not deliver me into the true fires of Hell, dear Lord…."

Most interesting in the telling of the tale is that the camera adopts Howie's point of view throughout, and the viewer is thus led to identify with the victim in true Hitchcockian fashion. Shaffer had actually worked with Hitchcock on the film *Frenzy* and picked up this trick of toying with audience expectations. But when Howie is executed, the film offers no comforting denouement. As the wicker man burns, the sun stands fixed in the sky, unknowing and unknowable. Howie's cries and prayers may have registered in the kingdom of God, but that view behind the veil is

7. The Return of Molech

neither offered nor suggested. In this, the film assaults the viewer in the troubling way that characterizes horror films after 1970.

Making the equation more complex is that while keeping the focus on Howie, the film makes him a bit of a boor in attitude and manner and so entices the viewer to side more and more in the ruse against him. When Willow dances naked in the adjacent room to tease Howie out of his virginity, she turns toward the camera to expose her endowments to the viewer as well as to the tormented police sergeant straining behind the door. Her invitation is to us, too. Likewise, the numerous scenes depicting pagan carnality lay open to the eyes of those watching in the theater as much as they do the protagonist. In fact, many such scenes open before Howie is present and linger after he has left the action.

In the context of this film, the assault is obvious. Howie may be the virgin king for a day to Summerisle and his revelers, but he is still the Christian patriarch, the righteous lawman, and the viewer is compelled to join in his humiliation and sacrifice as such. The film posits the ritual

Willow (Britt Eckland) tempts Howie out of his virginity in *The Wicker Man*. 1973. British Lion Corporation.

death of the old faith and the triumph of the older still. But while doing so, the film pulls no punches in finally describing what that older faith is all about. Howie, a good and righteous man who comes to the island to rescue a young maid, who plays the role of the Red Cross Knight, who withstands extreme temptation in the form of the lovely Willow, that Howie is mocked and sacrificed, crucified in a fashion, and with him Jesus, whom Summerisle says "had his chance and blew it." St. Boniface does not chop down the sacred oak and bring enlightenment to the land. He is rejected and his ax turned on him.

Once these narrative secrets are revealed, the film's trajectory arcs back and demands a re-viewing, in much the same fashion as a mystery story which needs a final interpretation of events already recounted. This is intentional, as Shaffer, who also authored the mystery *Sleuth*, designed the film with this device in mind as a way of adding a deeper layer of horror to a genre he and Robin Hardy felt needed some deeper layering. *The Wicker Man* does need to be seen twice.

A second viewing of the film makes plain all the subtle tells that Howie missed in his pursuit of Rowan Morrison. In the opening scene, for example, the old men who watch him embark from his plane show reluctance to offer any help at all, as do the men and women at the Green Man Inn who suddenly stop their song and dance when he enters the place. The behavior should have waved the red flag for him, but he persists. Likewise, it should have seemed rather odd that the innkeeper's daughter looked on him with such interest, while all others seemed scornful and even mocking. As the story unfolds and the events become more macabre, Howie likewise fails to recognize the threat posed to him as one man in uniform in a sea of potentially hostile natives. When he visits the local schoolhouse to inquire of Rowan's whereabouts, the teacher, who must stop a lecture of phallic symbolism to her class of young girls, seems nonplused at his threat to have her charged with the encouragement of lewd behavior and corruption of the young. When he finds an empty desk that must be Rowan's and that her name is in the class ledger, he opens the desk to find a beetle tied to a nail where it will go round and round to its death; the display is set up by a neighboring girl. Again, he seems oblivious to the obvious suggestion of his relation to the game.

Later this becomes even more explicit and unmistakable. In his May

7. The Return of Molech

Day search of houses, a girl plays dead and falls from a wardrobe at his feet, children with animal masks look down at him from windows, an old woman's burning hand is set as candle by his bedside. Finally, when he is garbed as Punch and participates in the May Day ritual, the women like witches prod and toy with him while Summerisle mocks his poor capering. He is teased with a display of a beheading and made to think his will be chopped, too. Yet he continues until he spots the real Rowan on a hillside, and even then thinks he can just sweep her up and away from the locals. He had found his plane sabotaged earlier, so one wonders at this point if he meant to swim her to the mainland with all the inhabitants of Summerisle watching like a herd of cows in a field.

This is not a herd of cows, however. These are committed pagans ruled over by a warlock laird and playing an elaborate spell to save themselves and their livelihood. The intentions are noble in their own terms, too, even if their vision has gone bad. Albeit with some fictional license and blending of older customs and beliefs, their created world has a unique integrity. The only gap one might find regards the laird Summerisle's own motivations. He knows the paganism has been imposed on the islanders for utilitarian purpose, yet he also seems to completely buy in as a true believer in the end. When Howie confronts him, saying he would be the next victim should the crops fail again, he answers that the crops will not fail, leaving his own inner thoughts somewhat ambiguous, although the viewer is inclined to believe he has indeed converted somewhere along the way. This would be the darker view in a film that leans toward darker views.

Along the way, the film whispers the truth behind Howie's back as much as it places it in front of his nose. The dinghy that brings him from his plane to the island has on it the image of an eye staring, an image that recurs later in the film when he returns to the boat and tries to fly out before the May Day celebration. That blank eye, something like a cold fish eye, suggests the motif of spying or voyeurism which plays throughout the story. We voyeuristically watch Willow dance. Howie travels through the land voyeuristically observing various fertility rights. When visiting the school house, Howie is first seen framed in the window, observed by the children. When in Summerisle's castle, waiting for the laird, Howie peeps through the window at lightly clad maidens in a neo-Druidic rite frolicking through a Stonehenge-like ruin. Then finally, of course, as Howie burns in the wicker man, all the locals form a circle around him and watch without emotion. The voyeur beholds from a distance for the purpose of sexual pleasure, objectifying the person or persons being watched. Howie fulfills that role of desired object in a weird way for the islanders; yet, his own participation in the role of "holder of the gaze," as feminist critics might call it, a role which the film spectator is invited to share, makes him somewhat complicit, or at least vulnerable. Let him who thinks he stands take heed lest he fall, as the Proverb warns. Howie should have "seen" it coming.

In fact, it's hard to understand how Howie missed the signs, at least apart from the suggestion that his own voyeuristic pleasure got the better of him. Death and sacrifice mark the island culture as much as its nubile carnality. Paganism and the occult run along similar tracks; in fact, the sixties, which marked the rise of neopaganism in youth culture, also marked the rise in Wicca. Heinrich Kramer, who wrote the seminal medieval treatise on witchcraft in 1487, the *Malleus Maleficarum* or *Hammer of Witches*, tied all forms of occult harm to a contractual relationship between the demon and the victim. Thus, Howie must come to the island and imbibe its culture through the exercise of "free will," as the women tell him in the end. Likewise, witchcraft was inherently sexual in Kramer's view; specifically it involved sexual congress with demons:

> Mark well, too, that among other things [witches] have to do four deeds for the increase of the perfidy, that is, to deny the Catholic faith in whole or in part through verbal sacrilege, to devote themselves body and soul [to the Devil], to offer up to the Evil One himself infants not yet baptized, and to persist in diabolical filthiness through carnal acts with incubus and succubus demons.[10]

Howie turns a blind eye to the occult signs on the island—the sacrificed animal (a hare in Rowan's grave), various jars with pickled animals and body parts in the chemist's shop, the prominence of sexually charged younger women, the complicity of the island's children, strange fertility rites performed in the old church graveyard, the prominence of fire and knives throughout, the many phallic symbols (from bushes to the bottles and taps in the inn to the maypoles and swords), and the burning hand candle. So, he turns a blind eye to the evil underneath the various seductions and becomes the final victim.

7. The Return of Molech

Another rather explicit motif in the film is power and authority. In the shorter version of the film, the first image that appears on screen is that of Howie's plane with propeller spinning and the word "POLICE" prominent on its tail. This iconography finds a match in the police uniform Howie wears throughout the film, at least until he willingly seals his own death by dressing as Punch and then is unwillingly dressed in a white frock for sacrifice. Howie walks like a police officer as well—stiffly and with chin up—and he continuously reminds people of the authority he brings to the island, warning the locals in the tavern, the school teacher and children, and even Summerisle of the threat his authority presents to their practices. However, no one on the island pays heed to these icons or to his assertions. In the very first scene, Howie, with megaphone, calls to a group of older men before the harbor master's dwelling requesting a dinghy. They casually reply that it is a private island, to which he replies, through the megaphone, "As you can see, I am a police officer...." The men stare blankly.

The camera furthers this motif through much of the film with Howie viewed from a lower angle on the plane and in various interior scenes or as he walks through town. Also, the camera remains fairly static when Howie is the subject. It will become more and more dynamic as the film progresses, and even with a Wellesian chaos, rapidly edited images taken from various angles and distances, in various scenes of the hobby horse and other mask players in the procession—at least until the very end when stability is restored through the sacrifice. From his point of view, he is given status by his uniform.

Unfortunately Lord Summerisle controls the island, and this, too, becomes evident in the way scenes are staged and shot. When Howie visits his castle, the space physically dominates him, as does Summerisle who is considerably taller and more natural in manner. The castle is replete with weaponry and emblems of traditional privilege. Howie must go up a staircase to get to the laird, and at first sees him sitting in a rather enormous chair turned away from the entranceway. Summerisle does not turn and rise to greet the officer. He is the laird. Summerisle controls the behavior of the women who fawn on him with more than vassal-like indulgence. In the procession, Summerisle appears and leads the various animal maskers with face paint and costume befitting a local shaman, which is what he is too. Howie misses this, blinded by his own sense of importance.

A Christian Response to Horror Cinema

What we have in the film, then, is a horror trap set by evil beings on an unwitting victim. Taken this way, the film is very much in the spirit of the oldest forms of the genre, think Jonathan Harker in *Nosferatu*. However, as has been said, the victim here gets no help from providence, as might be expected in stories with even a toe remaining in the older tradition. Thus, *The Wicker Man* is not only a film about pagan barbarity, but a film that suggests a world with a pagan god. The only real hope at the end is if by some chance the sacrifice of Howie may turn aside the wrath of Nuada and bring about a better harvest, thus ending the need for innocent victims, at least temporarily. History has shown that no amount of blood from bulls, goats, sheep, criminals, women, or children satisfies pagan blood lust for long.

Filtering all this through the sieve of questions that horror films prompt, *The Wicker Man* has even more to say. *What is the monster in this instance?* That would be the growing neopaganism in the culture Hardy and Shaffer saw developing in the youth movements of that day. The gigantic faceless wicker man that consumes Howie is the beast, a god without face or compassion, the god of the Druids, the ineffable sun and moon and sea gods. Summerisle is that beast's shaman, the suave idol ruler whose spell has turned the islanders into soulless clay.

And what is the monster's name? This again poses no challenge, as the wicker god, the personified image of Nuada who eats children is the old Molech waiting for the next victim to run through the fire so that the crops might grow, and teasing the old Hebrews into leaving the old revealed faith which waited for the final revealed sacrifice, the messiah born of human flesh to die a lamb. The film poses the very real threat that the culture developing in the 1960s was leaning toward beliefs and customs that would promise life and freedom, but at the price of random innocents, lost children, and with the secondary price of a lost innocence across the land. On this level *The Wicker Man* functions as a dark prophecy, which many would contend has been fulfilled in the past several generations.

Why are *these people* the victims of the evil? Why is Howie haunted and killed? These are the more significant questions. In the case of films like *The Mummy* or *The Thing*, one can see how scientists and soldiers who arrogantly promote some new world order to be achieved through

7. The Return of Molech

research and technology and military force might deserve the kind of fate suffered by Victor Frankenstein, whose relations are systematically destroyed by the thing his hubris created. But what has Howie done? To answer that question, consider again what Howie is.

We see Howie's faith played out twice in the film. The first instance occurs in the Green Man Inn on the first night during Willow's attempted seduction. The sequence begins with Howie kneeling beside his bed in prayer. A flashback shows him reading scripture as part of the Eucharistic celebration back home and then receiving the host himself. Interestingly enough, when Hardy and Shaffer wrote the novelization of the film in 1978 they expanded this back story, perhaps to underscore the importance of seeing Howie as a basically good character with religious integrity. As Howie prays, a guitarist begins to play in an adjacent room and Willow begins to sing and tap the wall inviting the officer to her bed. She will then continue with more provocative temptations. Howie sweats, prays harder, fights against his natural urges, and finally resists. The second display of his faith will occur in the end. When he sees the wicker man over the edge of the hill and thus finally understands his fate, he cries unequivocally, "Oh, God! Oh, Jesus Christ!" When inside his prison he pronounces judgment on all the beholders and makes the good confession, committing his soul to God, requesting mercy and grace, and singing the hymn, "The Lord's My Shepherd."

It is the alignment of the true believer with the authority he wields as enforcer of civil law that seems to be the problem. More pronounced than Howie's faith, which displays itself exclusively in these two trials, is Howie's rather arrogant insertion of his own importance and authority as a representative of civil law. That assertion of civil authority runs through every scene in the film. It might be said that the two trials bring out the real man and save him from the fate of the other. His martyr's death makes him a more winsome character. This is not to suggest that religious believers should not wield the sword of state, of course, but it does raise the question of whether Howie's social privilege had trumped and blurred his authority as follower of Christ. That would seem to be the large question Robin Hardy and Anthony Shaffer are posing, and it is a legitimate one. In the context of American or British popular culture, had the church become compromised by its own established authority and so lost its old power? The answer would seem to be yes given its failure to win that youth culture by and large and save it from the allures of neo-pagan revelry.

This leads to the most significant question in the context of *The Wicker Man*: what is the taboo that has been broken? Another way of putting this is: who sins first and do we see it? The answer to that is difficult only because it is so obvious. The sin is Howie's and what he represents, and might simply be expressed as *gullibility*. Howie is mind-numbingly gullible through the course of the story. Even the children can play him the fool, from Rowan's sister who tells him Rowan is a hare to the child who falls from the wardrobe playing dead to the children in animal masks watching him from windows throughout the town. His donning of the Punch costume and ridiculously inept capering in the procession is a ludicrous attempt to enact a rescue of the lost Rowan and appears all the more so when his antics are crosscut with shots of masked swordsmen forming a pentagram and chopping a false head from a child's costume. He is way out of his league and completely unprepared for what awaits him. When the thing is revealed, the village smith easily tosses him to the ground and puts him in an unbreakable headlock. He is carried to his fate like a helpless child, no heroic fighting to save himself; he is Fool for the Day, as the witch-like school teacher will tell him. The seductive Willow cuts him from his suit with a knife that seems very suited for her grip.

So the film seems to offer an indictment of a type of passive, religious gullibility, a lack of vigilance which has resulted in the old order losing real authority beyond the paper authority of temporal law, a human authority which can be easily overcome by greater human force. Although neither Hardy nor Shaffer confessed religious orthodoxy, the film stands as a warning that orthodoxy will not stand when held up by man's strength and not God's. Howie was blind to his danger because he hid behind a policeman's uniform and not behind the cross of Christ. He overcame Willow's temptations by prayer but did not overcome the force of Summerisle's devilry by that same prayer. He failed to heed Jesus' warning that some demons can only be exorcised through significant, committed effort.

Taken this way, the film predicts what actually occurred historically in the rise of the youth culture in the 1960s: the failure of the established church to read adequately the sign of the times and respond with an

7. The Return of Molech

authority equal to the challenge. Churches pandered to hold on to what they were losing and thus lost all the more.

The film also functions as lynchpin in the genre of horror. After *The Wicker Man*, horror film becomes considerably darker and more diabolical, playing much more with taboos like child possession, sadism, sodomy, and motiveless violence. It might be argued that the entire culture bottomed out by 1973 and that the film industry provided the most evident examples of how and why. The patriarch lost his place and was crucified again and cast out. The chilling conclusion of *The Wicker Man* likewise suggests that the unforgiveable sin had and has somehow been committed on a broad scale. Christ had been crucified again, and with this sin can come no redemption. He who holds back the tide of evil will move His hand away, as suggested in a Pauline letter.

The last question horror films prompt would be: how is the exorcism performed? In the climactic scene of *Wicker Man*, Howie calls on Christ and is led off with hands tied and then carried and forced into the wicker man. The camera adopts his point of view as the wicker structure shakes and seemingly approaches him. He falls to a knee en route beside a single barren tree. Behind him Summerisle walks mechanically, ritualistically with head high, no longer in face paint and costume, but as a warlock, the camera now imaging him from below, his hair blowing in the wind. An evil trinity of women follows, the new matriarchs of a world to be ruled by carnality and the impulses of cursed nature. Above them all towers the faceless wicker god, door open, ready to swallow the victim. In its arms and belly, sheep and goats and geese and other animals are also imprisoned, just in case Howie's life is not enough. Above is an indifferent sky with wisps of clouds drifting their silent courses. The men holding torches smile mockingly at the Fool for a Day, the man made as valueless or valuable as beasts or kegs of beer rolled into the sea. Summerisle, hair blowing in the wind, calls for the nature gods and goddesses to receive the sacrifice of the people and make the orchards fruit. The people watch silently. Howie pronounces judgment and prays. The locals are silent. The full sun in the red sky remains impassive. The gods and goddesses have no real faces. Summerisle drops his arm and the torch men light the reeds and the people play and sing a folk tune, swaying to its beat in the cold breath of the barren land. Summerisle looks mad. Howie prays, the ani-

Summerisle (Christopher Lee) calls upon the gods of the harvest while Howie (Edward Woodward) reaches for heaven's help to stay his coming martyrdom in the wicker man in the Robin Hardy film. 1973. British Lion Corporation.

mals scream, the camera pulls back. As the sacrifice is engulfed in flames, the singing of the locals drowns out the prayers and screaming; the faces around the circle are gleeful, mad. The camera pulls back fully, and the burning wicker man fills the screen. Its head breaks off from the burning and falls out of the frame, revealing the full burning, distant, indifferent sun. The credits roll.

There is no exorcism of the real beast. Christ himself is cast out. And so in *The Wicker Man* the genre of horror, which began with the paradigm of transgression, possession and then exorcism, turns away from the formula and welcomes the unchecked rule of evil. Subsequent films will make this entrance most explicit. Several will pit Satan embodied against the relics of a weakened church. Several others will suggest the old for-

7. The Return of Molech

mulas hold only momentary power. Yet the overall trajectory of the genre seems unmistakably turned toward a new formulation where the allure was no longer the carnival glimpse of the thing let loose with the safe bars holding it back and the gun with silver bullets loaded and aimed. The genre turned toward a voyeuristic display of the possibilities where Evil reigns and rampages, the Beast slouching toward Bethlehem is let loose and the ceremony of innocence is drowned for all to see.

What is the appeal, however, of this neopaganism, one might ask, or as Catherine Edwards Sanders pointedly phrased it: what is Wicca's charm?[11] Sanders suggests what John Ford once implied when he claimed the legend should be printed over the truth. A myth does not have to be true to be meaningful. And all people need a myth, even if it is nothing more than a revival of old, earth-bound matriarchy. The myth fulfills the need for dignity and the need for ritual and the need for rites of passage and the longing for Eden on Earth. Every human wants to feel the path toward the divine is open, even if that path be described as the green man, the oak king, and the holly king. For some, as Camus put it in *The Myth of Sisyphus*, "the struggle toward the summit suffices to fill the heart." Because "we are stardust, we are golden," a path to God will be described that attempts to satisfy our deepest longings. The old faith described such a path, and when that faith exuded spiritual power, then the church took care of those deepest longings. When the old faith, however, became and becomes as hollow as the wicker statue that imprisons Sergeant Howie, then it is marked for burning by those who long for more, and burned it will be without concern for what may follow, discarded the way a petulant, defiant child discards a favorite toy.

8

THE CORRUPTION OF THE VIRGIN
William Peter Blatty's *The Exorcist*

> *And there was there near the mountain a great herd of swine, feeding. And the spirits besought him, saying: Send us into the swine, that we may enter into them. And Jesus immediately gave them leave. And the unclean spirits going out, entered into the swine: and the herd with great violence was carried headlong into the sea, being about two thousand, and were stifled in the sea.*—Mark 5: 11-13, Douay-Rheims.
>
> *But Jesus taking him by the hand, lifted him up; and he arose. And when he was come into the house, his disciples secretly asked him: Why could not we cast him out? And he said to them: This kind can go out by nothing, but by prayer and fasting.*—Mark 9: 26-28

It should come as no surprise given the trajectory of the genre of horror and where on the arc of evil Hollywood had arrived by the 1970s that the Gadarene demoniac nearly triumphs in *The Exorcist*. As Father Damien Karras beats the possessed child Regan and demands the demon "take me," the most openly Catholic film in the genre staggers under the blows of Giant Despair and nearly succumbs. It doesn't, but it nearly does, and that seems a significant point.

Perhaps this might go unremarked if the film were not so unusually bold in its orthodox presentation of a bloody skirmish in the ongoing battle between Michael and the archangels and the powers and principalities of darkness. The film posits a literal devil and literal demons; real sacraments and real spiritual warfare. A young girl is possessed, in part because her loneliness over a missing father made her reach out for companionship through a Ouija board, but more because a demon is loosed from some temporal bondage during an archaeological dig, and it has

8. The Corruption of the Virgin

chosen this girl's body to lure and kill its real adversary, an older exorcist priest named Father Lankester Merrin. Being a demon, it craves the opportunity to corrupt human flesh and debase the sacred, which it of course does as the plot unfolds. So the real story of *The Exorcist* explores the twisted psychology of the powers of darkness, the physical spaces inhabited being somewhat accidental.

It is highly unlikely that film viewers saw this simple math of the film when it was released, or that many do even now. Several prominent critics in 1973, like Pauline Kael of the *New Yorker*, seemed to recognize *The Exorcist* for what it was and responded with measured scorn, not unlike what would be offered in larger shovels when Mel Gibson released *The Passion of the Christ* four decades later. *The Exorcist* did things never done before. It crossed lines. It displayed evil in the most vulgar of terms and brought it into a suburban house in Washington, D.C. But it also showed the face of a real demon and brought back what one critic called a feeling of "Old World contamination."[1] And it showed the face and the authority of the visible church, and not in a sentimental or excessively reverential way.

The film did other things, too, beyond foregrounding obscene images and utterances, matters that would have been taken up in an earlier age by the Legion of Decency. The film assaulted the viewer in new, subtle ways. *The Exorcist* showed that horror is not a genre defined only by narrative content, but by content plus mode of address. Whether intentionally or not, the film positioned the cinematic medium alongside the occult medium; it made of itself a Ouija board.

Midway through *The Exorcist*, a team of psychologists attempt yet another battery of tests on the girl Regan (Linda Blair) to prove that she is only sick, not possessed, despite substantial evidence to the contrary. They do not see because they will not see, an idea repeated throughout the narrative as it is in the Gospels. The girl is sitting up on a hospital bed and for a moment the camera adopts her point of view. Then, in a brief flash, a demon face appears in front of her and snarls. The film needs several viewings to catch it. Worse still, the girl shows little emotion, having become the Regan of her namesake in *King Lear*, watching the blinding of Gloucester with cold detachment. The same demonic face will flash in several other moments during the film in what amounts to subliminal

A Christian Response to Horror Cinema

The same demonic face threatening Chris (Ellen Burstyn) will flash in several moments during the film in a subliminal seduction of the viewer in *The Exorcist*. 1973. Warner Brothers.

seduction of the viewer. Since this first appearance adopts Regan's point of view, the effect is strong. The girl had been previously objectified as the thing to be studied, both within the context of the story by her mother and a battery of doctors and psychologists and also as monster in a monster movie. As such, the viewer has been offered a safe context. One knows the rules and might turn away anticipating what might come next. But here the viewers are teased and then assaulted, drawn within the girl only to have their eyeballs slit by a razor as in Buñuel's *Un Chien Andalou*.

With this scene it becomes apparent that *The Exorcist* is not only a film designed to tell a story about demonic possession, but also a film designed to plant images of demonism into the minds of viewers. All films leave images in the mind. All filmmakers try to plant images in the mind. But horror film exists as genre with a main goal of planting *certain kinds* of images in the mind—images of corruption, depravity, and mayhem. In this one film, the soul of the genre is revealed.

Two other film genres function this way. One is pornography, the most brazen and depraved type of carnival spectacle discussed earlier in the context of Karl Freund's *The Mummy*. The development of the cine-

8. The Corruption of the Virgin

matic medium offered a new possibility for the peep show, and the profiteers have been ringing up the change ever since. Feminist scholars like Virginia Wexman have rightly described pornography as a genre built around the pleasures of misogyny, a genre primarily designed to produce a physiological and emotional response independent of the aesthetics of narrative integrity or even cinematography. It is a genre designed to create disordered cravings and addictions. Pornography commits the unforgivable sin of looking at creatures made in the *imago dei* as base animals without souls. It devours both the object of the gaze, the woman typically, and the person gazing.

Ironically, the other genre which functions within a similar modality is the type of religious film best defined as "sacramental film." When the method of filmmaking changes radically at the end of Robert Bresson's masterpiece *Diary of a Country Priest* and the cross is emblazoned over a white screen as backdrop for the voiceover recounting the final days of a saint, the effect is to address and evangelize the viewer in a sacramental way. Take and eat. This is my body. Christ is communicated through physical elements, albeit not through the consecrating words of a priest or minister, but by filmmaker functioning as deacon, assisting the apostles and elders in the communication of the elements of faith.

Horror is a genre designed to produce a change in the viewer, independent of the specific themes and messages of individual films. It involves an explicit moral commitment of the human will. It invites a person to peep through the darkness at the obscene, by definition material that ought not be seen according to common standards of human decency. Then horror encourages vicarious participation in acts of violence and perversion. Finally, it implants those images of violence and perversion within the viewer for continued imaginative participation beyond the film. Horror employs celluloid amulets to conjure evil and then incarnate it within the viewer.

The paradox then with *The Exorcist* is that the story was apparently written and put onto film to lead people *toward* the faith. The root story came from an actual case of a fourteen-year-old boy in Mt. Rainier, Maryland, whom the church determined to have become demon possessed after playing with a Ouija board with his aunt. The boy spoke in languages he had not learned. Words appeared in scratches on his body, his bed vibrated, and objects flew around his room. The family was not Catholic, but the situation became so foul and so supernatural that priests were brought in to perform the rite of exorcism. The boy was delivered finally by Jesuits at St. Louis University. William Peter Blatty heard the story while a student at Georgetown. Possibly he obtained some original transcripts from the case. It stayed with him one way or another, and twenty years later, in 1971, he wrote and published the novel version of *The Exorcist* and saw it skyrocket to the top of the *New York Times* bestseller list and remain there for a year. Blatty, who would later write a saintly biography of his devout mother, claimed the novel served the cause of Christ by making evil real in an age where belief in good and evil as defined by the old faith had gone out of the culture.

The film would go into production while the book was still part of the cultural conversation. Unfortunately for Blatty, the chosen director, William Friedkin, celebrated for his hardcore realism in *The French Connection* (1971), was not a believer and wanted a film that left the audience wondering about its religious content. The result was a brilliantly realistic and well-paced narrative with strange theological ambiguities, especially in the final scenes. Blatty had designed a more consistent final cut but been overruled. Fortunately, a restored version was released by Warner Bros. in 2012, which cleared some of the ambiguities of the earlier version, and which met with both Blatty and Friedkin's approval. This will be the version discussed here.

One might compare Blatty's intentions in the film to those of Flannery O'Connor whose violent short stories typically resolved in a life-altering spiritual choice by the main characters. O'Connor believed that only violence would wake up spiritually slumbering modern readers and bring them to acknowledge their own souls hanging over the precipice of damnation. Walking over the pit of hell on a rotten covering is how Jonathan Edwards described the condition in his famous sermon. O'Connor saw the precarious life of unbelievers in sacramental terms and was not afraid to resolve her stories with bloodshed.

Whether the film woke up viewers up to examine their souls and turned fear of the real presence of evil in the world into real faith remains a matter of conjecture. The film certainly did and does terrify. And the images are not the sole reason. The horrific voices emanating from the

8. The Corruption of the Virgin

mouth of the possessed girl remain in the mind as well. In fact, those sounds were central to the ad campaigns promoting the film over the transistor radios of American teens in the early seventies. Especially chilling in retrospect in this new era of YouTube and social media is the similarity of those sounds to clips of real possessions caught on tape and distributed through the Internet, including part of the actual exorcism in the famous French possession case of Anneliese Michel, which would be transcribed through the 2005 film, *The Exorcism of Emily Rose*.

In his zeal to get the story of real demon possession out to a skeptical public, what Blatty did not seem to consider fully is the point central to this discussion: how the mechanisms of horror used in the horror film can have a powerful and dangerous influence on viewers, independent of the intentions of filmmakers. One might evoke Marshall McLuhan's assertions regarding the medium of modern media trumping its message. Even in Blatty's restored version of the film, with its explicit, redemptive resolution, a legitimate question remains regarding whether what will be taken from the theater will be the triumph of belief or the flash of the haunting face of a demon or the vile images and sounds that the fictional priests witnessed in Regan's bedroom.

Perhaps that question cannot be answered in a general way. Perhaps the matter calls for the kind of wisdom John suggests in his apocalypse when he describes the name of "the Beast" cryptically as 666. Still, the question must be asked both of the film and the person submitting to it. Are you aware? Have you considered? If the film itself suggests the haunting claim that real Evil can incarnate itself in real people who play with certain unholy objects and who invite the winds of alternative spiritualties, what makes any viewer feel immune?

Such questions tend to be deflected in the academy in favor of more banal issues, like the cultural causes for this sudden interest in dark spirituality in 1973. Was it the Vietnam War or the rise of social unrest on college campuses? *The Exorcist* cites both. Was it *angst* over absentee fathers? Regan has one. Was it "the mounting power of communism overseas," as one social critic stretched it?[2] Was it housewives watching the Watergate hearings, as another set of critic stretched it even further?[3]

Closest to the truth are the critics who follow the film's many references to Hollywood. Chris, Regan's mother (Ellen Burstyn), is an actress making a film about social unrest on a college campus. Burke Denning, Chris' lover, who becomes the worst victim of Regan's carnage, thrown out a window after having his head turned completely around, is a filmmaker. Father Dyer, a lapsed priest whose faith is restored at the end, wants to schmooze with celebrities in heaven. Lieutenant Kinderman, the inspector on the case, is a film buff who asks for an autograph from Chris while the daughter is upstairs blaspheming in backwards English.

Indeed, what made *The Exorcist* possible, more than any outside social factor, was Hollywood's economic collapse in the fifties which eventuated in producers willing to experiment with new filmmakers, new styles, and new rules of decency through the late sixties and seventies. More specifically, the most telling immediate context for Blatty's 1973 film would be the new industry profiting off growing cultural tolerance for pornography and violence. Behind *The Exorcist* was *Deep Throat* (1972), *The Wild Bunch* (1969), *Bonnie and Clyde* (1967), and *Rosemary's Baby* (1968). Those films broke new ground for the previously forbidden, and Hollywood saw a renewed revenue stream, as these new formerly taboo films were profitable, some fabulously so. *The Exorcist* followed suit, grossing over $8 million its opening weekend at the box office and over $350 million worldwide to date.

Rosemary's Baby (1968) offers the best context in terms of film content. That film, directed by Roman Polanski not long before his actress wife was viciously murdered by the demonic Charles Manson "family," opened the door for direct presentations of Satanism on screen. A woman acquires strange new neighbors who prove to be devil worshippers. Chosen to bear the antichrist, she is graphically raped by the Devil, bears the child, and remains mother to it in the film's disturbing conclusion—there is no defeat of evil, no redemption, just the triumph of the Beast and a cynical leer from the director.

So, the latent tendencies of the horror genre, its perversity and voyeurism and sadism and dread, had become legitimized in the new Hollywood by 1973. What had been anticipated already in the 1930s came to pass, as the new Enlightenment man, the child of logical science, had opened the door wide for the demonic while denying the power of the church to exorcise the thing itself. The genre had reached that point in 1973, and Blatty provided the material, although in a strange paradox of

8. The Corruption of the Virgin

providence, his material hung tight to those older religious formulas that the new society was moving away from.

The film makes no bones about the limitations and denials of the scientific age. While the viewer has been offered numerous convincing manifestations that Regan has been taken over—from the mild shock of a candle flaming up like a torch to a bed violently shaking without cause to deep guttural blasphemies emanating from the young girl to the girl-turned-monster spider-walking down a staircase—the medical community around the phenomena suggests cranial lesions or depression over a broken home. One of the most explicit sequences along these lines follows Regan's first full display of diabolical behavior in her bedroom. She has corrupted herself, spoken in a devilish voice, and been thrown wildly on and above her bed. The camera cuts from the mayhem to Chris' horrified face. Her secretary, Sharon, and two psychiatric doctors wrestle the girl-thing down and heavily sedate her. In the hall, the women huddle together in horrified silence. Out of the room come the doctors and after a canned speech about adrenaline-induced feats of strength, completely out of context, they restate their belief that the girl suffers from a lesion on the temporal lobe of her brain. As obvious as the point should be for the viewer, the camera reinforces it visually with a motif carried throughout the narrative—bars. Prominent in the shots outside the bedroom are the spindles in the railing. They visually imprison the women and the doctors and suggest the restrictions of scientific inquiry into spiritual matters.

Enclosed spaces with fences and railings are prominent throughout the film. The MacNeil house sits behind an iron fence. Numerous outdoor shots place characters within or without confined spaces. Kinderman will first talk to Karras (Jason Miller) against a long fence reminiscent of the atmospheric background fences in *On the Waterfront*, another film about minds chained to false allegiances. Chris is consistently shot while restricted within tight spaces, even in her own kitchen. Her conversations with doctors tend to occur in narrow areas. Likewise, Karras is typically shot very tight or positioned within a very limited space. And, more literally, Karras and Merrin wear collars as priests. When Regan kisses the restored priest, Father Dyer, she kisses his collar. Regan is bound not only by the demon, but consistently with straps and bandages and the armatures of machines. In an early scene establishing her innocence and the warmth of her relationships in the home, she steals food from the kitchen and is chased and wrestled to the floor by her mother and held there.

The binding of Regan through human means is ultimately ineffectual, of course. Ironically, in the scenes shot in the hospital where she is strapped in for tests, the binding appears cruel, especially as the camera lingers on the long needles and probes used on her by masked technicians. The scenes of outright demonic madness are in some ways easier to watch. So, medical science is presented as not only ineffectual, but ultimately callous, cruel, and detached. It compromises the character of Karras and deters his faith as he wrestles with his vocation as both priest and psychiatrist. The two find no easy harmony in him, and the discord makes him a prime target for the demon.

What *The Exorcist* posits on the surface is that the Enlightenment tendency to see human ill as a problem to be solved dehumanizes and ultimately degrades. In one moment of black humor in the film, when a psychologist hypnotizes Regan and commands the presence within to come out, the demon turns on the psychologist and attempts to emasculate him. The agonized doctor of science falls to the ground in a stylized manner that seems to quote the fall of Inspector Arbogast in *Psycho*, another Catholic story that mocks the seeming abilities of human reason to understand and remedy the condition of extreme human depravity.

The film dismisses the authority of the world's experts to address human hearts and replaces it with the need for divine intervention. The other dominant visual motif in the film beyond enclosures is of staircases. Both Burke Dennings and Damien Karras fall down staircases, the difference being that Karras is absolved by Father Dyer after his fall. Regan's room is at the top of the stairs. She spider-walks down and vomits blood. Numerous conversations throughout the film take place at the base or at the top of the stairs. Stairs most obviously suggest the direction toward heaven and hell, but they also suggest authority. He who ascends dominates. Thus, the demon–Regan, able to break its bandages and levitate above the bed, collapses down onto the bed and is eventually cast out and down from the house. Merrin is consistently shot from a low angle, accentuating his height and authority. When he stands against the demon figure in a scene from the film's prologue, a threatening red sun in the background, he stands taller than the thing.

8. The Corruption of the Virgin

This discussion leads to the aforementioned basic math of what the film poses as the mystery behind the girl's possession. In the opening scene in Iraq, which begins with the haunting sounds of the Muslim call to prayer, Merrin finds two objects at the site of an archaeological dig. From inside a small hole in a rock wall, he pulls out a Christian medallion and then a small demon head from a local idol, the Pazuza, demonic guardian of childbirth in Mesopotamian mythology. When he removes the demon head, an audible whoosh of wind follows, signal in several places in the film of the entrance of the demonic. Implied is that the icon had somehow imprisoned the demon which can now escape to steal, kill, and destroy. Apparently the demon has chosen the girl in Washington, D.C., as a way to lure Merrin and profane two sacred aspects of the faith, the virgin and the priest. The assault on Karras is calculated in this. The demon will tell Karras when he first arrives that the host inside the possessed girl is waiting for him to join them, a dark prophecy anticipating the film's conclusion.

The intent of the possession is stated during a conversation between the two priests. When Karras asks why this girl, Merrin responds that the goal may be to make them despair, "to see ourselves as animal and ugly." The scene, removed from the original version but restored in the restored version, has the priests shot in close-up on the stairway, with Merrin reflective at the top of the stairs and Karras troubled and frightened-looking down the stairs. Regan, the virgin, has been debased and made into an animal. The demon corrupts her in the vilest of ways, just as the demon has had her slip out and profane a statue of Mary in the local parish church. The assault on Regan through the possession is consistently a defilement of her femininity and virgin innocence. Seeing this corruption nearly breaks the already doubt-ridden, psychiatrist-priest Karras, especially when coupled with an assault on his own faithful mother. Karras couldn't provide his mother proper care in her old age, so she has died in the paupers' wing of a mental hospital. The demon taunts him through dreams, visions, and words. He abandoned his mother and let her rot. Now she's in hell ... his mother's voice comes accusingly out of the possessed girl. The thing even appears as his mother sitting in a haunting vale of light on Regan's bed.

The turning point for Karras comes in a break from the horrors of the exorcism when he finds his true self and assures Chris that Regan will not die in answer to the mother's question. He then re-climbs the steps of faith, the staircase to the girl's room, to rejoin Merrin. That affirmation of the power of God over the Devil, and its reiteration of the Roman rite the priests recite, signals Karras' renewed confidence in God, although he remains a flawed saint throughout the film. His comforting words to Chris derive from fundamental charity. God would not desire for a mother to suffer such losses without some larger redemptive purpose. Chris, too, is strangely beloved of the Lord in the biblical sense, and in the end she, too, will be restored.

When Karras returns to the room, Merrin is dead. The possessed Regan is unbound on the bed. Karras, rather than going in fear to bind Regan again as he has in a previous scene, fearlessly and forcefully tries to resuscitate the priest. It's another act of love. When he realizes the priest is gone and hears the diabolical giggles of the thing, he curses it, appropriately, and then throws it to the ground. While the demon growls like an animal, he beats it and cries, "Take me, take me." This, too, although disordered, is an act of love; his desire is to save the girl by substituting himself. The demon pulls a protective medallion from his neck, his protection, referencing the opening sequence with Merrin finding a medallion with the idol. Karras suddenly rears back and looks up at the curtains blowing in the window where he sees a brief image of his mother as a ghost, a special bit of demonic malice; then his eyes go green, like Regan's had been, and he is possessed.

This moment in the film may be most difficult to understand without the context of older spirituality. Karras has invited the evil into himself to save the girl; he has counted his own life worthless but channeled his rage toward the incarnation of evil, the demonic corrupter on the ground before him. Thus, his possession results from love. The viewer cannot gather this in immediately for the priest falls and rises with twisted face and hands positioned and moving to assault the helpless, now restored, Regan on the floor. The instant is shot from Karras' perspective so the viewer looks through the hands of the now thing-priest as it moves toward its ultimate goal of defilement and cruelty against the virgin girl. The demon has what it sought: opportunity to debase both priest and virgin together. The point-of-view camera device used becomes a staple in horror

8. The Corruption of the Virgin

films after *The Exorcist*, notably in the opening sequence of John Carpenter's *Halloween*. Carpenter, having obviously studied *The Exorcist* for this film, borrows several motifs, including the Halloween setting at the start of Regan's horror and the *Tubular Bells* opening music. This point-of-view device, placing the viewer in the mind and looking through the eyes of the psychotic killer, is likewise memorably employed in the climactic sequence of Jonathan Demme's *Silence of the Lambs*. The camera invites the viewer to watch the ultimate defilement from the perspective of cold evil. As Karras approaches the girl, he finds his last moment of humanity, cries "no," and throws himself through the bedroom window. Chris and Kinderman arrive in response to the violent sounds to find the freed child crying and cowering in the corner, Merrin dead as a martyr, and the window broken—Karras in the death throes of his martyrdom below. The demon has been cast down never to return. Bloody, grotesque, shocking—it is, nonetheless, a thoroughly orthodox and redemptive conclusion to a film that unequivocally affirms the power of love over the forces of darkness.

Once this complete story becomes clear, the film becomes much easier to read. More can be shown here by way of a close examination of two of the film's more recognizable scenes.

The first takes place at a party in Chris MacNeil's home early in the film. Present are several of her Hollywood friends, as well as other local celebrities, including an astronaut. The scene unfolds with the camera cutting among the participants, all wealthy, all drinking, and all posturing. The room is packed and chaotic. Regan has been showing the initial symptoms of the storm ahead, but is apparently sleeping upstairs. Downstairs the party resembles a gathering worthy of Screwtape and Wormwood. Burke Dennings, thoroughly drunk, begins to bait an older man by calling him a Nazi. The man responds that he is Swiss, but Dennings follows him into the kitchen and continues to heap insults on him until the man can no longer take it and goes to strangle the drunken film director. A fight breaks out which the women must break up. Jump to Chris upstairs after the ruckus checking Regan to see that she is covered. When Chris leaves, Regan opens her eyes in bed; the curtains are blowing in the open window behind her, a signal that the demonic has been released. Cut back to Dennings being ushered out of the house by Chris and Sharon to sleep it off.

He collapses into Chris' arms in a ridiculous love embrace before leaving. Chris, however, seems relatively unaffected by Dennings' depraved behavior, and she and Sharon glide into the parlor like intimate sisters with a secret to find another scene from the underworld unfolding. Father Dyer is at the piano leading a grouping of revelers. He looks up and says, ironically, "Hi Chris, it's a great party." The camera sweeps behind Chris to frame better the tableau as the worldly priest describes his vision of heaven as an eternal night club where he is headliner. It's a truly awful moment for anyone invested in the life and work of the church, punctuated when Regan comes down silently, tells the astronaut he will die "up there," and urinates on the floor. The obscene act functions as demonic commentary on the depravity the viewer has just witnessed, and it underscores Father Merrin's later words that the point of the possession will be to make "us" despair our humanity and see ourselves as animal and ugly. Needless to say, the girl's act addresses the viewer directly as much as it advances the narrative, being the first instance in the history of Hollywood film certainly where a child is put on screen for just such a purpose. Such taboo ground had been broken in the new Hollywood, however, in naturalistic films like Robert Altman's 1971 *McCabe & Mrs. Miller*. Regan's action simply fast-forwards the viewer to the end point of that moral slope in film history.

Still, by the end of the film, apart from the murdered film director, the main players in that diabolical scene will all be redeemed and restored to healthy human fellowship. Chris and Sharon, united in their terror at the horrors of the room containing the possessed child, come together after the ordeal and share a loving embrace in the film's resolution. Sharon will move on to different employ, but she hands Chris the medallion that the demon had pulled from Karras' neck before entering him. She found it in Regan's room, she says, which is a contextually rich comment. Chris will shortly afterward offer the medallion to Father Dyer before she is chauffeured off to her new home. Dyer closes his hand on it, signal of his restored faith, and then hands it back for Chris to keep. She likewise closes her hand on the medallion. After Chris departs and Regan has planted a kiss on the priest's collar, Dyer will walk to the stairs where Karras sacrificed himself for the girl. Above him is the boarded window of Regan's room. Dyer reflects on the scene and then walks up a hill where he will

8. The Corruption of the Virgin

meet Kinderman. The film will end in a warm exchange between the two. Kinderman asks about the girl. "She seems fine," Dyer tells him, and Kinderman reflects paternally, "That's important." They then banter about movies and go off to lunch together. The chaos and fear that had pulled everyone apart has been redeemed by the substitutionary act of the priest Karras, and human fellowship has been restored.

This restoration has been established earlier in scenes prior to and during the exorcism. In one such scene, Chris has offered Merrin brandy for his tea, which he accepts though the doctors have warned him against alcohol given his heart condition. The two smile at this secret admission. Karras and Chris share several warm and human exchanges. Likewise, Karras and Merrin share quiet moments of simple human kinship, expressed in humble questions such as, "Are you tired?" The purpose of redemption is to redeem the flesh, not dismiss it. People may be separated for holy use, but they are first brought into the redeemed community to share stories and meals.

The second recognizable scene that makes plain the film's larger intentions is less a scene than a short photographic montage. Merrin is ascending a leaf-covered hill in Woodstock, New York, a curiously chosen locale given its cultural history. He is reflective, and we have been told he is writing a book. Throughout the film, Merrin remains something of a holy mystery to the viewer, starting with his opening words: "There is something I must do." A novice runs uphill and hands him the letter directing the exorcism. He takes it and reads thoughtfully, the camera still at a distance below; then he continues slowly up the hill. The image dissolves into the demonic face of the girl-thing on the bed. This is the moment it had desired, the arrival of the enemy into the ring for battle. That horrible image is superimposed for a moment over Merrin arriving in a taxi at night. The cab pulls alongside a lamp post, quite suggestive in the context of the spiritual struggle, the light casting an aura over the grounds outside the MacNeil home. A bluish fog seems to pour from Regan's window. The priest goes out slowly and pauses in the lamplight in front of the house, a silhouette, his role as priest-exorcist defining him. It is a lovely and memorably poetic image, a sharp contrast to the demon face that the image will dissolve back into. Thus, the terms have been set—good versus evil, beauty and poetry versus chaos and vulgarity. Chris

A Christian Response to Horror Cinema

goes to the door and sees just the dark silhouette of Merrin. His face only becomes clear in the light of the foyer as he steps inside.

Throughout the exorcism, the demon will bait both Merrin and Karras into confronting the hidden, shameful details of their private lives. Merrin has cautioned Karras not to listen for the demon "is a liar" who will "lie to confuse us" and "mix lies with the truth" to make them more potent. When Merrin first enters the bedroom to begin the exorcism, he is abused with epithets of corrupted carnality. The demon calls him a faggot. The implication is obvious. Likewise, the demon torments Karras as a neglectful son and as a faithless priest. Karras succumbs. Merrin does not. Merrin knows that his humanity has been wrapped in a garment of sanctity through his faith and vocation. The man is protected, contained

The arrival of Father Merrin, God's messenger (Max von Sydow), in the most iconic shot from *The Exorcist*, sets the terms for the coming struggle in the bedroom. 1973. Warner Brothers.

8. The Corruption of the Virgin

as the medallion had contained the evil idol in Iraq. Human depravity and corruption is inescapable in society at large and within each individual, but the atonement of Christ, that consummate act of the love of God, has wrapped that flesh in a blanket and so made it holy for the day when full restoration will come. Regan proves to be the principle example. She is wrapped in blankets by her loving mother in several early scenes, but the demon consistently exposes her. She is covered by Karras later after the first part of the exorcism; then when she is restored after the sacrifice of Karras, her mother covers her again. A blanket of divine mercy continues to cover her after that, for the memory of her debauchery is erased. Her mother will lovingly escort her off to their new, clean home.

Still, despite all of this explicit theology in the film's storyline and visual canvas, this analysis must go one layer deeper and return to the place where it began, to the story of the Gadarene demoniac from the gospels. In Mark's vivid account in the fifth chapter of his gospel, Jesus comes to the place where the legion of demons has befouled a man. The demons cry in fear at his coming and bid him [send them] "into the swine, that we may enter into them." Jesus complies and the swine immediately plunge headlong off a cliff to the dismay of their owners. The motif is similar in *The Exorcist*; however, the power distribution has been altered. Karras barely recovers enough of himself to save the girl by casting himself from the cliff. The priests have struggled and have appeared to have lost the battle during the exorcism, as the demon seems able to resist their sacramental means and wield the greater authority. Now, this perception must be tempered by wider biblical context, for Blatty's account blends the story of the Gadarene demoniac with other episodes in the gospels. In an account in the ninth chapter of Mark, Jesus' disciples fail in an exorcism attempt and are told that "this kind can go out by nothing, but by prayer and fasting." Likewise in the thirteenth chapter of Luke's Acts of the Apostles, we find an account of demons beating some men who attempt an exorcism with only the formula but not the power and authority of the church: "And the man in whom the wicked spirit was, leaping upon them, and mastering them both, prevailed against them, so that they fled out of that house naked and wounded." These contextual additions to the root story of the Gadarene demoniac allow a better understanding of the problem Blatty's film raises regarding the church's spiritual authority in the modern world—this kind of Pazuza will not depart without a fight that demands a great sacrifice by those who have been purified.

The film also provides some challenging commentary to the modern conflict of good versus evil, even beyond this principle question of authority. First, *The Exorcist* does suggest that the old warriors of the faith are passing away as a class to be replaced by a generation of religious leaders who lack the faith and commitment to deal with the full-blown demonism that might be hovering at the edge of modern society. In an interesting recent article in *Commonweal*, an author recounts a relationship he had with a local parish priest of Sere-Lanso in the foothills of the Pyrenees. The curé was the local exorcist at Lourdes. A common man in most regards, he recounted an exorcism he performed on a nun that contained many of the harrowing details of the Mt. Rainier, Maryland, case. The curé was horrified by the incident; yet he took it as evidence of the strange powers of iniquity that operate alongside and through our own realm and that choose victims even from among the righteous. The writer celebrated the curé's simple faith in the "Victory of Christ over the Prince of Darkness," and concludes that the priest "lived in the simple radiance of that joy."[4] Unmistakable in the article is the author's intention that the accounts be taken in with a sigh of nostalgia. Ah, that we might all travel to remote French villages or have an opportunity to listen to account from missionaries in India to find the old faith in action. Such simple demonstrations of living piety accompanied by displays of real spiritual warfare, the real power of evil against the real power of God, have become growing anomalies in the modern world.

Second, *The Exorcist* suggests that very little holds back the tide of evil at the edge of modern society. In fact, the film suggests what I have asserted: that such evil is being energetically invited by the film industry itself. In other words, *The Exorcist* shows how dangerous a world we live in and how questionable our systems and agents of defense, while simultaneously demonstrating how profitable the display of demonic depravity and corruption can be in our world. Here again, an article which appeared in the *Journal of Religion and Health* in 2005 offers an insightful context. Therein, the author encourages psychiatric professionals to respond to the "growing evidence for demonic possession" through the means of psy-

8. The Corruption of the Virgin

chiatry. Among the conclusions is that the psychiatric powers and principalities "write grants for the tens of millions of dollars needed to further test the spiritual techniques that appear to be working."[5] In other words, fund research that uses the rite of exorcism to provide science a set of psychiatric techniques, and then package them for the use of private practitioners dealing with "mental disorders." From such and mountains of other evidence, we define the situation that the film and entertainment industry continues to rub the real genie's lamp while the academic and medical communities manufacture synthetic replacement lamps thinking these will be capable of sucking the genie back into confinement when the time comes. We are living the scene outside the demon-child's bedroom door with the two psychologists suggesting that Regan is turning her head all the way around and levitating off the bed because of a lesion in the temporal lobe that can be discovered with a long enough needle and cured by therapeutic intervention.

Third, *The Exorcist* not too subtly debunks the notion that the entertainment industry can wash its hands when it comes to the entrance of incarnate evil into the modern world. The weakest element of the film is the plot device that gets the demon from Iraq to Washington, D.C. It works only according to the logic of graphic novels, by shrouding exotic causality in blinding atmosphere. The scenes in Iraq are evocative and visually overwhelming. A clock stops while Merrin is examining the demon head. The priest is nearly struck by a car while rushing to a site where a larger version of the idol stands. The sun glows behind the eerie ruins in a giant ball of red as Merrin stands opposite a giant Pazuza. Wild dogs snarl and fight, making sounds eerily similar to some of those which will come from the possessed child. The point is made enough to suit the narrative—but still, why Washington, D.C.? Wouldn't an easier answer be that Regan lives in the center of a culture of decadence, her actress mother constantly taking the name of the Lord in vain and sleeping without remorse with a man other than Regan's father? She is raised in a godless home and is playing with an occult device, and she is longing for a deeper relationship with her familiar, identified as "Captain Howdy." Isn't the film moving naturally in the direction of subsequent films like *Ringu*, which link possession to modern entertainments, a videocassette movie in that case?

Finally, building on this last point and given the overall direction of the horror genre, it must be asked, did the filmmakers contribute to the immoral acts on display by building into the film's visual and auditory compositions numerous subliminal devices designed to get under the consciousness of viewers? Brush aside for a moment the sophistry of the production team denying that these were subliminal devices because the images can be seen for a moment. I previously mentioned the frightening scene when Regan sees a demonic face while she is on a hospital bed and we also see it. There are several moments like that in the film, employing devices borrowed from the portfolios of advertisers who write sex into the shadows of ice cubes in liquor advertisements. Chris walks into Regan's bedroom early into the haunting. The camera is positioned inside the room viewing her enter. Quickly across the door a demonic face flashes then disappears. The viewer sees it, albeit barely. Chris does not, for the image is on the other side and is designed to address the subconscious of the viewer, not the character. Later, Chris will walk through her kitchen, the lights flickering on and off in the house. The demon head briefly leers from off the range hood, again behind the woman. Later it will flash over Regan's face on the bed. In a dream sequence with Father Karras grieving his mother, Karras sees her at the top of a subway entrance. His medallion and chain fall slowly through space. The mother turns and the demon face appears, again for only a fraction of a second. These subliminal suggestions are clearly designed to spark fear during the film. Whether they do or not is a separate question. That they are designed to do so is the point.

As horror film entered its next stages, beyond this landmark from 1973, these devices of direct address became more blatant and artfully crafted. In addition, the motif of the implanted evil has become one of the driving plot elements—from *Alien* to the many science-fiction/horror films in which humans transform into grotesques via some viral carrier. One might add the *Nightmare on Elm Street* films in which the evil literally assaults its victims through the mind while they are sleeping. The graphic display of possession and demonic transformation may unfortunately be the principle selling point that the horror industry took away from *The Exorcist*, not the restatement of the older belief that the vampire can be killed by a stake through the heart.

And what does all this mean now? It means that the most consistent

8. The Corruption of the Virgin

and one of the best crafted films in the horror genre, the one with the most overtly religious content, may in fact be one of the most troubling. Modern horror had so far pulled from its origins in the realm of cautionary tale by 1973 that the way ahead seemed lost. No longer were these movies principally designed to illustrate what may happen when taboos are violated and demons unleashed. The new direction would focus on the mayhem caused and the inability of man, woman, or priest to stop it. No longer would the role of the church be to carry the elements, the stake and crucifix that kill the Beast. Now the authorities of the church would become the canvas upon which modern anxieties and weaknesses could be painted. The final question to be asked of the film is whether the images that remain in the mind afterward are of the saintly Merrin, the restored mother and child, the detective and priest in fellowship together; or rather, the images of a leering demonic face or the possessed and debased child performing graphic acts of indecency.

9

No Pleasure but Cruelty
John Carpenter's *Halloween*

> *"Jesus was the only One that ever raised the dead.... If He did what He said, then it's nothing for you to do but throw away everything and follow Him, and if He didn't, then it's nothing for you to do but enjoy the few minutes you got left the best way you can—by killing somebody or burning down his house or doing some other meanness to him. No pleasure but meanness."*—The Misfit in Flannery O'Connor's "A Good Man Is Hard to Find"

In Canto XXXII of Dante's *Inferno*, the most damned of souls appear locked forever in ice, as only "the remorseless dead center of the ice will serve to express their natures"; for they denied the love of "His Sun" and "all human ties," as poet John Ciardi explains.[1] The description might equally fit the ghouls haunting the circular descent of modern horror. Through the past century and a half, the genre has moved relentlessly downward toward greater displays of cold, remorseless treachery. The earliest beasts and monsters had motives beyond a ravenous appetite for evil; not so the brood of the latest generation. Whatever violation of taboo set the demons of the slasher film or the more recent child-possession film on their missions of destruction, few remain alive at the end to recount. The cultural clock has ticked the horror genre toward a fictional apocalypse of unmediated and irrational mayhem.

It didn't have to progress this way. The genre was at its birth wrapped in the cloth of belief. Many of the landmark films promoted human sympathy and resolved with an affirmation of the power of divine providence over evil, from *Vampyr* through *The Exorcist*, troubling though that film is, to the more recent *Exorcism of Emily Rose*. But the genre suggests the culture has turned a dark corner, and so half the formula, the half that suggests the efficacy of the sacraments, has mostly bled out. Julia Kristeva

9. No Pleasure but Cruelty

once suggested that behind the horror monster lays our "insatiable appetite" for destruction.[2] She had in view these newer, bloodier incarnations, and she spoke from the front of the line of the postmodern intelligentsia, assuming a progressive tenet that enlightened culture cannot decay, that people develop in fundamentally similar ways, and so when chaos does break out, it emerges less from evil choice or demonic activity than from some ripple in the pool of the id or the collective consciousness we all partly repress. Thus, the sadistic child molester or the mass murderer has just temporarily lost his or her way, and can be brought back to equilibrium through right thinking or drugs or therapy; at least, they can be rendered functional in some social context.

Yet, if horror is about *our* insatiable appetite, then logic would insist that the Beast is fully in each of us, and eager to break free; there lurks a hideous, hidden thing in every son of Adam and daughter of Eve. Such an explanation teases the fringe of the older Christian doctrine and appeals to the cultural materialism of many who write for the audience of academic professionals, but it would be considered heretical by the church, which has insisted historically that the propensity for evil, original sin, plagues all, but the conscience informed by grace restrains it, and the individual exercise of freedom draws its full shape. And this internal drama is complicated by the existence of a real, palpable pandemonium of evil beings surrounding all the sons and daughters of this present world, a realm of selves swirling beyond my desktop who apparently enjoy the flavor of the human soul. One human soul glimmers with sanctity in the battle and draws near the gates of Paradise. Another makes compact with some of these darker, other selves and is infected like Legion with a babble of contemptuous voices.

The older explanation on the surface would seem to align more with common experience. If we were to believe what the logic of modern psychology often suggests, that the full power of chaos bubbles under the lid of doctor, grocer, neighbor, and that fellow beside us on the train, then we should be daily tormented by fears that would make us mad. No fence would be secure enough, no human encounter ever altogether benign. But we do not want to believe the world is quite such a dreadful place. Common experience tells us to beware specific kinds of people, judged rightly or not, those whom we perceive to pose a threat because of their level of depravity; and we post guard against those particular threats that seem to have carried out the greatest commerce with the land of irrational evil.

The more colloquial approach then to the growing violence and despair in modern art and specifically here the popular cinematic form of horror, aligned with the older orthodox approach, will follow the logic of "once upon a time, we were certain life had some precious value: no longer."[3] That resonates. Something has grown foul in the land, and the air stinks from it. The culture has suffered a collapse, and many popular stories seem to provide the footage.

Just consider, for example, the turn toward sadistic violence represented in the slasher films that have become mainstream since their inception in the 1970s. No amount of pedantry or sensational news can possibly make us believe them artifacts of *ordinary* experience. Read a plot summary of Wes Craven's 1972 film *The Last House on the Left*, a film that promised theatergoers in its original advertisements that they might faint or lose their last meal before it was over. It features a gang of psychopathic killers who abduct two girls and then humiliate, rape, mutilate, and execute them. The killers are subsequently set upon by the parents and they mutilated and killed. That is the story. Then there is Tobe Hooper's 1974 cult favorite, *The Texas Chainsaw Massacre*, a film with a plot that makes the Grand Guignol seem more on the level of *The Twilight Zone*. A group of hippies break down near a house full of sadomasochistic killers. One by one they are bludgeoned, hung on meat hooks, tortured, humiliated, and then cut to pieces by a leather-mask-wearing butcher with a chainsaw; thus the compelling title. One girl escapes—presumably to tell the tale. Such films, the vast majority which will not be privileged here by name, remain "popular," but offer no redeeming merit or even well-designed scripts. They exist in the putrid air, one ledge up from a Mondo film like *The Faces of Death* (1978) and two ledges up from a snuff film, where real victims are butchered for voyeuristic pleasure.

The slasher film grew from a particular soil, that of the new Hollywood of the 1960s and early 1970s, when a dying industry determined anything lawful that would make a profit. They fed off something gone sick in the culture, a growing addiction to cruelty, obscenity, and death. They received their boost toward acceptance as legitimate art with the

9. No Pleasure but Cruelty

commercial success of one specific film, John Carpenter's *Halloween* in 1978—the film that will be discussed at length here. Carpenter gave the slasher film respectability the way *Oh! Calcutta!* and *Midnight Cowboy* did for porn.

The slasher film can be defined as a subgenre of horror in which the plot follows a series of executions,[4] usually of promiscuous young people isolated from the protection of loving parents. The foregrounding of alienated youth has provided the genre intellectual cover in that it allows critics to pass over the voyeurism and sadism explicit in the films and talk instead about issues like date rape, the problem of latchkey children, and the dissolution of the nuclear family. Yet these social issues have become red herrings, particularly as the films victimize and exploit the very young people whom culture critics imply the films indirectly tried to protect. The narrative form of the horror genre demands a violation of taboo, and these films suggest it is rampant, promiscuous teenage immorality. That works in the formal narrative logic. Yet the films don't hold up the deeper implications of such serious moral claims, as they are voyeuristic themselves and marketed toward the very class of people supposedly guilty of the crimes, the promiscuous teen crowd. So, the narrative ritual had become all form and no substance by the 1970s.

Slasher plots are principally directed toward the gruesome display of sadistic violence against young women, their boyfriends, relatives, and even children; the stories unfold as evil role-playing games that legitimize sadistic fantasies. *Halloween* set the pattern, and it proved wildly successful—shot in three weeks, costing roughly $300,000 and grossing well over $60,000,000 to date. And, paradoxically, it happens to be a masterful piece of filmmaking, unquestionably one of the best horror films ever made.

Like the more grisly bloodbaths described above, *Halloween* draws a simple and cruel plot. A soulless mass murderer escapes from an asylum and uncorks Halloween night demonic mayhem on the small town where he committed his first atrocity as a child. He executes four people in the course of the film and pursues a fifth before being temporarily stopped. He will step from the original to several sequels in order to continue his work. And, of course, each execution is a little more perverse and chilling, the gimmick of the slasher genre being how victims are dispatched.

What made *Halloween* stand out was the talent of filmmaker John

A Christian Response to Horror Cinema

Carpenter, who, like many of that era's young directors, was a product of a university film school, USC, where he studied and mastered the techniques of craftsmen like Alfred Hitchcock, John Ford and Howard Hawks. Carpenter's first film success was an update of Hawks' film *Rio Bravo* (1959), *Assault on Precinct 13* (1976), a small-budget action film involving an L.A. gang that lays siege to a police station as part of a mission of vengeance. *Halloween* follows a similar pattern of homage and violence. Numerous references to classic films are made throughout, from the theme music Carpenter wrote that echoes the "Tubular Bells" of *The Exorcist* to overt references to Hawks' *The Thing* to a subtle reference to the Lumières' landmark *Arrival of a Train at La Ciotat* (1896), an allusion that underscores the film's intention to disorient and frighten the viewer. Film philosopher Noël Carroll would famously criticize Carpenter and others of his generation for confusing allusion with style,[5] but the fact remains that Carpenter, despite a short career of successes, created in this one film something uniquely effective.

Perhaps the most interesting allusion in *Halloween* is to Luis Buñuel's *Un Chien Andalou* (1929). Buñuel, following principles of anti-bourgeois art described by Antonin Artaud in his experimental "Theatre of Cruelty," opened that film with the notorious slicing open of a woman's eye with a straight razor. The Carpenter film references wounds to the eye in several places, and clearly directs a similar scorn as Buñuel's toward viewers. The difference is that Carpenter leaped over Buñuel's Marxist intentions and went right for the gore.

The previously mentioned Grand Guignol of Paris provides further context. Founded by Oscar Metenier in 1894, the design was to stage dramatizations of cruelty perpetrated upon duped victims, a visual pleasure to satisfy those who perhaps enjoyed the work of the guillotine but who preferred such pleasures indoors with a roof overhead. The theater sat 285 against a smallish twenty-foot square stage, and with the optional amenity to purchase the intimacy of a booth. Productions featured graphic mutilations, eyeball gouging, rapes, and painful executions. They were short enough that three or four might be watched in an evening with more lighthearted sleaze thrown in for the release of dramatic tension. The Grand Guignol produced one work of lingering cultural significance, Gaston Leroux's *The Phantom of the Opera*, and did manage to hold an audi-

9. No Pleasure but Cruelty

ence until 1962, when it finally choked on its own bile. It would have been a familiar, whispered secret among the new generation of filmmakers who studied at the university film schools, and, of course, those who taught the film classes and enjoyed the luxury of university travel. The slasher films would borrow heavily from the gory aesthetic of the Grand Guignol, but with the advantage of the increased verisimilitude allowed by the cinema, which includes the greater intimacy granted the voyeur who may watch the carnage in the darkened multiplex or in the living room.

Halloween brings the viewer into the point of view of the sadist. It opens with a lengthy tracking shot of the boy killer, Michael Myers, walking toward his house, removing a butcher knife from a kitchen drawer and then slicing up his unsuspecting sister who is brushing her hair in her bedroom in the nude. He puts on a Halloween clown mask along the way, so the scene is displayed through the sightline of the mask and enhanced by the heavy breathing behind it. The motif has been a staple in the genre since, perhaps most recognizably in the climactic sequence of Jonathan Demme's *Silence of the Lambs* (1991) when Jodi Foster's character, Clarice Starling, is hunted through a dark basement by a serial killer wearing infrared glasses. The source of horror derives from the vulnerability of the victim, the suspense of the chase, and the allure of experiencing the events from the position of the killer.

Especially disturbing in this equation is the fact that the placement of the viewer in that active role parallels the positioning of female accomplices to sexually sadistic male killers in reality. A study printed in the *Journal of Family Violence* in 2002 described how women caught in such nightmare relationships later confessed that the "sadistic fantasy of the male [became] an organizing principle in [their] behavior."[6] The women caught in these nightmares remained compliant for a variety of reasons but uniformly slid toward patterns of greater debasement and increased participation with their sadistic partners. The disturbing truth is that this pattern of depraved complicity is iterated in the spectacle of the slasher film as the viewer is drawn into active alignment with a series of sadistic activities and is inevitably bonded to both the behaviors and the perpetrators. Although the victims of the carnage in the slasher film are both male and female, the iconography makes evident the stalker is a male sadist, a prowling beast who derives sexual satisfaction from dominance and cruelty. The sadistic monsters have tended to achieve the status of cult heroes as the analogy would predict, from Michael Myers to Leatherface to Jason to Freddie Krueger, and the personalities of those horror monsters has been subsumed by their iconic roles as perverted serial killers.

In sum, slasher film viewers are teased into enjoying portrayals of cruelty and debasement, and encouraged in the role-playing exercise to take the part of the sadist's accomplice. As might be predicted, the real-world consequences of this game have been borne out by research suggesting that "males exposed to sexually violent 'slasher films' increased their acceptance of belief that some violence against women is justified and that it may have positive consequences."[7]

The monster in the films is not human, despite the various pseudo-histories provided, but an *it*. In *Halloween*, he was described on set and in the credits as "the Shape," but he is called "it" by the psychiatrist pursuing him in the story, Sam Loomis, named after the boyfriend in Hitchcock's *Psycho*. The starlet who plays what critic Carol Clover aptly labeled the "Final Girl,"[8] the ultimate target of the *it*, is Janet Leigh's daughter, Jamie Lee Curtis, a casting choice that added another nod toward the Hitchcock film. *It* wears a mask, a blank face, and emerges from an anywhere house on an anywhere street in the anywhere of Haddonfield, Illinois. At the film's start, when the original clown mask is pulled from the boy, Michael, who has just slashed to death his sister, the child lacks any distinguishing features or expression. His parents likewise stand blandly to either side, impotent and irrelevant. This anonymity again subverts the older, more redemptive principles of the horror genre. The monster has no demonic name, just the "Bogeyman," the subject of irrational childhood fears, the *it*.

But, the *it* is still demonic, an agent of death with apparent immortality and nefarious purpose. By the film's conclusion, *it* will be punctured in the neck with a knitting needle, poked through the eye with a hanger, stabbed through the chest with a butcher knife, shot repeatedly, and launched off a second floor balcony, but *it* lives on. In the end, Sam Loomis searches the darkness for the monster while the Final Girl cowers whimpering in the corner. The camera flips through the various locations where *it* has previously emerged from some dark corner as the theme music sug-

9. No Pleasure but Cruelty

gests the evil still hovers within the spaces and that sound gets reinforced with an overlay of heavy breathing through Michael Myers' mask. In one of the film's most chilling scenes, after the Final Girl has stabbed *it* and imprudently turned her back, *it* sits upright on the floor like the damned souls tormented for graft in the eighth circle of hell who die only to rise again for more torment, except here the demon with the hook keeps getting up, not the victim.

As the monster is an *it*, so the victims of the mayhem function principally as types. They have few distinguishing features beyond their identification with stereotypical behaviors. The three murdered girls in the film are interchangeable. Their distinguishing marks are youth and promiscuity. The films underscore the promiscuity, but more as an analogue for their vulnerability. Girls alone with no weapons, no protectors, and little covering play the focused targets, with children providing secondary interest if needed. In *Halloween*, Final Girl Laurie Strode has a father who is seen briefly leaving for work in the morning. No mother is present. Annie, the first to be murdered on Halloween night, strangled in her car and then stabbed, has a police-officer father, but he is played as clearly ineffectual—he must be convinced of the danger Myers poses by Sam Loomis and has little control over his daughter, nor is he present for the attempted rescue in the conclusion when Loomis finally confronts Myers.

That the adults are not in the house gets loudly announced in one particularly chilling moment as Laurie stumbles from house porch to porch, having found her three friends murdered and been stabbed herself by Myers. She screams for help, but no one responds by opening a door, even in one residence where adults are visible through a front window. The scene recalls the Kitty Genovese case, the young woman brutally stabbed in New York in 1964 despite screaming and calling for help in a well-populated neighborhood where many neighbors heard but chose not to respond. In another film in the subgenre, *When a Stranger Calls* (1979), a sadist terrorizes a babysitter alone with children in a house, having already killed a sitter and children some years before. The police and the parents function as ineffectual recorders of the terror on the other end of the phone line. The girl victim is left alone like a goat in a lion's den.

The hunting game in the story of *Halloween* gets visual reinforcement in a cat-and-mouse tease that the camera plays throughout. Loomis, the

A Christian Response to Horror Cinema

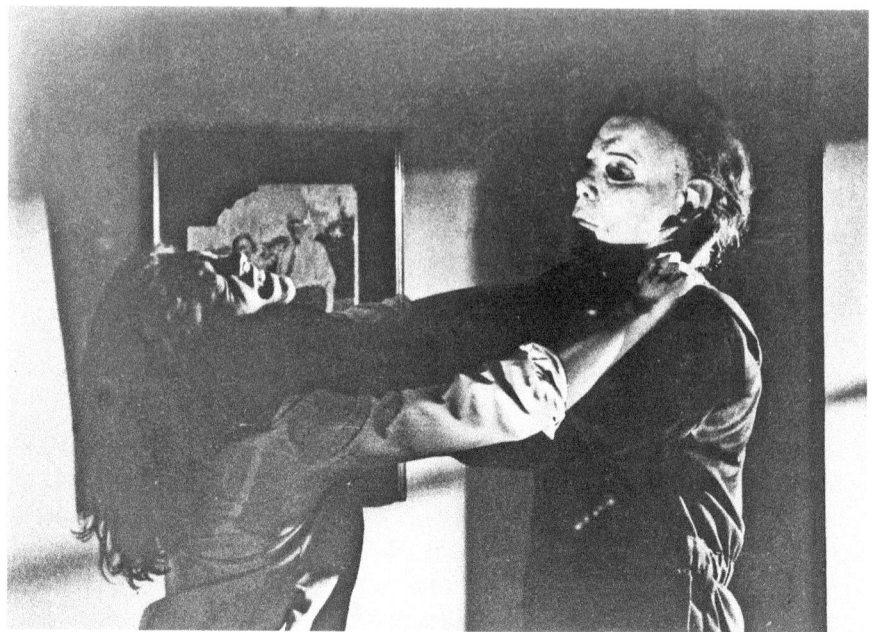

The "it," Michael Myers (Nick Castle), strangles Laurie (Jamie Lee Curtis) in front of a photograph of parents absent throughout the film and the genre. 1978. Falcon International Productions.

one strong male character beyond *it*, gets drawn into the game early to have his own ineffectuality put on display. Early in the action, he leaves a female nurse alone in a staff car after Michael Myers has let all the inmates of his asylum loose. This eventuates in the nurse being terrorized by Myers before he steals the car. Later, Loomis stands on a street corner surveying the walk in front of a hardware store Myers has robbed of supplies while Myers turns his stolen car and passes along the street directly behind him. The evil sees. Even the best of the rest are blind.

The viewer is brought into the tease as soon as Final Girl Laurie enters the action. As Laurie leaves her house in the morning for school, a long tracking shot suggests she is being followed, while the viewer is placed into the position of voyeur, the logical extension of the opening sequence documenting Myers approaching his house to murder his sister. When Laurie meets up with Tommy, the boy whom she will babysit, he

9. No Pleasure but Cruelty

warns her about the Myers house where Laurie is to drop off a key for her realtor father. As Laurie walks from the porch, "the shape" suddenly emerges beside the door and watches her leave. The camera adopts that position. Later at school, *it* will appear outside the stolen car while Laurie sits in a class only half listening to a teacher droning on about fate. She sees *it* but must stop looking through the window to answer a question. When she looks back, the street is empty. Later, on the walk home from school, *it* continues to stalk Laurie with the viewer carried along for the thrills as *it* appears beside bushes then disappears, and later appears again amidst sheets on a line in her yard.

A similar pattern will precede the murder of Annie, the first of Laurie's friends to be killed. Myers plays with her as she cleans her clothes in a laundry area, sometimes appearing behind a glass door but then disappearing. What makes this device psychologically difficult for the viewer is that what starts with the viewer identified with the killer ends with the viewer caught in the cat-and-mouse game and stalked along with the victim. The viewer never gets privileged with advance warning of where *it* will appear next.

This victimization of the viewer is what extends the film beyond the viewing experience, as the images and sounds of the film linger in the mind long afterward, a phenomenon like the phi phenomenon or that persistence of vision necessary to see moving images as seamless. The dread lingers in the subconscious mind and suggests that a portal to the demonic remains open, which it very well may. As much as horror film functions like nightmare, a projection of the darkest human fears and anxieties, it also becomes the stuff of nightmare. After Janet Leigh, the mother of the Final Girl actress, was slashed in the shower in *Psycho*, the shower became a dangerous space for women and men left alone. The genre has, in fact, systematically rendered unsafe numerous other zones of domestic comfort. Annie is stalked in the laundry room and then murdered in the driver's seat of her car. The other girlfriend victim, Lynda, is strangled with a telephone cord in the bedroom. The first victim, Michael's sister, was likewise in her bedroom. In numerous other films of this ilk, like *Scream* (1996) and *Ringu*, the kitchen is transformed into an unsafe space. In a subsequent *Halloween* film, it will be a hospital room. In *The Exorcist*, what might be termed a more redemptive horror film, the bedroom is defiled because the possessed girl occupies that space, but then the room returns to being a safe space when the evil is gone. In *Halloween*, the intention is to render unstable all safe spaces the viewer may enter after leaving the theater; the virus is taken home as it were.

Thus, the slasher film, propelled by its series of sadistic executions and its own voyeuristic propensities, compromises and assaults the viewer, both inviting complicity in perversion and murder and then turning the violence on the accomplices. And it corrupts and destabilizes a viewer's sense of security at home. But this is not all, as one component remains: the encouragement of heartlessness.

There are two male victims of the bogeyman in *Halloween*. One is a truck driver murdered for his clothes after Myers escapes from the asylum. The other is Lynda's boyfriend murdered by Myers in the kitchen going for a beer. Both cases underscore the film's strategy of encouraging emotional distance from the murder victim.

In the case of the truck driver, most troubling is that this victim is treated as irrelevant, even by Loomis who discovers his murder. The scene is set against the backdrop of a highway. Loomis has found an abandoned truck at the side of the road and calls the Haddonfield police to warn them of what is coming. He finds Myers' hospital garments on some branches and hurries back to his car while the camera meanwhile pulls from him to reveal the face and upper torso of the dead driver further into the brush. As Loomis hurries off with back turned, seemingly indifferent to the humanity lost behind him, the viewer is left to ponder the physical wreck of the nameless corpse. Especially interesting is that this marks the placement of the aforementioned quote of the Lumière film. A train has screamed past in the beginning of the sequence just to the left of the camera putting on edge the viewer, signaling through the allusion the film's rather callous intention.

The murder of Lynda's boyfriend is no less disturbing. It occurs in the silence of a dark kitchen. The youth opens the refrigerator to get the beer, oblivious to the evil in the closet behind him. Once Myers emerges, he grabs the boyfriend by the throat, lifts him off the ground and pins him to the cupboard with his knife. *It* then steps back and studies the victim with head slightly cocked, an intentional metaphor, one of the first images of the murderer seen in full figure, and a chilling one in the per-

9. No Pleasure but Cruelty

verse coolness it implies. *It* has "dead eyes, doll's eyes," Loomis has said. Prior shots were from a distance or with *it* just teasing the corner of the image and then disappearing.

The "reveal" of Myers follows the conventional striptease within the horror narrative. *It* is seen in full as a child and then only briefly as an adult, first leaping onto the back of the psychiatrist's car, then at a distance with the mask stolen from the hardware store. By the end of the film, *it* is more a presence, although when the mask is momentarily pulled off in a struggle with Laurie, the face is distorted and indecipherable. This, again, runs against the grain of convention, for the reveal had always been a reveal—be it of Frankenstein or the Wolfman or the Thing, or even much more recently, the Godzilla-like monster of *Cloverfield* (2008). Here, the reveal offers another razor swipe at the viewer's eye.

Halloween does something else characteristic of many of the more recent films of horror. It suggests authenticity and verisimilitude. "Haddonfield, Illinois, 1963," reads the script on the screen as the film begins. The device is repeated on the occasion of Myers' escape—"Smith Grove, Illinois, 1978." This is real, the title suggests, but with none of the whimsy of a film like *Fargo* employing the same device. You will watch real death in real time. More recent films have purported to be video recordings in real time. *The Blair Witch Project* (1999) advertised itself as found footage and played out as a succession of bits spliced together from the wreckage of a handheld camera. *Cloverfield* likewise presents the alien beast destroying New York through a camera held by one of the characters recording a party. *Paranormal Activity* (2007) displays the developing possession of a woman in her house through a security camera that stays on in the haunted bedroom. These plot and cinematographic devices are designed to both make the experience of watching all the more intense and the experience after watching all the more haunting.

The tagline for the sordid *Last House on the Left* was, "It's only a movie." Implied was the direction of the new horror toward realism, real Marquis de Sade-Charles Manson-Jeffrey Dahmer characters set in familiar contemporary places, not Egypt or Transylvania, and pursuing their blood lust for mutilation and execution with victims displayed in more detail than newspaper photos of gangsters killed in the '20s. That has drawn the crowds into the theaters. Haddonfield is played as Middle

A Christian Response to Horror Cinema

America with quiet suburban-style streets, except shot through a blue filter to render every corner ominous and cold. It is a familiar universe, but without God, with only the Devil and the poor souls left behind pulled along by some mechanical "fate," as Laurie's teacher drones on. The jaws of death gape wide, and the starved landscape tilts the victims that way.

The impulse to put on screen the grotesque and horrific, the carnival freak show discussed earlier, goes back to the earliest days of film when "peep show" was an accurate way to describe the potentialities of the new cinematic medium. Thomas Edison produced a sixteen-minute version of *Frankenstein* in 1910, and the genre has moved steadily forward and downward since then. Striking with a film like *Halloween* is how less stylized it is than the early Universal films which borrowed so heavily from German expressionism to suggest the elusive spiritual presences that surround material life. *Halloween* is skillfully crafted and *stylistic*, but not *stylized* in the old way, unless one is to suggest that the eerie blue filtering and shrill music equates to the hazy aura around Karloff's Mummy. It may just be that the removal of God from the visual aesthetics has pulled from the images any artistic beauty, that which always offered some hope amidst the horror.

The industry found a market in lower-budget gore festivals at a time when the market was needed. There may not be much different here in substance than in the concluding sequence of *Taxi Driver* (1976), in which Travis Bickle executes a gang of pimps and hustlers in a red-filtered montage of violence, except that Scorsese's sense of irony suggests some kind of moral universe. Whether or not those moral fibers have their roots tapped into the deep chambers is another matter. One should also consider that most narrative films, even especially violent ones like those of Scorsese or Peckinpah's *Wild Bunch* (1969) or Penn's *Bonnie and Clyde* (1967), do not set out to corrupt the viewer; the intention that sets the slashers apart beyond everything else is to degrade the innocent, humiliate the pure, and make heroic the sadistic, and not only within the confines of the screen, but outside in the clean night air and then inside in those formerly safe domestic spaces people typically run to for comfort and security.

The industry has marketed these films to women as well as men.[9] They feature female protagonists and storylines which follow standard

9. No Pleasure but Cruelty

romantic formulas. Will straight-laced A-student Laurie Strobe find some freedom in the love of a boy as have her friends Annie and Lynda? And will hers find a higher form, something less associated with high-school bathrooms? She will, of course, but in the closet and hallway alone with knife-wielding Michael Myers. And elementary school children are brought in, curious about the buzz in the conversation of their elder brothers and sisters. I first heard the storyline for *The Texas Chainsaw Massacre* when still a preteen. It was the secret the boys with experience shared with only their bravest friends.

How horror like this has been addressed within the university underscores the institutional move toward theoretical, scientific analyses and away from religious ones, specifically any that suggest a real presence of divinity in the world and the real presence of what the gospel writers termed the Evil One. To take one example, a prominent feminist theorist of the 1980s, notable for a long career exposing the forbidden territories where women have been exploited in the larger culture, could only come up with this when addressing the Final Girl victim of these new, hyperviolent horror films: "the woman encountered a monster whose deformed features suggested a distorted mirror-reflection of her own putative lack in the eyes of patriarchy."[10] So, all that bloodshed and mayhem just to make a gender statement about how men fear strong women? And, while we are at it, who in the predominately liberal film industry might be behind this vast conspiracy to display women's "lack"? That remains a great mystery. The uncomfortable fact that *Halloween* was heavily influenced by Debra Hill, a woman who assisted John Carpenter on the script and most other aspects of the production, seems to bear little weight in the scale of pedantry. One finally does need to say something, however, and the typical academic theories (such as the aforementioned feminist theory) do display a kind of mechanical soundness, at least in the rigor and consistency of their application. Unfortunately, by avoiding the larger moral and spiritual issues, the theories and theorists further a game of intellectual solitaire, offering little to explain the sadism and debasement involved in slasher productions or how one film emerged from a specific cultural moment or what has happened to the deep religious roots of the form through time.

I'd like to address those deep religious roots for a moment and carry the argument of this book forward regarding the subject at hand. What seems to have happened is that horror film has shifted not so much in its affirmation of the real presence of evil, but in its belief in the real presence of God, both as benevolent providence and as the agent of salvific intervention; namely, the Savior who rescues those who cry out for help. When Laurie cowers whimpering in the corner at the end of *Halloween*, no one hears. Loomis looks around the house for *it*, but not for help. His gun was his crucifix, and the gun might as well have fired blanks. Noteworthy is that the children have disappeared from view in the final scene, a vestigial decency perhaps, for they stand to be the first devoured when the bogey man returns.

Equally telling is that the film concludes with the viewer left alone in the house. No indication is given as to where *it* might have gone. No security is offered for when the nightmares come later. So, Dante has been led down to the frozen ice at the bottom of hell and has seen the Beast devouring the treacherous Judas and Brutus and Cassius. He has seen the unimaginable and felt the tingle of fear down his spine; then as he follows Virgil over the hairy flank of the frozen king of pain, the yellow eye turns his way, and the guiding poet disappears.

Where can the horror genre go after this, one wonders? As mentioned, the attempts at greater and greater verisimilitude will come, fol-

Absent in *Halloween* and the slasher genre is "the Savior who rescues those who cry out for help," as Laurie does throughout the entire final sequence. 1978. Falcon International Productions.

9. No Pleasure but Cruelty

lowing André Bazin's theory that film will always pull along that rope. Better depictions of bloodletting, better latex technologies, better camera lenses that allow more evil to play in corners of the screen, richer sound—all this, certainly, and with more talent behind and before the camera (think Anthony Hopkins as Hannibal Lecter), and with more bits of reality spliced in (actual images from the photo journals of death perhaps or graphic, unedited video streams from the new journalists). And perhaps one day, real cutting and bleeding, controlled at first and stylized, but real, and then...

The world depicted must also grow colder and darker. The representatives of the old church must be made to seem more villainous and more complicit in what the society chooses to label immoral. Priests and ministers must be played as child molesters. Holy water and crucifixes and even prayer are to be cast as superstitions left over from a dangerous medieval era that depended for its existence on ignorance, prejudice, the subjugation of women, and all other heinous expressions of social injustice.

10

LORD OF THE WORLD
Hideo Nakata's *Ringu*

"And the dragon stood on the sand of the seashore. Then I saw a beast coming up out of the sea...."—Revelation 13: 1 NAS

There is something appropriate that the latest wave of horror has emerged from Japan given the history of that nation over the past hundred years. Hideo Nakata's 1998 film *Ringu*, an adaptation of a novel by Koji Suzuki, quickly became that country's highest-grossing film the year of its release and triggered something of an international sensation in the horror community, resulting in several sequels and remakes in Korea and America. In America the best-known film in this category would be Gore Verbinski's remake *The Ring* (2002) and the hugely successful *The Grudge* (2004). The films feature viral ghosts of the Japanese yūrei variety which haunt and kill the unwary, by means of a videocassette and television set in the original. Thus, the films link an unpredictable demonic entity bent on revenge and mayhem with various components of contemporary urban life.

A few summary comments should be advanced at the start of this chapter regarding this new turn and the overall direction of the horror genre. What has remained a constant in horror, from its inception in nineteenth-century Gothic literature and its earliest formations in narrative film, has been the presence of the demonic, although the demons have been more pernicious and unpredictable in recent films; Sadako, the yūrei in *Ringu*, is much more frightening than the Golem and its reincarnation in hulking monsters like Frankenstein. Also constant is a plot structure built around the understanding and naming of the particular haunting demon and the search for the means to exorcise it. What has changed is, first of all, the environment in which the haunting takes place.

10. Lord of the World

Early horror was set in exotic locations: the polar regions north of Europe, a forest somewhere near Frankfurt, a steamy Welsh ancestral estate, a desert area in Egypt; even some later films maintain this original tendency, *Alien* being set in a ship in deep space, for instance. The new beasts dwell in affluent suburbs, trendy urban neighborhoods, and Middle America. They step into the world of mortals through ordinary television sets and telephones and the back seats of sedans. Also changed are the means to exorcise the beasts. Early incarnations were limited in range by some divine dispensation that allowed the haunting but also provided the formula to the secret elixir by which the things could be eventually dismissed. The newer demons have shaken off all divine shackles and cannot be exorcised, only appeased. In *Ringu* the appeasement is revealed to be part of a cruel game the demon plays to determine its next victims. It will in fact never be stopped.

In *Ringu*, the Japanese yūrei demon kills via the evil eye. The gimmick that moves it from victim to victim is similar to the passing of the rune in Tourneur's *Night of the Demon*: a videocassette the thing has made psionically as an expression of its wrath over how it was sent from this world to the next. Thus, the overall mood is dark and relentlessly ominous. When the film ends, the viewers realize they have watched the cursed video along with the demon's on-screen victims and might likewise be marked for haunting in the days to come.

The clean-lined plot of *Ringu* runs as follows. Two teenagers discuss an urban legend of a cursed videocassette while alone in a house in Tokyo. One claims to have seen such a tape recently on a weekend with friends in the coastal town of Izu. The girl, Tomoko, tells her friend the legend that after seeing the tape and receiving a phone call, the victim has seven days to live. Tomoko got the phone call in the cabin in Izu, and this is the seventh day. Predictably, when her friend goes out of the room for a few minutes before leaving to return to her home, the television in the living room mysteriously turns on and Tomoko is killed horrifically. What the viewer sees is the girl turning to see something over her shoulder and then gasping.

The girl's cousin, Reiko, a reporter for a local television station, goes to the funeral and hears from Tomoko's mother the awful nature of the death and that the other girl has gone mad and will not venture near a television. Then she hears other schoolgirls discussing the urban legend of the death tape. She begins to investigate and finds that all the teens who went to the cabin died mysteriously. When she accesses some photos they took, she discovers that their faces are distorted in the developed pictures. Reiko drives to the cabin in Izu, finds the mysterious tape, and plays it.

After some initial static, a series of grainy and disorienting images appear: a threatening moon, a woman combing her hair in a mirror, then another mirror showing briefly a creepy younger girl with black hair, Japanese characters from newsprint that shift and dance over a white screen spelling "eruption," men and women staggering and crawling slowly up a hill, a man with a towel covering his head pointing to the ocean, an evil eye with the characters spelling "Sada" etched in, and then an ominous-looking well in a clearing amidst leaves. The video terrifies Reiko and the viewer, and even more so when an image of the creepy girl shows in the blank television set after Reiko turns it off, and the phone rings. When she picks it up, she hears no voice but otherworldly demonic sounds and realizes she has seven days to live.

Reiko elicits the assistance of her ex-husband, Ryuji, a university professor with some psychic abilities. He watches a copy of the tape she has made and agrees to help decipher it, and together they determine the tape is a message inviting someone to find its hidden message. After some research, the story begins to come together. Some decades earlier a psychic woman named Shizuko had predicted the eruption of a volcano. A university professor interested in psychic phenomenon, Dr. Ikuma, discovered her and decided to put her on display to prove the validity of ESP, and to make money. At a public demonstration, a reporter who challenges the validity of Shizuko's skills was suddenly struck dead. Shizuko attributed the death to her daughter, Sadako, purportedly the illegitimate child of the psychic and Dr. Ikuma who has powers greater than her mother and is "a monster." Reiko and Ryuji then discover that Shizuko committed suicide after the scandal by throwing herself into the volcano and that Dr. Ikuma took Sadako away and killed her with a blow to the head, then throwing her body down a well. On Reiko's last day, Ryuji takes her to the cabin where she saw the tape determining that it was built over the sealed well. They find the well and go down to the body, discovering by streaks

10. Lord of the World

of blood on the walls that Sadako was still alive when she hit bottom and died a slow and terrible death. Reiko finds the body, or it finds her, and the two come up and turn the evidence over to the police.

But the story does not end there. Back in Tokyo, Reiko makes plans to get her son from where she had left him at her father's house. Ryuji goes back to his apartment. While there, his television turns on mysteriously to show the last scene in the cursed video. Sadako crawls out of the well, then walks to and through the television screen. She moves eerily toward the terrified Ryuji and kills him by the evil eye. When Reiko is notified, she comes to the apartment and questions why he had been killed and not her. The ghostly man with the towel on his head from the video appears and points her to Ryuji's bag, in which is the copy of the tape she had made. Reiko realizes she was spared not by finding Sadako and giving her a proper burial, but by copying the tape and passing along the virus. In the last scene, she is driving to pick up her son Yoichi from her father's house, apparently with the intention of passing the tape through her son to her father and then on until Sadako has another victim.

In many ways, *Ringu* is a perfectly designed little film, reminiscent of *Halloween*, from which it borrows the motif of teens with absent parents haunted by a force far above their powers to understand. It likewise has a female protagonist willing to go into the bowels of hell to protect the children, her son Yoichi in this case, and a monster that cannot be destroyed. Most similar to the John Carpenter film may be *Ringu's* sense of intentionality; at ninety-six minutes the film is all lean and no fat by modern standards.

Beyond its tight plot, *Ringu* has a genuinely haunting quality. The images of evil are uniformly upsetting. Likewise the demonic sounds that come through the phone and then recur intermittently throughout the events have a chilling effect akin to that of the growling sounds coming from the upstairs bedroom in *The Exorcist*. And *Ringu* manages to linger in the mind without need for gore or excessive violence. The symbols of demonic oppression are more than enough.

The image that most recall from watching *Ringu* occurs with the demon Sadako crawling out of the television screen and into Ryuji's apartment. The trick is accomplished via clever editing and a weird backward walk by the kabuki-trained actress playing the demon child. Its novelty gets an extra boost from a surrealistic dream: the beast attacking the viewer directly through the theater screen.

What critics have talked about most in the film other than this plot surprise, is the actual cursed video with its disturbing images and sounds. Imagine a brief film composed by a denizen of the underworld with the purpose of luring victims to explore it and be damned. Then add to that the sounds that one might hear from a distance were a window in hell opened. That is the video, both in Nakata's original and in Gore Verbinski's remake. Scholars have described both in great length and compared them to show the cultural differences distinguishing the visual art of East and West.[1] But largely missed is the function of the video as analog to the larger task of modern horror.

The video hints at components of the surface mystery of the plot. The original woman in the mirror is the mother Shizuko. The girl in the other mirror is Sadako. The people crawling up the hill apparently suggest victims of the volcanic eruption Shizuko had predicted. The man with the towel on his head is some ghostly servant suggesting the viewer needs to be guided on the way toward some truth, perhaps the well where Sadako was murdered. However, all of these initial conclusions get undermined by the time the story ends. The controller of the video is really Sadako, who wants the viewer to read it logically and think of the evil eye deaths as part of a problem to be solved, the modern way of looking at the realities of a fallen world. In truth, however, she apparently didn't need her body found. She didn't need a real burial. She wasn't after closure. The video is simply a disease, and the design is to lead to a false diagnosis, apparently from no real purpose other than the perpetual expression of malice. At one point in the film, a suggestion is made that Sadako is not the illegitimate daughter of Shizuko and Dr. Ikuma. Shizuko had sat for hours by the sea and spoken to it in a language not human, we are told. The child may actually be the progeny of the witch and a sea demon, which would be why local fishermen hated Shizuko and blamed her for their losses. When Reiko and Ryuji analyze the tape, they hear a phrase spoken in dialect, which Ryuji translates as, "Frolic in brine. Goblins be thine." Ryuji will then later interpret these words to mean something cryptic but explicable: if you play in the sea, you may drown. By the end, it seems to be a demonic incantation: the goblins will come and play with you.

10. Lord of the World

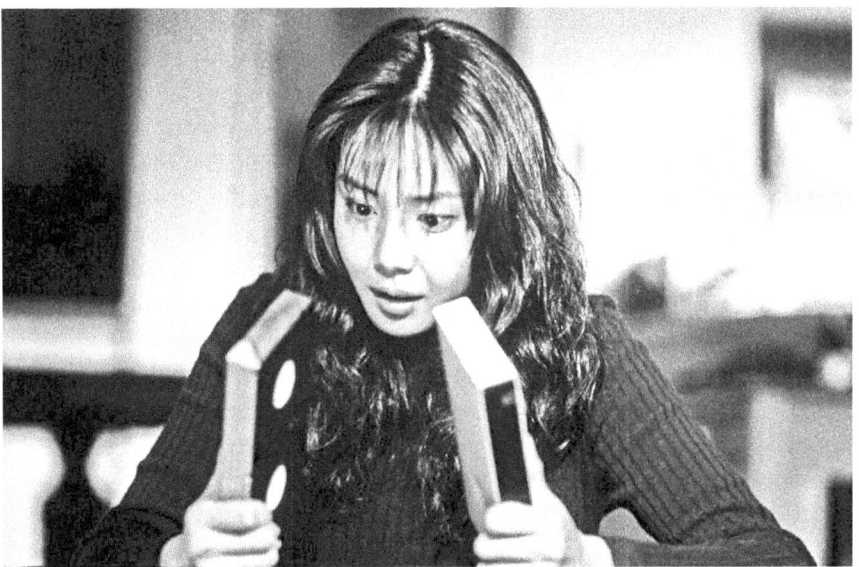

The reporter Reiko (Nanako Matsushima) realizes the video is a contagion with "no real purpose other than the perpetual expression of malice" in *Ringu*. 1998. Toho Company Ltd.

Both of the novelties in *Ringu* have to haunt contemporary viewers. The image of the girl demon emerging from the comfortable appliance of television seems so apt. Beyond a gnawing guilt over the genocides of the twentieth century, those ugly unintended consequences of the enlightened myth of progress, a horror that might indeed be imaged through the men in the cursed video crawling up some tier in hell, the century had also produced more martyrdoms than any other in the Christian era. Antonio Socci put the number at 45.5 million,[2] a full 65 percent of all martyrdoms since the time of Christ. There is something tragic in the fate of Shizuko whose public crime was to testify that she saw what others could not. Although her face-saving suicide, leaping into the live volcano, does run toward Oriental pulp fiction, her exploitation at the hands of science and victimization by the masses and the "press" inspires sympathy.

Another component to tack on here might be the trajectory of twentieth-century abortion rates. Worldwide, abortions were performed at the end of the twentieth century at a rate of 40 to 50 million per year.

A Christian Response to Horror Cinema

The population of America's largest city, New York, is well under 9 million. Sadako, the "demon child," is in the way, and thus killed and put out of sight. That she does not die immediately is suggestive. Furthering the motif of the unwanted child is the absence of active parents throughout the story. Reiko's son, Yoichi, is constantly being shuttled off into the care of someone beyond his mother. Although she calls him frequently and expresses her love, it tends to be while arranging that he stay at a distance—with friends or family or home alone. Likewise, the father, Ryuji, indicates surprise that the boy is in elementary school already. He has been busy with his own life; we learn he has a student assistant as a paramour and that he is being haunted by the girl Tomoko who died in the initial scene, a curious attachment in that the girl, no longer Tomoko as he says, chooses to haunt him primarily. The children have been used or moved out of the way throughout the story, and although they die horribly, the grief expressed by the adults seems rather muted. At one point in the action, Reiko asks Ryuji to stay with her when she dies. He expresses disdain at the question because the friend of Tomoko had gone insane by seeing what happened so why would he want that. For Yoichi's sake she implores him, but he responds that perhaps it would be better if they all die, including Yoichi.

Given this context, the initial meeting of father and son, Ryuji and Yoichi, deserves some closer scrutiny. It's raining and both have umbrellas. They meet outside Reiko's apartment, the child on his way to school, the father to see the distressed mother. No words are expressed. In the rear of the shot is a fence suggesting the barriers between them. They stare at one another, and then Yoichi walks past his father. It is a moving portrait of an abandoned child grown cold toward the distant abandoner and writing him off.

It is tempting to take this moment as suggestive of some intentional message in the film. One could easily argue the "repressed other" in the story is the unwanted child, and Sadako is emblem of the repressed returning. Perhaps Tomoko likewise is returning and perhaps Yoichi will one day, too—he is able to see her ghost and she has told him to watch the video to experience what she has experienced. And so perhaps in the unwanted child's return some measure of just vengeance is meted out and the culture repressing such crimes is given a nightmare warning that the

10. Lord of the World

time has come to address their sins and repent. The film presents a hopeless relational world when you get down to it. Even in the more peaceful scenes with Yoichi's grandfather, the grandmother is absent. There are no intact and happy family circles in *Ringu*.

The immediate context of the story is the tradition of the Japanese yūrei tale, which dates back before the seventeenth century to numerous myths and folk tales in the kaidan tradition. These typically feature an innocent woman murdered by a man who returns to the land of mortals to exact some vengeance or at least ensure through supernatural means that her body receive the appropriate rites so her soul may be allowed a place in the spiritual world of ancestor protectors. The cause of the yūrei's haunting is specific to a crime, and the yūrei seeks resolution and release. An analogy might be to Madison Elizabeth Frank in the Zemeckis film, *What Lies Beneath*, that began this study. The yūrei in Japanese lore would appear in shadowy form as a woman in white clothing, suggesting her innocence, and with long black and disheveled hair, apparently a reference to Japanese funeral tradition when women let their hair down.

Sadako would be the traditional yūrei who has been misunderstood and then abused by her father, Dr. Ikuma. Having been thrown down the well, her body obviously did not undergo the sacred rites preparing it for life with the ancestors. So, she created the video with clues to the crime in hopes that some sensitive person would unravel the mystery and find her corpse. This is what Reiko and Ryuji do. However, the film does not end with this resolution. Instead, Sadako seemingly has interest in her body being recovered only as a cruel trick played on Reiko, who gets the pleasure of diving into the well to recover the rotten corpse and then having her ex-husband whom she still seems to love killed and her son, Yoichi, next on the hit list.

In the cold logic that emerges at the end, Sadako is revealed as anything but an innocent victim. She doesn't even show particular malice for her murderer. Likewise, the girl Tomoko, who is killed in the opening sequence, has an ambiguous mission. The motives of evil are not as clean as the tradition would suggest. The vengeful Sadako may have begun her wrath in some directed fashion, but her course unfolds differently. The sequels of *Ringu* suggest that the video is a literal virus that Sadako created to populate the world with beings like herself.

A Christian Response to Horror Cinema

In *The Exorcist*, Father Merrin tells Father Karras that the demon wants the priests and all others involved in the possession nightmare to despair of their humanity. Its ultimate goal is the corruption of faith. In *Ringu*, the intentions of Sadako seem less defined, for there is no immediate theological context for the story. The tape is a postmodern game of arbitrary murder. There is no logic to who dies next, and that is a mechanism toward fear, not despair. As Reiko and Ryuji travel by boat from Tokyo to the island where Sadako had lived, Reiko wonders where the urban legend got its start. Ryuji offers two possibilities: that some tension in a culture birthed it, the premise of modern scholarship regarding the subject of horror, or that no human started it. At this point in the story, Reiko is still of the naïve opinion that she can rescue herself and her son through some noble means. Ryuji—who shares some measure of Shizuko and Sadako's psychic powers—senses something more malevolent at work: no human started it.

In *Ringu*, the background religion of the horror genre merges with the traditional kaidan tale into something much darker than the genre had previously exhibited. In Oriental thought, a cosmic equilibrium directs the interplay of events on earth and in the nether world. The wandering yūrei in the kabuki tradition are not all malevolent, much in the same way that the spirit Manitou of American Indian folklore produces life. The yūrei has the honorable task of restoring cosmic equilibrium. Sadako does not. In fact, her malevolence runs counter to the reserve of the Japanese culture she inhabits; Reiko and Ryuji remain reasonably calm and polite through the entire ordeal, even in the end as Reiko calls her father with the intention of somehow infecting him with the cursed tape. So, in *Ringu* the Oriental revenge tale has been itself infected by two dark elements from a collapsing Western Christianity: the dysfunctional family, with abandoned children, and the demon with little motive beyond chaos and mayhem.

At this point it is fair to propose that the horror genre in its current transformation might be aptly termed *cinema diabolique*. It certainly stands as an anti-tradition to what Western writers offered in the redemptive literature of the mid- to late-nineteenth century. Although Raskolnikov murders a wretched pawnbroker and inadvertently her godly sister in *Crime and Punishment*, though he splits their skulls in most gruesome

10. Lord of the World

fashion, his subsequent journey is toward humility and confession. He will kiss the ground where the main roads meet and submit to the nursing mercies of a broken-down prostitute, and then he will reach under his pillow in Siberia and pull out a Testament; reading that book will begin his new life. Likewise, in a symbolic variation, although Jean Valjean descends into the Paris sewers through a drain and nearly drowns in the black waters under the city, he emerges again into the light carrying his daughter's lover to safety and overcoming his chief adversary, Javert, by the power of his self-effacing love and integrity. The tradition of literature developed in the late medieval period continued in a purposeful and redemptive direction until the dawn of the twentieth century, when it began to crack and disintegrate. In the older tradition, chaos was overcome by grace guided by providence. The blows and arrows of the righteous found their targets. So, Tolkien writing under the cloud of Mordor, still has Bard's final black arrow hit the one unprotected spot of Smaug's armored belly. The Gothic tradition, too, despite its tormented romanticism, maintained the overall theological assumptions about the triumphs of grace and providence. Even in *Frankenstein*, Walton the ship captain repents his decision to pursue the North Pole and risk losing his crew after hearing the mad scientist's awful tale. Likewise, the earliest horror films looked backward to paradise lost but heaven promised. Those who persevered to the end would be saved. But not so in the anti-genre of modern horror where the tape of redemptive history is backward masked like a satanic prayer. The one man left standing the grotesque night with the zombies in *Night of the Living Dead* is shot in the head by an idiot sheriff's deputy who thinks him also a zombie.

The seeming intention of this modern horror, this *cinema diabolique*, is to suggest that grace and providence are mythic. What exists in the world of flesh is will, and the strongest wills are those inclined toward evil. Creatures of virtue or culture, like Reiko in *Ringu*, cannot begin to understand the will to evil that governs the new world. Thus, when the veil is pulled aside to reveal the thing, they do not think to look for a stake and hammer; their response is servile appeasement. Reiko will become the agent of Sadako if it means she and her son will be saved. So, the viewer of the horror film is taunted with a similar doubt—why even cry out when no one cares to listen? The films break down religious hope and

A Christian Response to Horror Cinema

simultaneously break down any confidence in the certainty of categories of cause and effect and good and evil. It is both troubling and ironic that Sadako would go on to become a character in a popular video game and that many teen fans of the Japanese films have practiced and sent into the cloud renditions of her chilling walk from the television set.

The effects of this type of film experience are quite difficult to measure, although it is easy enough to trace the causal lines between twentieth-century political and moral horrors and the changes in the genre. It is undeniable that the new century had already been marked by a rash of inexplicable, random violence, mass shootings at camps and malls and theaters and elementary schools, and by individuals with unclear motives beyond the will to mayhem. Attempts to explain away these events fall flat, as do the typical political solutions posed by those whose power depends upon the impression of understanding and competence response.

In the cryptic video that Reiko and Ryuji watch and attempt to interpret, two images remain ambiguous even after Sadako's real nature is made clear. One is the man with head covered and the other is the image of people climbing up a hill. The man with head covered has no clear explanation, especially as he will appear in Ryuji's apartment to direct Reiko to the bag that contains the video copy she made for her ex-husband. Is he Dr. Ikuma? Has he become the servant of the witch, like the peg-legged soldier in *Vampyr*? Is he a benevolent spirit protecting his own eyes from Sadako's evil eye and so insinuated into the video to help those who can still be helped? Can we trust our understanding of them? Likewise, the second ambiguous image, the people crawling and staggering uphill, might be suggestive of those caught near the blast of the volcano and so are as lost and disoriented as the surviving victims of Hiroshima and Nagasaki were. Here, too, however, the explanation is problematic, for why are they climbing uphill? What is the hill? Perhaps they can be better understood as denizens of hell like Sadako shambling toward some opening that will give them access into the world of daylight?

The effect of these disorienting images and their interpretive ambiguity is to disintegrate the viewer's understanding, just as the effect of the mood of horror is to disintegrate feelings of stability and security. In the American remake, *The Ring*, the demonic video is more overtly designed toward this purpose. That one includes intestines extending out of a gaping mouth, wriggling maggots filling the screen, and a finger impaled on a nail. All of these additions suggest the subjective reality of the demon girl trapped in the well, but with a surrealistic, disorienting arrangement that brings the viewer into the mind of chaos. Put simply, the tapes are designed to corrupt. Once in the mind, like the viral videocassette itself, they remain there and form impressions within the outward reality perceived thereafter, and around the behaviors those impressions incite.

If art is directed toward the creation of beauty and conveyance of truth, then modern horror might be logically termed "anti-art." Likewise, if the spirit of the older faith sought to guide the artist in some fashion, as Tolstoy argued, toward infectious art that somehow inspires fellowship and sympathy, then modern horror is antithetical to the older understanding of the function of art. If art mimics the original creative enterprise, as Dorothy Sayers suggests in her *Mind of the Maker*, if an orthodox Trinitarian character of God is somehow metaphorically suggested by the Artist who conceives an idea as the Father, of the craftsman who composes like the Son, and of the infectious Spirit who applies the ideas to the heart and mind, then modern horror could be said to be antithetical to the Christian understanding of the character and purposes of God.

But most would say that modern horror is simply a projection of the mind of the modern artist functioning in the world of celluloid invention. Still, even if only that is maintained, the modern artist must be observed as following a current much deeper and faster than anticipated, one headed around some bend toward a cataract that roars but cannot quite be seen. The individual artist functions in the modern imagination like the Great Man invented by Thomas Carlyle and other romantics who saw giant individuals directing the currents of history. The auteur director who produces something enduring is celebrated as important and even virtuous in an artistic sense, for that artist has marked time and shaped those who sculpt it in the future. If the artist creates new words and others write them on new blank tablets, then the artist is a genius to be revered. Forget for a while what those words say. This is the way we are taught to think.

Yet the Great Man notion of history has been largely debunked, as it was even in its own day. Victor Hugo argued that the prototypical Great Man, Napoleon, irritated God, and so providence eventually spit him out.

A Christian Response to Horror Cinema

Tolstoy portrayed that same Great Man as a great fraud, a byproduct of hubris and tragic history, a character himself just as bound to the cause and effect machinery of human events as the peasant pulling a cart or the naïve girl stepping into the hall for her first ball. So, what of this notion that the artistic history of film transcends the currents of history and should be traced through the emergence of new styles and techniques and the geniuses who shape them?

It might be helpful to point out here that very few of even the more memorable horror films have come from directors considered first rate. Hideo Nakata will not find his place beside Yasujiro Ozu or Akira Kurosawa in the pantheon of Japanese filmmakers any more than will John Carpenter and Karl Freund have their names placed alongside Orson Welles, John Ford, and Francis Ford Coppola. Many horror directors seemed to share Aaron's experience with the golden calf. The genre somehow found them and whispered in their ear and guided their hands. Film genres in themselves come from places that very few critics and philosophers have been able to identify easily.

Consider, for example, one of the more eerie effects of *Ringu*, the demonic sounds that emanate from the phone and the videocassette and punctuate the scoring of non-diegetic effects in the film. Why does it get so deep under the skin? When Reiko hears it, her face opens in terror much as it does when she watches the disorienting images on the video. When the viewer hears it, a similar terror follows, but not cued by the character. The sounds are enough, like the sounds played backward on Father Karras' audio recording of the possessed Regan. Every time that sound occurs, the effect is produced. Reiko has traveled to the cabin at Izu where the teens stayed prior to their mysterious deaths and searches in vain for clues. She finds none in the cabin and lies on the sofa in dismay. The camera views her from above, as if watched. She is vulnerable and marked. Then she goes to the main desk and asks the custodian if he has seen the teens in a picture she shows him. While he looks, she notices a shelf of videos with colorful art on the boxes, and then one lone unmarked box at the end of a shelf. She hears, and we hear, the unearthly growling sounds. She knows. We know. From that moment on, the viewer feels as pulled along by occult forces as the woman in the story. To whom or what do we attribute this experience?

10. Lord of the World

Genre theory teaches that groupings of texts arise at particular historical moments and that they are open systems related to other parts of the system but flexible and subject to modification once other texts enter the system. Critics and scholars place barriers around genres in order to categorize and evaluate specific members by a form of touchstone theory, the better films determining the value of the lesser.[3] Likewise, producers market certain films and encourage the creation of other like films when a market is identified for what the "genre" seems to offer. Yet none of this adequately explains what a genre really is and why it works. Academics have tried explanations, most often through psychoanalytic theory or through structuralist systems of binary terms—chaos versus order, foreign versus familiar, dark versus light, etc. But these explanations simply offer a primer for language games used to engage the texts. The genre itself always defies those games in the end and like larger historical and artistic movements refuses to be easily pinned down. Too many disparate elements are involved, as are too many moral choices and unforeseen consequences.

Who made the initial decision to try to replicate the sounds of demonic possession and reproduce them in a marketed form and why? Does it matter? And who can explain fully why one particular generation determined such a choice and the game invented around it to be both acceptable and desirable? What terrifies any human viewer and listener in those moments when Reiko sees the sights and hears the sounds of hell is a troubling intuition that we all secretly long to see and hear the infernal as a contractual obligation connected to some old destiny. And the awareness of this secret desire to know hell is terrible to consider. The same applies when the demon Sadako crawls from the screen. The audience understands that visitation as the perfect, most logical extension of what the film and the entire larger genre has invited. Her coming fulfills an internal logic long awaited. It satisfies deeply and thus horrifies deeply. If only the demon girl will stay in the final area of confinement, within the narrative imprinted on the celluloid and run through the flickering machine. But she won't, of course. She will live in the minds and souls of many who walk away whether they will it to be so or not. Forces beyond the individual creators have willed it.

Recent studies on the effects of watching horrific or excessively vio-

A Christian Response to Horror Cinema

lent media content have revealed two interesting facts to go alongside these conclusions. The first is that those who watch great amounts of a certain kind of visual programming do not necessarily enjoy those programs watched. They watch out of habit, and not even necessarily the addiction to a specific form. Those most affected by the content do, however, tend to enjoy the forms more.[4] The conclusion is, then, that a line exists, perhaps the final line, between those who watch without knowing quite why and who have, therefore, given up the power of choice, and those who watch and have taken back the will to choose and who assent to the full experience. The research suggests that the more dangerous group in terms of the potential social consequence is the latter. So, watching is aligned like all moral behaviors—the trajectory is from allure to indulgence to addiction to full assent, at which point one might argue the soul is lost and there can be "no more repentance" and very bad things may result. The second interesting fact is that recent research has also shown that there is a significant relationship between the amount of media viewing one does during the teen and young-adult years and the likelihood of acts of aggression and violence later in life; this is driven by the types of content the majority of teens and young adults tend to watch in these years.[5] So, addiction to the behavior of watching chaos and cruelty leads again to an assent to the behaviors watched which finds its outlet in the actual exercise of the chaos and cruelty.

In *Ringu*, this trajectory might be mapped through the character of Reiko. She hears the story of the haunted video and is lured into the cursed activity by what she believes is her moral responsibility to investigate and find the truth about her cousin's death, but this goes against her greater responsibility to raise and protect her son, Yoichi, who is perhaps most at risk of all the young people. She leaves him alone repeatedly and is indirectly the cause of his taking and playing the video. She cannot keep herself from watching the television news of the strange deaths, then the weird photos, then a video image of the teens taken dead from their car, then the cursed video, and then a copy of the cursed video with Ryuji. Once hooked, she doubles down on the behavior, leaving Yoichi for an extended period while she explores the home of the psychic witch Shizuko, the photo of the woman's past life, and then the dark waters of the well. In the well, Reiko embraces the demon girl; actually, as she is

10. Lord of the World

fishing in the muck to find her, Sadako grabs her by the wrist. Later, when taking the video to her father as witting ally of the demonic, she seems content, smiling as her car speeds off toward some distant mountains shrouded in luminous gray clouds.

Consistent in *Ringu* is the suggestion that those who believe they are watching are actually the ones being watched. Again, Reiko is the main player here. In the cabin, she stares intently at the cursed images, but once the television goes off she is horrified to discover that Sadako is behind her, the image reflected in the darkened screen. This is presaged several

The "old and powerful" yūrei Sadako (Rie Ino'o) haunts Reiko and for a nefarious purpose. *Ringu* 1998. Toho Company Ltd.

scenes earlier. When she goes to Tomoko's house for the funeral and walks upstairs to investigate, the camera adopts a position of distance and height. She is walking into a trap. A paper blows on Tomoko's dresser though no windows are open; it is the photo receipt which will take Reiko farther into this forest. Likewise, Ryuji has psychic powers but is at their mercy. They can't predict as Shizuko's could; they can only sense when he is being watched. So, he sits on a bench looking down at his work when he senses the approach of the demon that was Tomoko and looks up slightly to see her legs and dirty white shoes, but he does not need to look up further to see her face, for he knows it is her. Likewise, Shizuko's cousin, who still owns the property where she lived with Dr. Ikuma and Sadako, lives in constant terror because Shizuko could read his secret thoughts, something that Ryuji reminds him of during their encounter.

Once again, this plot device functions as the perfect metaphor for what the viewer senses to be the truth. What if the horror-watcher has been watched? Or even worse, what if the watcher is known personally and followed home later? What if a reflection will appear in the dark lens of the bedroom television or if a set of malicious eyes will peer through the blinds? Who can say for sure *when* in the course of reading the secret scroll of Thoth the entity is allowed to enter in? And once the entity arrives, will God still respond to those who have mocked the danger of the chilled air blowing through the room?

And what if the film itself is an amulet, a Ouija board? Will the demon be, if not exorcised, perhaps appeased when the viewer invites friends over for a second viewing with pizza or if, as with the girls in the beginning of *Ringu*, the tale is retold to companions eager to defuse the tension in the room? In *Ringu*, such appeasement proves ineffective. Tomoko's friend who laughs at the story of the tape and Tomoko's exploits in the cabin goes insane. You can only stop the thing by doing what it says. What will it say?

The not-so-subliminal message of *Ringu* is that we mere mortals had gone too far already. The demons we had toyed with are old, powerful and too evil to be challenged; and the thing which got us in trouble is in every room of every house. This brings to mind the memorable original ending of Don Siegel's *Invasion of the Body Snatchers*, when Dr. Miles Binnell runs into a road to get help to fight the pods that have infected

10. Lord of the World

his hometown only to find trucks loaded with pods already driving the disease throughout the land. But now the pods are not filled with a political idea, like the spread of Marxist thought; the pods really have something living inside.

In the Gore Verbinski remake, the character akin to Reiko finds that while watching the cursed video a fly in the image somehow crawls out and onto her finger. It is a foreshadowing. In *Ringu*, a date appears at the start of each sequence marking the days after Reiko and then Ryuji watch the film. It starts with 5 September 1997 when Tomoko sees the film and then jumps to 13 September with Reiko. It reads "21 September" when Sadako appears to get Ryuji. But then again, as the film ends, with Reiko driving toward the mountains, the script appears before the credits. The cycle continues on and on. The device originated in *film noir*, the sense of doom evoked by the voice-over narrative that tells the story. It entered horror in *Halloween*, when the first date of Michael Myers' murder is offered and then the date of his return to Haddonfield. This evil is scripted. In *Cloverfield*, the date is that of the recording device showing the monstrous beast from space rampaging through New York. It is the marker for reality constructed by will and not individual choice, and it works perfectly in this film so dependent on the metaphor of evil will dominating individual choice in a world driven by digital reconstructions.

Verisimilitude moves the devices of filmmaking toward greater constructions of space and time. The machine goes faster, makes less sound, and produces twice the product of the older version; it must be purchased and used. So, the story moves harder forward as well, and must be written.

Where is all of this headed in the new century and beyond? The question is intriguing, although the primary function of the present study is to be analytical, not predictive. The horror genre evolved through the twentieth century into a form that put on display the will to evil. Its appeal became the appalling design of the artifacts of that will. Thus, it became a genre built upon the allure of what had been formally taboo and still remains taboo on the surface of "polite society." Horror depends on the allowance of a temptation played out, something Poe once termed the "imp of the perverse." What if we take character X and lead her toward a bridal altar only to have the face of her groom transform into a ghoul at the last minute and then have her laid on the altar as a victim of devilish sacrifice instead of blessed bride going to her husband? Nobody has done that, have they? Act on the impulse. Think of all the unspeakable, obscene atrocities that have haunted our worst thoughts. Now put them on screen for effect.

I have a colleague who returned to her faith when she heard the Devil speak to her, as she puts it. She was working in New York for a major network, had three Emmys on her shelf, and was on the fast elevator traveling upward, but she felt herself losing her way from her Catholic upbringing and fretted over the inevitable personal consequences of her success. One day she was standing on a subway platform when, in her words, she heard an evil voice that came from outside and behind her. It said, "Push him onto the tracks." The "him" was a man who stood in front of her at the edge of the platform. She was horrified at the impulse, the voice, but had to exercise all her will to resist, which she says she barely managed. Later in the week, she heard a breaking news story that a man had just been pushed onto the tracks on that very subway platform and horribly mangled. Interpret this how we may, she returned to the church and soon left New York to pursue a career in teaching.

Why not make a movie of that, but remove what some would regard as the contrived and sentimental ending. A killer randomly kills. The film will offer no explanation but many images of the gore and mayhem. It might end with a villain caught and brought down by a resourceful police detective. All could seem resolved, except that when the detective returns home that night his family has been brutally murdered. There actually was a film made like that some years back, of course, called *Seven* which ended with a police detective finding his wife's head in a box. So some minor changes would need be made to our story.

And so moves the overall direction of modern horror as it has been handed from the past century to contemporary filmmakers—unresolved chaos and demonic brutality with a teasing narrative that suggested evil can be stopped but the contradictory subtext that it really cannot, so join in.

The refreshed genre already emerging in films like the *Paranormal Activity* (2007) series and *The Cabin in the Woods* (2012) and *The Conjuring* (2013) has already, and will undoubtedly continue to, follow the logic of

10. Lord of the World

narrative verisimilitude and present more and more graphic displays of the overtly demonic, a drive to incarnate fully that thing itself, something analogous to the older attempts in religious films to incarnate the divine— the creepy display of Sadako's emergence into the world of flesh gets close in *Ringu*, her evil eye somewhat less so, a detail that led Gore Verbinski to actually image the demonic face in his 2002 version. Note also that there is no equivalent attempt to find ways to better show sanctity or the realm of the angelic in contemporary film.

Another logical development in the genre of horror, one more technical than narrative, will be greater attempts to plant the film images and sounds permanently inside the viewer. This might be done through creative subliminal suggestion, perhaps a new kind of rapid montage effect. Underground film might encourage watching while under the influence of specific drugs. That behavior has been going on informally since *The Rocky Horror Picture Show*, but it would seem that a more sophisticated alignment between certain hallucinogens and certain kinds of film experience may inevitably be explored.

In the actual business of film production, a logical development might be the use of more amateur footage to increase verisimilitude, something akin to the video footage in *Paranormal Activity* and *Cloverfield*. Dark sequences and images exist in the cloud of public domain that can easily be brought into the constructed realities of film narratives to heighten their effect. And perhaps some performers will allow some dramatic effects to be more literal. It has long been common practice for actors to starve themselves or go days without water or run to exhaustion to enhance their performances. Actress Farrah Fawcett produced a television documentary tracking her own final illness. Robert De Niro feasted and fasted to achieve the heightened representation of Jake LaMotta's rise and descent in *Raging Bull*. Would an actor or actress be willing to take a moderate wound, just a small cut to start, if paid sufficiently and if it made their performance really stand out for the judges of the Academy or Cannes? The direction of the horror genre may very well head that way on the fringes of the industry.

On the other side of the speculation, can an entire culture be put in retreat if a consensus is formed that the culture has taken too hard a turn and has started rolling down a dangerous hill? This is a question Nikolai

A Christian Response to Horror Cinema

Gogol posed at the end of the first section of his masterpiece *Dead Souls*, peering ahead with skeptical humor at where the Russian motherland was speeding toward in the progress of the nineteenth century. I'm also reminded of the end of Hilaire Belloc's *The Servile State*. After pages of analysis describing the shift in Western culture toward a capitalist system so misbalanced from the abuses of the sixteenth century that a return to serfdom in the modern world seems inevitable, Belloc suggests that it is always possible for an intervention of grace to occur to restore the lost perspective and lead to choices countering the dangerous current. He offers that one glimmer of hope in less than a single page at the very end of the book. It is always possible for the mysterious to intervene and for shifts to occur that seem possible only in dreams, but rare.

Looking at the genre from a distance, there would seem to be no easy mechanism to temper the more troubling developments in the form of horror if only because it is so difficult to identify what type of images and sounds and stories are to be controlled. The Production Code successfully kept certain kinds of content off the screen for three decades and insisted on certain kinds of resolutions, but that code of regulation governed during an era when Hollywood existed as a monolithic entity and when American films dominated the world market, other countries tending to follow our lead. Those conditions no longer exist. The American film industry has fragmented. Students at universities can check out sophisticated equipment and make low-budget films in a matter of weeks that could go viral overnight. Films can be made in developing countries beyond any local regulations and distributed through telephone technology. Communities of faith currently laud these technological advances as they make it possible to create simple evangelistic films carried on mobile devices and then projected on walls in underdeveloped areas, so would even people of faith agree to welcome restrictive regulations? And who would be on the censorship committees and would these be regional or international? Likely international committees would need to be formed. And who would create the standards? Likely the standards would be a set of values determined by the discretion of the most powerful minds and wills on such committees. That frightening prospect suggests the cure might lead to far worse than the initial disease, as tends to be the case more often than not when regulations are imposed on artistic content and form.

10. Lord of the World

Stay away from the woods, especially late at night when creatures unspeakable come out and wait for naive travelers as here during the climax of *Cabin in the Woods*. 2012. Lionsgate.

A Christian Response to Horror Cinema

The best response might just be the old one, the simple warning offered in the grim and cautionary folk tales—stay away from the woods, especially late at night when unspeakable creatures come out and wait for naive travelers. Don't be foolish. But also take ease in the metanarrative that evil has been already defeated by a champion and though the camp seems hopelessly surrounded by hostile enemies, greater forces surround them.

In the context of the labors of this book, this last allusion brings to mind Christina Rossetti's brilliant and haunted poem "Goblin Market," in which a naive girl is tempted in the woods by the voices of goblin men who offer sweet but cursed fruit. Laura cannot resist and goes and eats and falls into a slumber and illness that tips her toward death. Her beloved sister, Lizzie, however, determines to save Laura by offering herself. Lizzie steals off at night in a horrific ministry of love and is accosted by the goblins who try to force her to eat, wiping their food all over her face and pushing it against her lips. She resists heroically and returns to her sister at daybreak, offering the food on her face sanctified by sacrificial love as antidote. Laura eats and is restored.

There would seem to be no easy cure for an image stuck in the mind that debases a person's view of a woman or a child, no magic eraser to wipe the interior screen clean. Similarly, there is no removing the sound of the demon's voice from a real exorcism that starts to play when you are alone in the dark or in one room while your wife and children are in the next. There may especially be no easy cure when you have already given the nod to powers of chaos. An appetite, once developed, demands an occasional feeding. So, pilgrims need to heed the signs and warnings, and may at times need real help.

Still, some inoculation of horror might be necessary in a world that creates so much horror around us—if the vaccine offers the disease in a pure form, with a short trigger and quick set of stages that resolve in the eradication of future danger. All the best vaccines come with that warning.

Conclusion

If the world has not come to an end, it has reached a major turn in history, equal in importance to the turn from the Middle Ages to the Renaissance. It will exact from us a spiritual upsurge. We shall have to rise to a new height of vision, to a new level of life ... —Alexander Solzhenitsyn, Harvard Address, June 8, 1978

The danger of writing a book like this is that friends and family and, perhaps worse, unknown readers may assume the author holds a special affection for the subject. That would not be true, although this haunted terrain has offered many provocative views. The genre of horror, in keeping with the tradition of all creative art, has provided a canvas for real artists to ply their craft. And as horror has roots in theological soil damp with the blood of redemption and damnation, many films of this type prove intellectually and emotionally engaging, especially when approached as a measure of cultural change. Of the ten films described in the preceding chap-

Older pilgrims would have insisted that some journeys are bruising, and call for courage, companionship, and perhaps a guide, as Ofelia discovers in *Pan's Labyrinth*. 1973. Warner Brothers.

Conclusion

ters, six can be watched without first carefully reading the warning label, the exceptions being *The Wicker Man*, *The Exorcist*, *Halloween*, and *Ringu*, all of which contain elements genuinely disturbing. Three of the ten, *The Mummy*, *Vampyr*, and *Pan's Labyrinth*, are, on the other hand, classic films rewarding for any mature audience by any measure.

Yet it is hard not to conclude outright that the genre of horror has moved in a troubling arc through the past century, and that a large number of contemporary films in the genre should simply not be watched indiscriminately, and especially not by the unprepared and young. Some of them may really be dangerous, controversial though that claim may now be. By definition at least, the entire genre flirts with danger, if only because it plays in the yard of the diabolic.

Yet a virtue of the horror genre is frankness. The films do not dissemble about what they are and what they may do, for good or ill. This dark forest has marked trails. When the bat flies through the window and transforms into a man, the viewer ought to know that death has arrived.

So, like many elements in this mysterious, haunted world, the horror genre demands a viewing strategy and an honest assessment of the potential consequences to the person handling the material. I do not know that I will be leaving this labor a better person than when I removed the books and tapes from the house a decade ago. Perhaps we all secretly lean heavily on mercy.

Older pilgrims have insisted that some journeys call for courage, companionship, and perhaps a guide. I do hope, then, that these words at least provide theological scaffolding for those interested in some stable structure to withstand and measure the heavy winds of the culture emerging from the unsettling changes of the past century. The great fear that drives horror, after all, is not specifically the fear of the things that go bump in the night, but fear that we will be left alone and defenseless when those evil things bump our way.

I further hope that what the reader discovers behind all the historical and cultural artifacts laid out on these shelves, not to mention the bulky machinery, is the gold coin of the story. Horror, whether of the older variety found in folk tales or in the crippled children of Mary Shelley's troubled dreams, reminds us that the struggles of our darkest nights are

Conclusion

matters of the flesh and the spirit, for we are both. And horror likewise brings to mind the centerpiece of an ancient wisdom: when all words have been spoken and all images and actions pass and our transient struggles come to a final end, only one force in the battle can be left standing, with a great multitude of wounded survivors gathered round hoping to raise a cry of gratitude, not despair.

Chapter Notes

Chapter 1

1. Out of the pockets of Freud's "The Uncanny" have come wads of critical interpretations of the horror genre and of individual films, all of which identify the monster's entrance into the narrative as a "return of the repressed." Feminist and gender theorists have paid particular attention to the sexual violence embedded in the horror formula, a type of interpretation that would see *What Lies Beneath* as a response to perceived cultural oppressions. See, for example, Barbara Creed, *The Monstrous Feminine: Film, Feminism, and Psychoanalysis* (New York and London: Routledge, 1993); or, see Rhonda Berenstein, *Attack of the Leading Ladies: Gender, Sexuality, and Spectatorship in Classic Horror Cinema* (New York: Columbia University Press, 1996).

2. Gustav Aulén argues convincingly that the triumph of Christ over Satan is the most ancient Christian understanding of redemption, the buying back of the saints from demonic bondage. See *Christus Victor: An Historical Study of the Three Main Types of the Idea of the Atonement*, trans. A. G. Herbert (New York: Macmillan, 1969). See also Jaroslav Pelikan, *The Christian Tradition: A History of the Development of Doctrine* (Chicago: University of Chicago Press, 1971), especially volume I, 141–71.

3. Romans 1: 18.

4. After dismissing standard explanations of the appeal of the horror genre, Noël Carroll convincingly argues that "we are attracted to the majority of horror fictions because of the way that the plots of discovery and the dramas of proof pique our curiosity, and abet our interest." We derive pleasure in the fascinating pursuit of the grotesque that underlies horror plots, a morbid pursuit of that which "problematizes standard cultural classifications." Horror gives us pleasure then, according to Carroll, both as chase and pursuit narrative sport, as well as in its almost pornographic construction of images forbidden by the larger culture, which the rules of the sport allow us to temporarily access. While I assume many of Carroll's positions here about the forbidden allure of the horror narrative, I differ on an historic and metaphysical level. Although the genre seems open to postmodern play, and has drifted into its own self-parody in films like *Scream* (1996), its roots are in romanticism, not modernism. As such, its roots are deeply religious, and the indices of horror point, therefore, to the metaphysical realities of the angelic and demonic. In direct terms, whereas Carroll and the vast majority of contemporary critics do not seem to believe in the bogey man, the genre does. See Noel Carroll, *The Philosophy of Horror, or Paradoxes of the Heart* (New York and London: Routledge, 1990), 158–95.

5. Noel Carroll's trend-setting argument is summed up as follows: "Thus, to a large extent, the horror story is driven explicitly by curiosity. It engages the audience by being involved in the processes of disclosure, discovery, proof, explanation, hypothesis, and confirmation. Doubt, skepticism, and the fear that belief in the existence of the monster is a form of insanity are predictable foils to the revelation (to the audience or to the

characters or both) of the existence of the monster." Noël Carroll, "The General Theory of Horrific Appeal," in *Dark Thoughts: Philosophic Reflections on Cinematic Horror*, eds. Steven Jay Schneider and Daniel Shaw (Oxford: Scarecrow Press, 2003), 4.

6. S. S. Prawer most clearly articulated the premise that our fascination of the uncanny is central to the development of the horror genre, describing "the uncanny" as "everything which should remain mysterious, hidden, latent, and has come to light" (S. S. Prawer, *Caligari's Children: the Film as Tale of Terror* [Oxford: Oxford University Press, 1980], 111).

7. For example, Kracauer writes that "both films [*M* and *The Blue Angel*] bear upon the psychological situation of those crucial years and both anticipate what was to happen on a large scale unless people could free themselves from the specters pursuing them" (*From Caligari to Hitler: A Psychological History of the German Film* [Princeton: Princeton University Press, 1947]), 222.

8. http://www.catholicdoors.com/prayers/english/p01975b.htm.

9. Cynthia Freeland makes much the same point in her conclusion to *The Naked and the Undead: Evil and the Appeal of Horror* (Boulder, CO: Westview Press, 2000). She writes, "Most of all, horror movies are about the very picturing of evil" (275).

10. I borrow the term with much respect from E. Michael Jones, who correctly traces the Gothic tradition to the "Enlightenment's continuing attempt to destabilize morals and replace them with biology and hygienic technology" (*Monsters from the Id* [Dallas: Spence Publishing, 2000], 140).

11. Despite Charles Derry's assertion that the older type of horror film "keeps its distance from man both aesthetically and metaphysically," the psychological and spiritual effects of the genre have remained fairly constant (see Charles Derry, *Dark Dreams: A Psychological History of the Modern Horror Film* [New York: A. S. Barnes, 1977], 17). Shifts in the immediacy of the genre, which are the logical developments of the form toward greater and greater verisimilitude, do not alter the basic equation of what the generation is in and of itself, nor do they alter in essence the experience of the viewer.

12. Sir James Frazer, *The Golden Bough: A Study of Magic and Religion* (New York: Macmillan, 1958), 260.

13. It is significant that in the Mosaic Law, offerings must be made for sins intentional and *unintentional* (Leviticus 4:2–3), for ignorance of sin is a mark of depravity, not a barrier against sin's consequences.

14. Quoted in Henry Ansgar Kelly, *Satan: A Biography* (Cambridge: Cambridge University Press, 2006), 305.

15. In *The Devil's Bride: Exorcism— Past and Present* (New York: Harper and Row, 1974), Martin Ebon writes, "Depending on one's outlook, the underlying sameness of possession and exorcism may either be interpreted as proof of the universal presence of devils, demons, or possessing spirits, or as clear indication of the basic identity of the human psyche" (12). The majority of previous studies of the horror genre assume the latter.

16. Taken again from 1999 *Roman Rite of Exorcism*.

Chapter 2

1. *Center for Holocaust and Genocide Studies*, University of Minnesota. Web. February 10, 2013.

2. A summary analysis offered as anecdote in his forward to Elie Weisel's *Night*, trans. Marion Weisel (New York: Hill and Wang, 1958), xvii–xviii.

3. Jones, *Monsters from the Id*, 8.

4. "I'm tired of hearing that the best horror movies are the ones that don't show the monster. I'm from the school that likes to show the creatures," quoted in Jaime Perales Contreras, "The New Master of Horror Movies," *Américas* 61 (March/April 2009), 61.

5. Rosa Montero, "The Silent Revo-

lution: The Social and Cultural Advances of Women in Democratic Spain," in *Spanish Cultural Studies: The Struggle for Modernity*, ed. Jo Labanyi (Oxford: Oxford University Press, 1995), 381.

6. Benedict XVI, *Spe Salvi*, November 30, 2007, http://www.vatican.va/holy_father/benedict_xvi/encyclicals/documents/hf_ben-xvi_enc_20071130_spe-salvi_en.html.

7. 1 John 2:15-16.

8. See Marsha Kinder and Beverle Houston, "Seeing Is Believing: *The Exorcist* and *Don't Look Now*," in Gregory Waller, *American Horrors: Essays on the Modern American Horror Film* (Urbana: University of Illinois Press, 1987), especially their discussion of sound in *The Exorcist*, 56ff.

Chapter 3

1. C. S. Lewis, "The Weight of Glory," in *The Weight of Glory and Other Addresses*, ed. Walter Hooper (New York: Macmillan, 1962), 19.

2. David Bordwell, *The Films of Carl-Theodor Dreyer* (Berkeley: University of California Press, 1981), 93-116.

3. Bordwell, 116.

4. See, for example, Alison Peirse, "The Impossibility of Vision: Vampirism, Formlessness, and Horror in *Vampyr*," *Studies in European Cinema* 5, no. 3 (2008), 161-70.

5. Sheridan Le Fanu, *Carmilla*, 1872, chapter 7, Google Book Search, Web, June 10, 2011.

6. Ibid., chapter 15.

7. Susannah Clements, *The Vampire Defanged* (Grand Rapids, MI: Brazos Press, 2011), 26.

8. Thomas Fleming, "The Five Good Reasons," *Chronicles* 35 (January 2011), 10.

9. Douglas Cowen suggests that the entire genre might be categorized as a form of "eroticism" in *Sacred Terror: Religion and Horror on the Silver Screen* (Waco, TX: Baylor University Press, 2008), 13 et al.

10. Romans 1: 28.

Chapter 4

1. The Michigan penal code, for example, added a law in 1931 that "any person who shall so expose in museums or elsewhere diseased or deformed human bodies, or parts thereof, or representations of the same, which would be indecent in the case of a living person, except as used for scientific purposes before members of the medical profession or medical classes, shall be guilty of a misdemeanor" (Act 328, section 750.347).

2. Old loyalty compels me to offer a nod to my former professor Linda Williams who quirkily, yet astutely, coupled horror and pornography together as "body arts" in *Hard Core: Power, Pleasure and the Frenzy of the Visible* (Berkeley: University of California Press, 1989).

3. Michael Brunas, John Brunas, and Tom Weaver, *Universal Horrors: The Studio's Classic Films, 1931-1946* (Jefferson, NC: McFarland, 1990), 52.

4. Cited in Mark Vieira, *Hollywood Horror: from Gothic to Cosmic* (New York: Abrams, 2003), 58.

5. The name sounds like, and may well have been, a jest about the film's storyline, "*angst* and amen."

6. The comment is actually part of an astute photo caption from the introduction to Halliwell's casual study of the genre, *The Dead that Walk* (New York: Ungar, 1988).

7. Halliwell, in fact, traces the source materials for Balderston's play to stories by Poe and Doyle, 212-13.

8. David Sklar explains how the reaction of "the angry villagers," the moral groups in the culture, created a buzz around the Universal horror films, which were made after the Production Code was written. However, the Code addressed overt sexuality and violence in realist narratives, but was not designed to unpack the "sneaky" subcodes of the horror genre. In *The Monster Show: A Cultural History of Horror* (New York: Norton, 1993), 161-209.

9. Cited in *Universal Horrors*, 52.

10. This technique of separating head from hands as a way of describing the modern denial of moral responsibility was, of course, later perfected by the French Catholic director Robert Bresson in films like *Pickpocket* (1959) and *Une femme douce* (1969).

11. It might also be a little joke directed toward the censors as well.

12. Conchita Gonzalez in a letter of June 2, 1965, published in *Journal de Conchita*, a French annotated translation of documents relating to the Garabandal events still under examination for authenticity, although deemed consistent with Roman Catholic teachings. G. du Pilier (Paris: Nouvelles Editions Latines, 1967), 52.

Chapter 5

1. "I make films on the supernatural and I make them because I believe in it." Cited in Chris Fujiwara, *Jacques Tourneur: The Cinema of Nightfall* (Jefferson, NC: McFarland, 1998), 242.

2. Quoted in Fujiwara, 246.

Chapter 6

1. From M. Karecki and S. Wroblewski, *Franciscan Spirituality: Franciscan Study Guide Series*, vol. 1 (Jeppestown: The Franciscan Institute of South Africa, 2000).

Chapter 7

1. Robin Wood, *The American Nightmare: Essays on the Horror Film*, eds. Robin Wood and Richard Lippe (Toronto: Festival of Festivals, 1979), 7–32.

2. Wood, "What Lies Beneath?" *Senses of Cinema*. Film Victoria, July 18, 2001. Web. July 31, 2012.

3. David Skal, *Screams of Reason: Mad Science and Modern Culture* (New York: Norton, 1998), 33.

4. John Kenneth Muir, *Horror Films of the 1970s* (Jefferson, NC: McFarland, 2002), 36.

5. Ibid., 156.

6. Mikel Koven, "The Folklore Fallacy: A Folklorist/Filmic Perspective on The Wicker Man," *Fabula* 48, nos. 3–4 (2007), 280.

7. Robin Hardy, from interview with David Bartholomew, *Cinefantastique* 6, no. 3 (1977).

8. C. Julius Caesar, *Caesar's Gallic War*, trans. W. A. McDevitte and W. S. Bohn (New York: Harper and Brothers, 1999 rpt.).

9. G. K. Chesterton, *The Everlasting Man* (New York: Image Books, 1955), 243.

10. Heinrich Kramer, quoted in "Carnal Knowledge: the Epistemology of Sexual Trauma in Witches' Sabbaths, Satanic Ritual Abuse, and Alien Abduction Narratives," *Preternature: Critical and Historical Studies of the Preternatural* 1.1 (2012), 100–129. Project Muse. Web. July 31, 2012.

11. Catherine Edwards Sanders, *Wicca's Charm: Understanding the Spiritual Hunger behind the Rise of Modern Witchcraft and Pagan Spirituality* (Colorado Springs: Shaw Books, 2005).

Chapter 8

1. Tony Williams, *Hearts of Darkness: The Family in the American Horror Film* (London: Associated University Presses, 1996), 108.

2. Nick Cull, "The Exorcist," *History Today* 50, no. 5 (May 2000), 46–51.

3. Marsha Kinder and Beverle Houston, "Seeing Is Believing: *The Exorcist* and *Don't Look Now*," in *American Essays on the Modern Horror Film*, ed. Gregory Waller (Urbana: University of Illinois Press), 44–61.

4. Jerry Ryan, "Legacy of a Country Priest: My Friend the Exorcist," *Commonweal* 138, no. 17 (October 2011), 18–21.

5. Betty Stafford, "The Growing Evidence for 'Demonic Possession': What Should Psychiatry's Response Be?" *Journal of Religion and Health* 44, no. 1 (Spring 2005), 29.

Chapter 9

1. See his introductory notes to the canto in *The Inferno*, trans. John Ciardi (New York: Penguin, 1982), 266.
2. For a discussion of this as it applies to horror, see Jonathan Lake Crane, *Terror and Everyday Life: Singular Moments in the History of Horror Film* (London: Sage, 1994).
3. Crane, 154.
4. The phrase belongs to Ian Conrich, *Horror Zones: the Cultural Experience of Contemporary Horror* (London: Taurus, 2010), 179.
5. See Noël Carroll, "The Future of Allusion: Hollywood in the Seventies (and Beyond)," *October* 20 (Spring 1982), 55–81.
6. Janet I. Warren and Robert L. Hazelwood, "Relational Patterns Associated with Sexual Sadism: a Study of 20 Wives and Girlfriends," *Journal of Family Violence* 17 (March 2002), 75.
7. See Ron Tamborini and Kristen Salomonson, "Horror's Effect on Social Perceptions and Behaviors," in *Horror Films: Current Research in Audience Preferences and Reactions*, eds. James B. Weaver III and Ron Tamborini (New York: Routledge, 1996), 184.
8. Carol Clover, *Men, Women, and Chainsaws: Gender in the Modern Horror Film* (Princeton: Princeton University Press, 1992).
9. Feminist theorists in debt to Laura Mulvey, who suggested the male gaze was all that really mattered in Hollywood, have masked this crucial fact for well over three decades. The truth is that producers and distributors aimed many of these films specifically at the audience of teenage girls and young women. See Richard Nowell, "'There's More Than One Way to Lose Your Heart': The American Film Industry, Early Teen Slasher Films, and Female Youth," *Cinema Journal* 51 (Fall 2011), 115–40.
10. Linda Williams, "When the Woman Looks," in *ReVision: Essays in Feminist Film Criticism*, eds. Mary Ann Doane, Patricia Mellencamp, and Linda Williams (Frederick, MD: University Press of America, 1984), 91.

Chapter 10

1. For example, see Valerie Wee, "Visual Aesthetics and Ways of Seeing: Comparing *Ringu* and *The Ring*," *Cinema Journal* 50 (Winter 2011), 41–60.
2. *I Nuovo Perseguitati* (Casale Monferrato: Piemme, 2002).
3. See, for example, Ralph Cohen, "History and Genre," *New Literary History* 17 (Winter 1986), 203–218.
4. Marina Krcmar and Linda Godbold Kean, "Uses and Gratifications of Media Violence: Personality Correlates of Viewing and Liking Violent Genres," *Media Psychology* 7, no. 4 (2005), 399–420.
5. Patricia Cohen, Jeffrey Johnson, and Elizabeth Smailes, "Television Viewing and Aggressive Behavior during Adolescence and Adulthood," *Science* 295 (March 2002), 2468–71.

Bibliography

Aulén, Gustav. *Christus Victor: An Historical Study of the Three Main Types of the Idea of the Atonement.* Trans. A. G. Herbert. New York: Macmillan, 1969.

Benedict XVI. *Spe Salvi.* Libreria Editrice Vaticana. November 30, 2007. http://www.vatican.va/holy_father/benedict_xvi/encyclicals/documents/hf_ben-xvi_enc_20071130_spe-salvi_en.html.

Benson, Robert Hugh. *Lord of the World.* South Bend, IN: St. Augustine's Press, 2011.

Berenstein, Rhonda. *Attack of the Leading Ladies: Gender, Sexuality, and Spectatorship in Classic Horror Cinema.* New York: Columbia University Press, 1996.

Bordwell, David. *The Films of Carl-Theodor Dreyer.* Berkeley: University of California Press, 1981.

Brunas, Michael, John Brunas, and Tom Weaver. *Universal Horrors: The Studio's Classic Films, 1931–1946.* Jefferson, NC: McFarland, 1990.

Carroll, Noël. "The Future of Allusion: Hollywood in the Seventies (and Beyond)." October 20 (Spring 1982), 55–81.

———. *The Philosophy of Horror, or Paradoxes of the Heart.* New York and London: Routledge, 1990.

Chesterton, G. K. *The Everlasting Man.* New York: Image Books, 1955.

———. *Orthodoxy.* San Francisco: Ignatius Press, 1995.

Clements, Susannah. *The Vampire Defanged.* Grand Rapids: Brazos Press, 2011.

Clover, Carol. *Men, Women, and Chainsaws: Gender in the Modern Horror Film.* Princeton: Princeton University Press, 1992.

Cohen, Patricia, Jeffrey Johnson, and Elizabeth Smailes. "Television Viewing and Aggressive Behavior during Adolescence and Adulthood." *Science* 295 (March 2002), 2468–71.

Cohen, Ralph. "History and Genre." *New Literary History* 17 (Winter 1986), 203–218.

Conrich, Ian. *Horror Zones: The Cultural Experience of Contemporary Horror.* London: Taurus, 2010.

Contreras, Jaime Perales. "The New Master of Horror Movies." *Américas.* 61, no. 2 (2009), 60–61.

Cowen, Douglas. *Sacred Terror: Religion and Horror on the Silver Screen.* Waco, TX: Baylor University Press, 2008.

Crane, Jonathan Lake. *Terror and Everyday Life: Singular Moments in the History of Horror Film.* London: Sage, 1994.

Creed, Barbara. *The Monstrous Feminine: Film, Feminism, and Psychoanalysis.* New York and London: Routledge, 1993.

Bibliography

Cull, Nick. "The Exorcist." *History Today* 50, no. 5 (May 2000), 46–51.

Dante Alighieri. *The Inferno.* Trans. John Ciardi. New York: Signet Classics, 2009.

Derry, Charles. *Dark Dreams: a Psychological History of the Modern Horror Film.* New York: A. S. Barnes, 1977.

Doane, Mary Ann, Patricia Mellencamp, and Linda Williams, Linda, eds. *ReVision: Essays in Feminist Film Criticism.* Frederick, MD: University Press of America, 1984.

Ebon, Martin. *The Devil's Bride: Exorcism—Past and Present.* New York: Harper and Row, 1974.

Eisner, Lotte H. *The Haunted Screen: Expressionism in the German Cinema and the Influence of Max Reinhardt.* Trans. Roger Greaves. Berkeley and Los Angeles: University of California Press, 1969.

Fleming, Thomas. "The Five Good Reasons." *Chronicles* 35 (January 2011), 10.

Fraser, Peter. *Images of the Passion: the Sacramental Mode in Film.* Westport, CT: Praeger, 1998.

Frazer, Sir James. *The Golden Bough: A Study of Magic and Religion.* New York: Macmillan, 1958.

Freeland, Cynthia. *The Naked and the Undead: Evil and the Appeal of Horror.* Boulder, CO: Westview Press, 2000.

Freud, Sigmund. *The Uncanny.* Trans. David McLintock. New York: Penguin, 2003.

Fujiwara, Chris. *Jacques Tourneur: The Cinema of Nightfall.* Jefferson, NC: McFarland, 1998.

Halliwell, Leslie. *The Dead that Walk.* New York: Ungar, 1988.

Jones, E. Michael. *Monsters from the Id.* Dallas: Spence Publishing, 2000.

Karecki, M., and S. Wroblewski. *Franciscan Spirituality: Franciscan Study Guide Series.* Vol. 1. Jeppestown: The Franciscan Institute of South Africa, 2000.

Kawin, Bruce. *Horror and the Horror Film.* London: Anthem Press, 2012.

Kelly, Henry Ansgar. *Satan: A Biography.* Cambridge: Cambridge University Press, 2006.

Koven, Mikel. "The Folklore Fallacy: A Folklorist/Filmic Perspective on The Wicker Man." *Fabula* 48, nos. 3–4 (2007).

Kracauer, Siegfried. *From Caligari to Hitler: A Psychological History of the German Film.* Princeton: Princeton University Press, 1947.

Kramer, Heinrich, and James Sprenger. *The Malleus Maleficarum.* Trans. Montague Summers. New York: Dover, 1971.

Krcmar, Marina, and Linda Godbold Kean. "Uses and Gratifications of Media Violence: Personality Correlates of Viewing and Liking Violent Genres." *Media Psychology* 7, no. 4 (2005), 399–420.

Lasch, Christopher. *The Culture of Narcissism: American Life in an Age of Diminishing Expectations.* New York: Norton, 1978.

Le Fanu, Sheridan. *Carmilla.* Syracuse: Syracuse University Press, 2013.

Lewis, C. S. "The Weight of Glory." In *The Weight of Glory and Other Addresses.* Ed. Walter Hooper. New York: Macmillan, 1962.

Bibliography

McDevitte, W. A. *Caesar's Gallic War.* Trans. W. S. Bohn. New York: Harper and Brothers, 1999.

Montero, Rosa. "The Silent Revolution: The Social and Cultural Advances of Women in Democratic Spain." In *Spanish Cultural Studies: The Struggle for Modernity.* Ed. Jo Labanyi. Oxford: Oxford University Press, 1995.

Muir, John Kenneth. *Horror Films of the 1970s.* Jefferson, NC: McFarland, 2002.

Nowell, Richard. "'There's More Than One Way to Lose Your Heart': The American Film Industry, Early Teen Slasher Films, and Female Youth." *Cinema Journal* 51 (Fall 2011), 115–40.

Peirse, Alison. "The Impossibility of Vision: Vampirism, Formlessness, and Horror in *Vampyr.*" *Studies in European Cinema.* 5, no. 3 (2008), 161–70.

Pelikan, Jaroslav. *The Christian Tradition: A History of the Development of Doctrine.* Chicago: University of Chicago Press, 1971.

Prawer, S. S. *Caligari's Children: The Film as Tale of Terror.* Oxford: Oxford University Press, 1980.

Ryan, Jerry. "Legacy of a Country Priest: My Friend the Exorcist." *Commonweal* 138, no. 17 (October 2011), 18–21.

Sanders, Catherine Edwards. *Wicca's Charm: Understanding the Spiritual Hunger behind the Rise of Modern Witchcraft and Pagan Spirituality.* Colorado Springs: Shaw Books, 2005.

Schneider, Steven J., and Daniel Shaw, eds. *Dark Thoughts: Philosophic Reflections on Cinematic Horror.* Oxford: Scarecrow Press, 2003.

Shelley, Mary. *Frankenstein: A Norton Critical Edition.* Ed. J. Paul Hunter. New York and London: W. W. Norton, 1996.

Skal, David. *Screams of Reason: Mad Science and Modern Culture.* New York: Norton, 1998.

Sklar, David. *The Monster Show: A Cultural History of Horror.* New York: Norton, 1993.

Solzhenitsyn, Aleksandr Isaevich. *The Nobel Lecture.* Trans. F. D. Reeve. New York: Farrar, Straus, Giroux, 1972.

Stafford, Betty. "The Growing Evidence for 'Demonic Possession': What Should Psychiatry's Response Be?" *Journal of Religion and Health* 44, no. 1 (Spring 2005), 13–30.

Tamborini, Ron, and James B. Weaver, eds. *Horror Films: Current Research in Audience Preferences and Reactions.* New York: Routledge, 1996.

Tolstoy, Leo. *War and Peace.* Trans. Constance Garnett. New York: Modern Library, 1994.

Vieira, Mark. *Hollywood Horror: From Gothic to Cosmic.* New York: Abrams, 2003.

Waller, Gregory, ed. *American Horrors: Essays on the Modern American Horror Film.* Urbana: University of Illinois Press, 1987.

Warren, Janet I., and Robert L. Hazelwood. "Relational Patterns Associated with Sexual Sadism: a Study of 20 Wives and Girlfriends." *Journal of Family Violence* 17 (March 2002), 75–89.

Wee, Valerie. "Visual Aesthetics and Ways of Seeing: Comparing *Ringu*

Bibliography

and *The Ring.*" *Cinema Journal* 50 (Winter 2011), 41–60.

Weisel, Elie. *Night.* Trans. Marion Weisel. New York: Hill and Wang, 1958.

Williams, Linda. *Hard Core: Power, Pleasure and the Frenzy of the Visible.* Berkeley: University of California Press, 1989.

Williams, Tony. *Hearts of Darkness: The Family in the American Horror Film.* London: Associated University Presses, 1996.

Wood, Robin, and Richard Lippe, eds. *The American Nightmare: Essays on the Horror Film.* Toronto: Festival of Festivals, 1979.

Worland, Rick. *The Horror Film: An Introduction.* Oxford: Blackwell Publishing, 2007.

Index

Alien 12, 62, 106, 150, 169
All Quiet on the Western Front (film) 66
American Nightmare 113–14
Antichrist 29, 41, 73, 94, 138
Aquinas, Thomas 57, 104
Arrival of a Train at La Ciotat 156
Aulén, Gustav 7, 228

Balderston, John 65–66
Bazin, André 90, 167
Belloc, Hilaire 188
Ben-Hur 40
Benedict XVI 28, 32
Benson, Robert Hugh 28
Beresford, Bruce 115
Bierce, Ambrose 80
Black Robe 115
Blade 46
Blair Witch Project 163
Blatty, William Peter 22, 132, 136–38, 147
The Blob 73
Boniface 122
Bonnie and Clyde 138, 164
Bordwell, David 44
Bresson, Robert 81, 135, 198
British Lion 116, 121, 130
Browning, Tod 60, 65
Buñuel, Luis 134, 156
Burns, Robert 116
Byron, Lord 47, 83, 101

Cabin in the Woods 186
Cabinet of Dr. Caligari 13, 65
Caesar, Julius 117
Caligari's Children 196
Campbell, Joseph 115
Camus, Albert 131
Carlyle, Thomas 179
Carmilla 44–46, 57, 64

Carpenter, John 6, 62, 99–100, 143, 152, 155–56, 171, 180
Carrie 15
Carroll, Noël 156, 195–96
Cat People 81, 89, 106
Celtic paganism 115–20, 123–26, 131
Chaney, Lon 60, 62
Chekhov, Anton 80
Un Chien Andalou 134, 156
"Christmas Carol" 80
Christus Victor 7, 22, 49, 195
Cicero 117
Clements, Susannah 47
A Clockwork Orange 28
Clover, Carol 158
Cloverfield 163, 185, 187
Coleridge, Samuel Taylor 101
Conan Doyle, Arthur 74, 197
The Conjuring 186
Coppola, Francis Ford 103, 180
Craven, Wes 154
Crime and Punishment 81, 176
Crowley, Alistair 82

Dante 10, 23, 98, 152, 166
Day the Earth Stood Still 105
Dead Souls 188
Deep Throat 138
del Toro, Guillermo 26–27, 29, 31, 34
Demme, Jonathan 93, 143, 157
demonic possession 3, 15, 24, 44–46, 49, 63, 84, 100, 111, 129–37, 141–52, 163, 175, 181, 196
Derrickson, Scott 22
Diary of a Country Priest 135
Dickens, Charles 80
Dr. Spock 22
Dostoyevsky, Fyodor 81
Dracula 22, 29, 47, 60, 65, 73, 100, 103, 108
Dreyer, Carl 42, 43–59, 73, 75, 81
Druids 117, 126

Index

Eckland, Britt 117, 121
Eliot, T.S. 104
Ellison, Ralph 72
"Ethics of Elfland" 35, 110
Event Horizon 101
exorcism 3, 15–25, 45–48, 52, 56, 59, 74, 84, 93, 96, 107–11, 129–30, 136–52, 190, 196
Exorcism of Emily Rose 22, 137, 152
Exorcist 3, 22–25, 106, 132–52, 156, 161, 171, 176, 192

Faces of Death 154
Fatima 76
Faust 5, 101
feminist theory 21, 124, 135, 165, 195, 199
"Final Girl" 158–65
Flannery, Seamus 116
Fleming, Thomas 56
Ford, John 131, 156, 180
Franco, Francisco 31–32
Frankenstein (film) 10, 22, 60, 62, 71, 99, 108, 163
Frankenstein (novel) 47, 92, 97, 101, 109, 114, 127, 164, 177
Frazer, Sir James 18, 116
Freaks 60
Freddy Krueger 74
French Connection 136
Frenzy 120
Freud, Sigmund 2, 6, 9, 96, 195
Freudian criticism 6, 44, 67, 113, 195
Freund, Karl 23, 60–74, 99, 134, 180
Friedkin, William 22, 136
From Caligari to Hitler 13

Gadarene demoniac 132, 147
Gance, Abel 80
Garabandal 76–77, 198
genocide 26–27, 107, 173
Genovese, Kitty 159
genre theory 181
Giovanni, Paul 116
"Goblin Market" 190
Godfather 44
Godwin, William 47, 113
Godzilla 10, 22, 106, 108, 163
Goethe 5
Gogol, Nikolai 188
Golden Bough 18, 116
Golem 29, 168

Gonzalez, Conchita 198
Gospel According to St. Matthew 63
Gothic tradition 46, 48, 80, 97, 168, 177, 196
Grand Guignol 154, 156–57
The Grudge 168

Halloween 6, 23, 66, 84, 99, 143, 152–67, 171, 185, 196
Hamlet 38, 48, 53–54, 59
Hammer Studios 106, 115
Hannibal Lecter 29, 61, 167
Hardy, Robin 113–18, 122, 126–28, 130
Hawks, Howard 95–103, 106, 108, 110, 156
Hill, Debra 165
History of the Gallic Wars 117
Hitchcock, Alfred 5–6, 8, 16, 22, 68, 120, 156, 158
Hitler, Adolf 26
Hooper, Tobe 154
Hugo, Victor 179

I Walked with a Zombie 81
"imp of the perverse" 185
Invasion of the Body Snatchers 11–12, 73, 98, 106, 184
Invisible Man 72
Isis and Osiris 63, 65–66, 70, 72, 74

Jackson, Shirley 119
James, Henry 80
James, Montague 82
Jaws 22, 164
Johann, Zita 75–76
John Paul II 28
Jones, E. Michael 28, 196

Kael, Pauline 133
Karloff, Boris 60, 62–63, 66, 69–71, 75, 99, 164
Keaton, Buster 69, 81
King Kong 89
King Lear 27, 88, 133
Kracauer, Siegfried 13, 196
Kramer, Heinrich 24, 124
Kristeva, Julia 152
Kubrick, Stanley 28
Kurosawa, Akira 180

Laemmle, Carl 65–66
Lasch, Christopher 28, 96

206

Index

Last House on the Left 154, 163
Lee, Christopher 15, 130
Le Fanu, Sheridan 44–48, 57
Legion of Decency 133
Leigh, Janet 22, 158, 161
Leroux, Gaston 156
Lewis, C.S. 28, 42, 73, 107
Lewton, Val 81
Lord of the World 28, 168
"The Lottery" 119
Lumière films 156–162

Malleus Maleficarum 24, 124
Manson, Charles 138, 163
martyrdom 39, 130, 143, 173
Marx, Karl 32
Marxism 32, 113
May Day 120, 123
McCarthy, Cormac 28, 93
Metenier, Oscar 156
Michel, Anneliese 137
Midnight Cowboy 155
Milestone, Lewis 66
Milton, John 7, 29, 109
Mind of the Maker 179
Mitchell, Joni 116
Molech 113, 117–18, 126
Monsters from the Id 18, 196
Mulvey, Laura 199
The Mummy 10, 23, 60–77, 98–99, 108, 126, 134, 164, 192
Murnau, F.W. 22, 49
Myers, Michael 6, 23, 74, 99, 114, 157–65, 185
Myth of Sisyphus 131

Nakata, Hideo 168, 172, 180
Napoleon 27, 129
narcissism 96–98, 104, 111
Narcissus 96
Navarrete, Javier 40
Nebuchadnezzar 87–88
neopaganism 115, 124, 126, 131
Night 26
Night of the Demon 78–94, 96, 98, 100, 169
Night of the Living Dead 1, 11, 18, 29, 102, 106, 177
Norman Bates 6, 8, 18, 22
Nosferatu 12, 27, 49, 126
Nuada 120, 126

nuclear bomb 10, 92, 95, 108
Nyby, Christian 96

O'Connor, Flannery 136, 152
Oh! Calcutta! 155
The Omen 73, 106
Ordet 46, 48–49, 54–55, 59
Orthodoxy 78
Ouija 13, 19, 24, 98, 111, 132–33, 135, 184
Ozu, Yasuhiro 180

Pan's Labyrinth 26–41, 98, 191
Paradise Lost 55, 177
Paranormal Activity 84, 163, 186–87
Pasolini, Pier Paolo 63
passing the rune 82–85, 93, 169
La Passion de Jeanne D'Arc 43, 49
Pazuza 141, 148–49
peep shows 12, 21, 63, 74, 76, 135, 164
Phantom of the Opera 60, 156
Pickpocket 81, 198
Planet of the Apes 73
Poe, Edgar Allan 73–74
Polanski, Roman 138
Polidari, John 47–48, 101
pornography 15, 21, 61, 134–35, 138, 197
Prawer, S.S. 196
protoevangelium 22, 34
Psycho 5–6, 8, 18, 22, 140, 158, 161
psychoanalytic theory 181

Raging Bull 187
Red Cross Knight 122
Reign of Terror 26
"Rime of the Ancient Mariner" 101
The Ring 2, 6, 13, 168, 178
Ringu 12, 84, 93, 149, 161, 168–87, 192
The Road 28
Rocky Horror Picture Show 187
Roman Rite of Exorcism 15, 24, 136, 149
Rosemary's Baby 73, 84, 106, 138
Rossetti, Christina 190

The Sacrifice 28
sadism 12, 129, 138, 155, 165
St. Francis 95, 111–12
St. Paul 7, 39, 58, 93, 129
Sayers, Dorothy 179
Scanners 15
Schaffer, Anthony 115
science fiction 72–73, 90–107, 150

207

Index

Scorsese, Martin 164
Scott, Ridley 62, 106
Screwtape Letters 143
Servile State 188
Shakespeare, William 34, 53, 88
Shelley, Mary 47, 92, 97–101, 113–14, 192
Shelley, Percy 47, 97, 101
Sherlock Holmes 74
Shyamalan, M. Night 99
Siegel, Don 98, 109, 184
Signs 99
Silence of the Lambs 66, 143, 157
Silvestri, Alan 40
slasher film 66, 152–58, 162–66
Snell, Peter 116
Solzhenitsyn Alexander 191
Spe Salvi 31, 197
Stevenson, Robert Louis 80
Stoker, Bram 47–48, 114
structuralist theory 181
Suzuki, Koji 168

taboos 18–24, 43, 56–57, 61, 67, 75, 84, 128–29, 138, 144, 151–55, 185, 190
Tacitus 117
Tarkovski, Andrei 28
Taxi Driver 164
Texas Chainsaw Massacre 1, 102, 154, 165
The Thing 62
Thing from Another World 95–112, 126, 156, 163
Tobis-Klangfilm 45, 50–51, 58
Tolkien, J.R.R. 28, 107, 177
Tolstoy, Leo 27–28, 179–80
Tourneur, Jacques 78–83, 86–90, 93–94, 104–05, 109, 169
"Tubular Bells" 143, 156
Twilight 46

Universal Studio 10, 60, 62, 65–66, 72, 75, 103, 164, 197

vampires 12, 44–53, 57–59, 64, 98, 114, 150
Vampyr 42–59, 64, 73, 75, 81, 98, 100, 152, 178, 192
The Vampyre 47
Van Helsing 47, 74
Vendée Wars 26
Verbinski, Gore 2, 6, 168, 172, 185, 187
verisimilitude 63, 90, 157, 163, 166, 185, 187, 196
Victor Frankenstein 10, 92, 97, 101, 109, 127
Vietnam 137
voyeurism 22, 70, 72, 123, 138, 155

War and Peace 27
Watergate 137
"Weight of Glory" 42
Weisel, Elie 26
Welles, Orson 125, 180
Wexman, Virginia Wright 135
Whale, James 60, 71, 99
What Lies Beneath 2, 5–25, 39–40, 61, 98, 175, 195
When a Stranger Calls 159
Who Goes There 103
Wicca 124, 131
Wicker Man 113–31, 192
Wiene, Robert 65
Wild Bunch 138, 164
Wilde, Oscar 80
Williams, Linda 197
Wolf Man 12, 163
Wood, Robin 113
Woodstock 115–17, 145
Woodward, Edward 115, 130

yūrei 168–69, 175–76, 18

Zemeckis, Robert 2, 5, 7, 22, 175

www.ingramcontent.com/pod-product-compliance
Ingram Content Group UK Ltd.
Pitfield, Milton Keynes, MK11 3LW, UK
UKHW042000140426
5217IPUK00015B/902